DAVE GROHL

FOO FIGHTERS, NIRVANA & OTHER MISADVENTURES

Books are to be returned on or before
the last date below.

This edition published 2008 by
INDEPENDENT MUSIC PRESS
First published in 2003.
Independent Music Press is an imprint of I.M. P. Publishing Limited
This Work is Copyright © I. M. P. Publishing Ltd 2003

Dave Grohl – Foo Fighters, Nirvana And Other Misadventures
by Martin James

British Library Cataloguing-in-Publication Data.
A catalogue for this book is available from The British Library.

ISBN 978-1-906191-05-4

Every effort has been made to contact and credit correctly the photographers
whose work has been used in this book - however a few were unobtainable.
The publishers would be grateful if those concerned would contact
Independent Music Press.

Cover Design by Fresh Lemon.

Printed in the UK.

Independent Music Press
P.O. Box 69,
Church Stretton, Shropshire
SY6 6WZ

Visit us on the web at: www.impbooks.com
and www.myspace.com/independentmusicpress

For a free catalogue, e-mail us at: info@impbooks.com
Fax: 01694 720049

DAVE GROHL

FOO FIGHTERS, NIRVANA
& OTHER MISADVENTURES

by Martin James

Independent Music Press

About the Author

Martin James has been a popular music culture journalist for almost thirteen years. He has held editorial positions at various magazines including *Melody Maker, Vox* and *Flipside*(UK). He regularly contributes to *The Independent* and has also written for *The Independent on Sunday, The Guardian, Mojo, Uncut, Dazed and Confused* and many others. Martin also holds a PhD in popular music journalism. He is the author of biographies on Moby, The Prodigy, Fatboy Slim, as well as studies of jungle and French music. He currently lives in the frozen north east of England, in the city of Sunderland with his partner Lisa, and three children, Ruby Blue, Felix Drum and Bella Pearl.

Read Martin's blog at http://st8ofbass.blogspot.com/

Acknowledgements

I would like to thank the following people for their invaluable help; Gemma Price for the research on the first version (you're a star), Victoria Segal, Ian Winwood, Stevie Chick and Keith Cameron for the interviews, Ben Myers, Anton and Paddy at Bad Moon Publicity (and John, get in touch mate). Everett True for being himself. To Grohl for being himself. All of the people who agreed to be interviewed but asked to remain anonymous! Geordie from Killing Joke, Queens of the Stone Age, David Galgano and Liam Howlett. The guys at Southern and all of the photographers and writers whose work is featured in this book. I would also like to thank Manateebound.com and unomas.com for some of the best Grohl stuff to be found anywhere. Respect and thanks as always to Martin and Kaye at Independent Music Press, as well as Dave Hanley, who did such a great job on this second version.

And finally, thanks and eternal love to my family and above all to my fantastic gang, Lisa, Ruby Blue, Felix Drum and Bella Pearl – I love you all more than words ...

Martin James, Sunderland, England March 2008

DEDICATED TO

TO LISA, RUBY BLUE, FELIX DRUM AND BELLA PEARL

A DRUMMER JOKE

A drummer in a world famous band decides to record some music as a solo artist. He needs some equipment so he goes shopping in the local mall. He walks up to the sales assistant and explains what he wants to buy.

"I'll take a guitar, a bass, some keyboards, a mixing desk, some nice effects and a microphone," he declares as he hands over his credit card.

"You're a drummer aren't you?" replies the assistant.

"Yeah… how did you know?" the drummer asks.

"You're in McDonald's."

Drummers don't make great albums on their own. Drummers don't make great drummers on their own. Drummers wear those stupid head mics when they sing. Drummers always want to add a bit of jazz. Drummers secretly admire Phil Collins for stepping from behind the drum stool and making a career out of being a singer. Drummers think Animal from *The Muppets* is cool. Drummers think *The Muppets* are cool. Drummers are the butt of almost every joke to have emerged from the music industry. Drummers hit things for a living… how dumb is that?

INTRODUCTION

Dave Grohl flashes a boozy grin across the plastic tables that adorn the backstage area. Superfly sideburns and gigolo-chic hairstyle frame his thin, chiselled face, slightly drained from intensive touring.

As he talks, plumes of smoke billow from his nose and mouth. He takes another drag, laughs at events that are unfolding around him and smoke again floods his face, licking around its angular contours. He takes a swig of beer. It's the latest in a line of beers he's downed since his band, Foo Fighters, played their mid-afternoon set. He's in a triumphant mood. He's talkative, animated and just relaxed enough to let his oft-claimed insecurity take a back seat.

I tell him my drummer joke. He's heard it before. An English journalist had told him it a couple of days before. But he likes it. In fact he loves drummer jokes. He even regularly checks out a site dedicated to drummer jokes. This joke was new to him a couple of days ago. Now it's second hand. But he laughs. In fact he laughs a lot, beer splatters down his chin and smoke pours from his mouth. He leans forward, stubs out yet another cigarette and starts his own line in drummer jokes. Dave Grohl is proud of his drumming roots.

"How many drummers does it take to change a light bulb?" he asks. "Just one, but the roadie has to get the ladder, set it up and put the bulb in the socket for him! How can you tell a drummer's at the door?" he continues, barely stopping for breath between punch-line and guffaw. "The knocking speeds up."

Twenty minutes later, we're all side-of-stage for the headlining act, the Prodigy. Dave Grohl loves the Prodigy as much as he loves drummer jokes. To him they embody everything that he worships about adrenalised punk rock, despite their dance beginnings.

A couple of years earlier, Grohl had witnessed the Prodigy play at Scotland's T In The Park festival. "That's one of Nirvana's songs they've sampled," he'd declared to local television personality Ewan Macleod. He went on to explain that they let the Prodigy use the sample of Nirvana's 'Very Ape' on the track 'Voodoo People' because "they're the best fucking rock 'n' roll band in the world, man. Better than Nirvana ever were."

Some might argue with that statement. But on this late summer evening in Leeds, it is easy to see what Grohl meant by the claim. And it's obvious he still feels this way by the look of unadulterated, excitable admiration on his Cheshire cat grinning face.

As the Essex stormtroopers turn up the heat on the festival crowd, Grohl is overtaken by sheer energy. "I FUCKING LOVE THIS!" he screams. In a sudden burst of hyperactive energy, he jumps on to the speaker rigging and starts to scramble up like a marine. He's followed by one much less fit journalist who seizes the moment to get a better view of the heaving crowd. Sadly, I'm not as fast as Grohl and security quickly drag me from my pursuit, clawing me as far away from trouble as possible. Then they go for Dave. They pull at him and he wriggles. They drag him and he laughs. Eventually they bring him back to Earth. And he just giggles.

Much later, as the Prodigy's road crew busied themselves with clearing the stage, the security guards could be heard boasting about the event like cabbies bragging about a recent fare ("you'll never guess who I 'ad in 'ere just now…").

"Ere, that was that geezer from Nirvana you nearly decked."

"Fuck off, he's dead. Even I know that."

"Nah you twat, he was the drummer."

"Shit, the drummer in Nirvana…. Wait till I tell me mates. I loved that band. What was his name then?"

"Fucked if I know. Just the drummer."

Except Dave Grohl isn't "just the drummer from Nirvana." He never was *just* the drummer for anyone. Or the guitarist. Or the singer. Dave Grohl is, in fact, the embodiment of the multi-skilled DIY ethic at the centre of punk rock. An attitude which translated in 1977 into the punk slogan as declared in London fanzine, *Sniffin' Glue*, "here's three chords, now form a band."

For many though, this ethos begged to be taken further. It

translated as an uncompromising, nothing–ventured–nothing–gained approach to all instruments. It was about pure excitement and wonderment. A love of how each instrument sounded and a desire to experience everything, regardless of ability. As such, Dave Grohl's natural exuberance and refusal to place self–imposed obstacles in his own way have seen him move from guitar to drums to multi–instrumentalist to front man with the kind of ease usually associated with your average Renaissance man. The punk rock Leonardo De Vinci whose dumb–assed antics belie an intelligence and wit that see him tackling all new instruments with a rare verve.

It's this adaptability that has marked out his career. A life in which he has jumped into the recently vacated stools of at least two well–respected bands – one of them on the verge of going global. This adaptability has also helped propel him into the stadium rock icon he is today. Not that he would agree with that description. Typically, he would call himself a guy from Nowheresville who got lucky. Very lucky.

Dave Grohl then is the archetypal punk kid who devoted his life to the band ethic. On the road, in the studio, sleeping in vans, squats and fleapit rooms, he's done the lot. But more than simply being that punk kid made good, he is the epitome of punk rock itself. From its energetic DIY grassroots to the corporate investment it is today. He represents the essence of punk's journey from outsider force to mainstream genre, backroom to stadium, a few copies of a demo tape sold out of the back of a van to million of albums shifted all over the world.

But Grohl's story isn't one of a simple sell–out. He's remained true to his own ideals throughout. He was never the political activist like his Washington DC straight edge counterparts (and mentors) in his early days with punk bands Mission Impossible, Scream etc. Similarly, he was far less fazed than his band mates when Nirvana was hit full force by the onslaught of fame. Since he first started pouting out records, Dave Grohl has been accused of ditching his friends for his heroes, trying to co-opt the legacy he helped create by copying his old band's sound and moving from the anti-star standpoint of his punk rock days to embracing a celebrity lifestyle in the gossip columns. He's been described as a megalomaniac; someone who has always wanted to be a star and a hypocrite who drops ideals as quickly as band mates.

By contrast, he's also been described as the nicest man in rock. He is critically lauded as one of the finest rock drummers on the planet. Just ask Queens of the Stone Age whom he drummed for in 2002 and the legendary Killing Joke, whom he turned in a powerhouse performance for on their 2003 album *The Death and Resurrection Show*. If that's not enough, he's also dropped one or two astounding songs... not only with Foo Fighters, but with bands in previous lives like Nirvana, Scream, Dain Bramage, Mission Impossible and Freak Baby.

So, far more than just the drummer in Nirvana, Dave Grohl is someone who has walked the punk rock path from its snotty-nosed, oppositional beginnings to the corporate advertising soundtrack it is today. A man with a history as exciting as his present day, and a future that looks brighter than a metal furnace.

1

FROM FREAKBABY TO *FUMBLE*

ANOTHER DRUMMER JOKE
What's the difference between a chiropodist and a drummer?
A chiropodist bucks up your feet.

In 1969, the Stooges released the definitive collection of punk classics with their eponymous debut album. A series of three-minute songs that punched, spat and kicked against the pricks, but above all pointed an accusatory finger at the middle-class indulgences of the West Coast's hippy scenesters and the arty habits of Warhol's Factory fops and their New York cool.

In the Stooges' unique world was Iggy Pop, a singer who could move like a tiger on Vaseline (as Bowie would have it) and croon like Sinatra on amphetamines. Legend has it that the Stooges got their deal after Iggy jumped on a Sony Records boss' desk and delivered his finest Sinatra rendition. "I'm not sure if he signed us because he was impressed or scared," Iggy told me in 1999.

With that debut album, the Stooges delivered a blue-print in trail-blazing, guitar-frenzied punk rock attacks. "It's 1969 OK, war across the USA," sang Iggy. The war he referred to had little to do with Vietnam. It had nothing to do with the fight that Dr Timothy Leary and the rest of the élite intelligentsia were embroiled in by attempting to liberate LSD. The Stooges war was all about society's real outsiders versus the mainstream middle-class, the middle Americans that dominated the culture of the time. This was the punk rock manifesto. A celebration of the outsider, a body of people who would eventually become defined as Generation X.

In the same year eulogised by the war-mongering Iggy and his Stooges, a young couple from Warren, Ohio called James and

Virginia Grohl had a son. It was their second child. The first, Lisa, was born three years earlier. Their new addition was given the name David Eric. He was born on January 14.

The Grohl family moved to Springfield, Virginia when Dave was three. Thanks to his parents' shared love of music, their young son quickly developed a desire to play an instrument. His mother had been a singer in a band and his father was an accomplished flautist, so making music was a normal part of Grohl family life. There was always a guitar lying around the house, so by the time Grohl was ten he'd already started to pick out tunes like Deep Purple's 'Smoke On The Water'.

"I was always really good at figuring out songs by ear," Grohl said in 1995. This natural aptitude was complemented around the age of eleven by formal guitar lessons. He also spent hours practising with his friend, Larry Hinkle. The duo called themselves the H G Hancock Band.

"I always had a guitar wherever I went around my house growing up. Sitting on the couch watching TV, I'd always have it in my hands," he explained to Eric Brace of *unomas.com* "My mom was like, 'Put down that guitar and do your homework!' I'd play along to records on this portable record player my mom would borrow from the Fairfax County public schools. We'd bought a few Beatles records and this K-Tel album that had Edgar Winters' 'Frankenstein' on it, which I thought was the coolest thing in the world. That was my favourite." [1]

James and Virginia separated when their son was only seven. Dave Grohl's father was a journalist for the Scripps-Howard newspaper chain. Following the spilt he moved back to Ohio, with the children staying with their mother in Virginia. "I was so young I didn't understand it (his parents' divorce). And by the time I got a hold of the situation, it was too late for me to have a freak-out," explained Grohl. "It just seemed abnormal for all my friends to have a father. I thought growing-up with my mother and sister was just the way it was supposed to be." [2]

Following the divorce, Virginia took on three jobs to support

Dave and his sister Lisa. She worked as a High School teacher and also in a department store at night. On the weekend she did estimates for a carpet-cleaning company. "She worked her fingers to the bone just to make sure we survived," says a proud Grohl.

Grohl got his first electric guitar for Christmas when he was twelve. It was a 1960s Silvertone with the amp built into the case. A classic in fact. Unfortunately, the young Grohl's hyperactive personality soon saw the end of that guitar. While messing around one day, he dropped and broke it. It was only a few months old. The heartbroken youngster soon got a replacement however, this time in the shape of a black Memphis Les Paul copy.

With the discovery of distortion pedals and a growing confidence in his own ability, Grohl soon joined a local covers band specialising in faithfully recreated copies of songs by The Who and The Rolling Stones. When the band was invited to perform at a local nursing home, Grohl was to experience for the first time the adrenalised joy of performing live. One song that stands out in his mind from this show was their version of 'Time Is On My Side', simply because the audience actually danced.

A seed had been planted in Dave Grohl's psyche that would grow with increased rapidity over the following years. At first this newly focussed love of being in a band manifested itself with him having drum lessons at high school. However the first subcultural focus for Grohl's rock 'n' roll aspirations came when he was thirteen. It was the summer of 1982 and his family took their annual holiday to Evanston, Illinois to visit his cousins. In the year since they'd last visited, Grohl's cousin Tracey had undergone an image transformation that would leave Dave speechless. In twelve short months, she had become a fully formed punk rocker.

"I was greeted at the front door by Tracey," he explained in 1995. "But this wasn't the Tracey I had grown to love, this was punk Tracey. Complete with bondage pants, spiked hair, chains, the whole nine yards. It was the most fucking awesome thing I had ever seen."

This unassuming family holiday subsequently made an indelible mark on the fledgling rock icon's view of the world of music. Through Tracey, a door to an entirely new world had been opened. Until then punk rockers had been something that Grohl had only ever seen on television and in the media. They were alien to his hometown, simply not a feature of his life and consequently, as was the case for so many people living through this period, punk rock had taken on an almost virtual image. A scene that existed somewhere else entirely.

Until that was, the day he saw Tracey. With her outlandish looks and feisty passion, punk rock was suddenly wrenched out of the TV screen and crash-landed into the reality of Grohl's life. His previously blinkered eyes began to feast upon the huge network of underground labels, fanzines and bands as slowly he began to relate to the innate sense of alternative culture and history that punk represented.

In addition to this Tracey had amassed a huge record collection from all over the world. During that summer break, Grohl developed a love of the sounds that would remain with him throughout his musical career. Indeed, many of these seminal records in Tracey's collection would later be regularly referenced by Grohl in his own bands.

Perhaps more significantly for an artist who would make his name as an invigorating performer, it was during this time that Grohl took in his first live show. It was at a venue called the Cubby Bear and featured Naked Raygun and R.O.T.A. (two Big Black-affiliated punk bands from Chicago). The gritty, in-your-face rawness of this low budget gig filled the gig virgin Grohl with intense wonderment. He felt an immediate affinity with the surrounding vibe and any thoughts of continuing with covers bands and playing live in nursing homes left his mind. His ambitions instantly converted to a punk-rock-only currency. However, at this stage he didn't even have a band.

By the time Grohl had discovered punk rock, the subculture was already eight years old. US bands like The Ramones had delivered the paradigm of the three chord, high speed attack as far back as 1975, while the UK had developed the style via a group of art students and their friends a year later, reaching its zenith with the Sex Pistols (but therein lies another tale!).

In 1983, however the punk dream was all but dead in the notoriously fickle UK. New Romantics, techno pop and the hip hop/electro movement had dominated the limelight since the turn of the decade, although the post-punk alternative rock scene proudly continued the DIY ethic. Punk's angry dream was still encompassed by political activist groups like Crass, but generally the punk scene was by this time largely derided as a stagnant movement fuelled by cheap strong cider and bereft of its original fire.

By contrast, the US had continued to develop its own unique scene, spawned by a myriad of underground fanzines and disseminated by people with a fervent energy. Where early US punk inspirations like The Ramones, Patti Smith and Television had delivered respectively the high speed rush, the unorthodox poetry and the edgy dissonance that would herald the arrival of punk rock, it was with bands like The Cramps, Black Flag and Dead Kennedys that the US truly started to reclaim the punk crown from the UK.

Grohl had started travelling further afield to root out his favourite punk bands. Luckily, Washington DC was within easy reach of his hometown and he quickly hooked into that city's burgeoning scene.

Washington DC had been one of the earliest US cities to develop its own distinct style – indeed, it had already been noted as early as 1979 by figures like Dead Kennedys' Jello Biafra as being far more extreme in its approach to punk than other cities.

One of the most influential DC bands was Bad Brains, a group of Rastas who combined The Clash's political fury with hard and heavy rock songs, laced with a strong reggae vibe. Bad Brains emerged from the ashes of jazz funk outfit Mind Power in 1977.

Inspired by the Sex Pistols' *Never Mind The Bollocks* album and The Clash's early experiments with punk and reggae the four piece became an almost immediate success within the DC punk rock fraternity, essentially delivering a blueprint for the fast and tight sound known as hardcore that was to follow.

Having read about The Clash's intention to play free gigs on estates in the UK, Bad Brains started to arrange impromptu gigs in Washington's poorer neighbourhoods. Their actions brought fans from all walks, but also attracted intense interest from the police who even started a surveillance operation on their house.

When the police saw one of the band shooting rats with a small air pistol, they used it as their excuse to storm the building. All they found was that air pistol and a lone marijuana plant in the living room! Disgusted by the police's actions, Bad Brains decided to relocate to New York where they would have an equally huge impact on bands such as the Beastie Boys and also the nascent Big Apple hardcore scene.

Prior to leaving DC however, Bad Brains recorded a demo at Don Zientara's home-based studio, Inner Ear in Arlington, Virginia (Zientara would go on to engineer and/or produce most of the early records on Dischord). These demos eventually saw the light of day in 1996 as the *Black Dots* album on Caroline Records. In 1981 they delivered an album for the legendary ROIR cassette series, which showed both the band's intensity and also their newfound Rastafarian faith. 1983's *Rock For Light* showed the band introducing a greater reggae influence, while the following years *I Against I* has become regarded as one of the defining moments of US hardcore, thanks to its super-tight, high speed arrangements and eclectic approach to sound.

Although Bad Brains would never again reach the same level of blistering intensity (their last for Caroline, *Quickness* was nearing mainstream rock, while major label albums for Epic and Maverick saw them delivering blanded-out versions of punk and reggae), their influence on the international punk and hardcore scene cannot be over-stated. Certainly their initial three years of intense gigging in Washington DC had a huge and lasting effect on the area's growing mass of young punks.

Subsequently, Washington DC quickly marked itself out as a punk capital, albeit not through the radical politics of Bad Brains, but through the emergence of a highly motivated so-called 'teen-punk' scene. These punks, too young to go to the club venues, had taken a stance that was in direct opposition to the older generation of punk rockers, many of whom were derided for their neo-hippy, drug-taking lifestyles. These teen-punks were staunchly united in their anti-drug stance.

With this teen punk scene - marked out by an 'X' written in marker pens on their hands and uniformly shaven heads - there was a near-rejection of the values upheld by the punk originals. Furthermore, these DC teenagers would stand their ground through any means necessary – which invariably meant violence at the gigs.

At the forefront of this scene was The Teen Idles who counted among their numbers one Ian MacKaye, a hyperactive skate kid who respected rock legend Ted Nugent for his total rejection of drugs. He quickly recognised a similarly contrary stance in punk and increasingly adopted the musical ideologies of bands like the Sex Pistols.

The Teen Idles split when MacKaye decided he wanted to be the main songwriter - however their posthumously released eponymous single did mark the beginning of the famous Dischord label, which became a ground zero for hardcore fans. MacKaye immediately returned to the limelight as vocalist in the seminal hardcore act Minor Threat - so called because they were all below twenty-one years of age and because their threat to the status quo was considered negligible.

The teen punk scene did represent a threat to the punk hegemony however. Their ethos was more on the edge, more confrontational more... harDCore - as the DC teens punks started to spell the word. By 1980, the violence that surrounded the Washington DC harDCore scene had begun to overshadow the music itself. However, in bands like Minor Threat, there was something quite unique and different from the punk that was being created elsewhere. Sure there was a heavy influence from the UK scene, especially The Clash's debut album, but they were delivering their sound at breakneck speed, with clear and precise dynamics.

With the arrival of the debut eponymous Minor Threat EP, the third release on Dischord, there also came an ideology which marked out the DC teens. The eight track EP included the cut 'Straight Edge' which, although not intended to provide a philosophy for the scene, succeeded in doing exactly that. Straight Edge thus became signified by the 'X' mark (as previously used to identify the teen punk scene and used on every Dischord release to date) and represented an ideology that embraced anti-drugs and anti-alcohol beliefs, even the abstinence from underage sex. The DC teen punks were flying directly in the face of the easy liberalism of the 1960s' hippy generation.

Ironically, however, the Straight Edge harDCore scene didn't regard itself as political. Lyrically the songs of Minor Threat *et al* were far more about personal beliefs and observations. Inevitably, this meant that their fury was vented in the direction of small targets. Thus the older generation of punks would get it in the neck, as too would the venues that didn't admit underage punks. On the surface then, this hardly appeared to be an establishment-scaring manifesto, but it was a stance that became crucially important to this increasingly élitist group of teens.

The Straight Edge philosophy found its way into MacKaye's lyrics for Minor Threat's second and final EP in 1983 - *In My Eyes* - specifically on the title track 'Out Of Step' which found the vocalist proclaiming "Don't smoke/Don't drink/Don't fuck/At least I can fucking think". It was a totalitarian philosophy that by this time had unfortunately found favour with right-wing skinheads. Straight Edge was turning into a major threat.

Following Minor Threat's split, MacKaye ventured to England to roadie for Black Flag (in support of clueless punk band Chelsea and proto-Oi! band Exploited). Here he met Crass and was introduced to a much wider political viewpoint. During this period he was able to redress many of his earlier beliefs, but remained nonetheless extreme in his standpoint.

By late1983 then, when David Grohl first started to venture to Washington DC, there was a vibrant scene that was gaining an international reputation. MacKaye and friends had continued with their Dischord label putting out the definitive harDCore compilation *Flex Your Head* in 1982 as well as later records in 1983 by bands including Scream, SOA, Faith, Void and Marginal Man. Minor Threat's *Out of Step* EP also heralded the start of a partnership with John Lober of Southern Studios in London (who had also put out the Crass records).

In the summer of 1984, Dave Grohl trekked to DC to see a show by local harDCore band Void. At this show he met fellow teenage punk Brian Samuels. Grohl's new-found friend, it turned out, was in a band called Freak Baby and they were on the lookout for a guitarist. Grohl jumped at the opportunity and an audition was hastily set up.

Freak Baby consisted of Samuels on bass, David Smith on drums, Bryant Mason on guitar and Chris Page on vocals. The gaggle of young punks was impressed by Grohl's six string abilities and invited him to join as second guitarist. The wheels of Grohl's punk rock career were thus set in motion and in the six months that followed, Freak Baby played a number of gigs at a local high school and even gained a following of about six skinheads. A start of sorts had been made, although it is a fact that such allegiances were hardly unusual at a time when the harDCore scene was becoming over-run by skinheads who'd latched onto the Straight Edge scene's ideology.

Freak Baby then recorded a demo in local studio The Laundry Room, home of engineer and producer Barrett Jones, who would go on to be a regular feature in Grohl's recording life. Jones's set-up was located in Arlington, Virginia, and so-called because the studio had originally been in the washing room of Jones's parents' house.

The Freak Baby demo represented another turning point in Grohl's life. Far from the cassette recordings of old, this was a fully-fledged four-track studio and in Jones he had discovered a musical compatriot whose own multi-instrumentalist approach to the DIY punk rock ethic would continually inspire Grohl to write and record his own songs.

Of the Freak Baby tracks recorded, one stood out. It was called 'Different' and it displayed the band's rough-around-the-edges approach to punk. Stuffed to the gills with adolescent anger, but somewhat lacking in the precise power of punk at its best. However, despite its obvious energy, when placed in context against the big punk bands of the time, Freak Baby seemed only one small step away from being that covers band in Grohl's past. Their sound was too loose, especially in the rhythm department, so the power was dissipated through inability. Furthermore, the band's sound was mostly a transparent pastiche of their heroes. Nonetheless, local record store Smash was impressed enough by the demo to stock it and even sold a couple of copies!

Freak Baby remained with this line up for only six months until, one day after a rehearsal Grohl sat behind the drum kit and started bashing out a rhythm. As mentioned, Grohl had started drum lessons at Fairfax County High School, but he didn't possess his own kit. Instead he would practice by employing a pair of enormous marching band drumsticks to hit out rhythms on everything within sight in his room while the radio blasted. It was during this time of hitting pillows hard enough to hear a beat that he learned to strike the drums with the intensity he is renowned for today.

With Grohl finally ensconced behind the kit, hitting the drums like a man possessed, usual drummer David Smith took the opportunity to pick up Samuels' bass - Samuels had already gone home. The bass guitar was, it turned out, Smith's favoured instrument. The only reason he had taken up drums in the band was because he owned a kit and, as was obvious on the band's demo, his drumming abilities were limited.

When Grohl and Smith started jamming together they immediately produced a supertight, powerhouse sound. Bryant Mason picked up his guitar and started playing along and Chris Page took up the mic. It was immediately obvious that this was a vastly improved version of Freak Baby.

Rather than continue under the same name however they split up and reconvened without Brian Samuel but with a new moniker – Mission Impossible. "That new band was a super-fast hardcore delight," explained Grohl ten years later. "A chance to try out all the tricks I had learned from my growing record collection, on a real drum set even! I hadn't the slightest idea how to set the fucking thing up, but I sure loved beating the shit out of it... we actually wrote songs that had little breaks in them so we could jump just like the pictures we'd seen in (the magazines) *Maximumrocknroll* and *Flipside*. It was 1985 and I was living my hardcore dream."

Mission Impossible set about playing shows in an ever-widening circle of venues –including one show opening for the legendary Washington Go-Go act Troublefunk at a high school prom (Washington Go-Go was a dance sound which linked 1980s tech-funk and late 1980s house) - before going back to The Laundry Room studios to record some new material and a few vastly improved Freak Baby tracks. Among these was a vastly superior take on 'Different', on which the rhythm section tightened to a singular, pounding unit, pushing the song with a hitherto unseen power.

"I saw Dave when he was in Mission Impossible," explained Dante Ferrando to Eric Brace of *unomas.com*. Ferrando, part-owner of the Black Cat nightclub (of which Grohl is also a partner) and past drummer in such Washington area punk bands as Iron Cross and Grey Matter, was clearly impressed by his friend's ability as a teenager. "He was pretty young, and the stuff he was playing was simple but he did it with so much power and precision." He continued, "I remember someone telling me he'd only been playing live about eight months and could I believe it? I was envious because I'd been playing for years and couldn't play like that." [3]

Soon after they recorded their demo, Mission Impossible developed an association with Washington DC hardcore band Lunchmeat (later to become known as Soulside – one of the more interesting bands to emerge from the Washington DC scene). Over the course of the next few months, the two bands would play gigs together in front of a growing fan base.

1985 had seen a wave of new harDCore bands which had taken over from the original acts including Rites of Spring, Kingface, Beefeater, Fire Party, Dag Nasty, Embrace (Ian Mackaye's first post-Minor Threat band), and, of course, Lunchmeat and Mission Impossible. Impressively, Ian Mackaye publicly declared his love for Grohl's band and their gigging partners.

"Lunchmeat and Mission Impossible were totally inspiring to see, high school kids playing again," he continued. "Their whole scene was similar to how ours was in early Minor Threat and Teen Idles days." [4]

MacKaye's faith in both Mission Impossible and Lunchmeat was eventually realised when a split single between the two bands was released. Although it appeared on the band's own Sammich label (which was started by Amanda MacKaye and Eli Janney), it received huge help and support from Dischord records. Two earlier releases from Mission Impossible had appeared in the shape of 'Helpless' and 'I Can Only Try' on the WGNS/*Metrozine* compilation *Alive And Kicking*. Together the releases displayed Mission Impossible's brand of super fast hardcore. However, their combination of jazz-fuelled guitar and Grohl's often-intricate patterns saw them stand out from many of the other bands on the DC scene at the time.

Although many of the bands of the era were involved in political benefits, Mission Impossible were far less active than most. This led to suggestions that they were apolitical at a time when it was deemed vitally important to show your colours. Yet for Mission Impossible, punk and harDCore was more about playing the music and walking the walk, rather than talking up political activism.

Yet, only a year after the foursome had first formed, Mission Impossible played their last show in the summer of 1985 at Fort Reno Park in Washington. Two members of the band – Bryant and Chris – had opted to go to college and were thus forced to quit life in the punk rock fast lane. It was an act that was mirrored throughout the relatively youthful hardcore scene as many bands split in favour of the education system.

1985, the year of Mission Impossible, was also notable in DC history for being a time when the political side of the harDCore scene found a fresh direction. One of the more energetic forces was Amy Pickering, who had coined the term 'Revolution Summer', to capture the spirit that she set about distributing via hastily photocopied Situationist slogans (a tack used to great effect some years later by the Manic Street Preachers).

With many people now rejecting the narrow, and some would say misogynistic Straight Edge philosophy, the DC scene also found a unified and increasingly loud voice through a political activist group called Positive Force DC, a collective that would become increasingly important to Grohl in his future dealings with DC bands.

Around the same time as Mission Impossible disbanded, another local Springfield band of some repute had also split up. They were called A.O.C. and they drew their sound from a much artier area of the punk rock lexicon. Their axis spun around the intricate but abrasive structures of bands like Television and the post-punk funk sounds of Gang of Four. Central to A.O.C. was an extraordinary bassist called Rueben Radding. Grohl invited him to jam with the remaining former Mission duo of himself and Dave Smith in his living room.

The combination of the two Daves' hardcore energy and Radding's inventive bass explorations immediately gelled and the trio wrote four songs in that very first jam, with Radding improvising the vocals. The questionably-monikered Dain Bramage was thus born.

"We started writing song after song at an alarming pace," stated Grohl. "Playing shows around town, whenever we could get them, usually to the hardcore kids' dismay. This band was where I really started to utilise my growing interest in songwriting: arrangement, dynamics, different tunings, etc. We were extremely experimental, usually experimenting with classic rock clichés in a noisy, punk rock kind of way."

Dain Bramage played their first gig in December 1985 at Burke Community Centre in Virginia. As Grohl explained, it was to the dismay of the hardcore crowd that the ex-Mission Impossible/Fast duo had gone in such an arty, experimental direction. However, despite the negative response of much of the crowd, the band did impress a few of the more eclectically-minded punks, after which Dain Bramage slowly built up some fanatical support.

Somewhat inevitably the band enlisted the support of the aforementioned producer Barrett Jones, vanishing into his Laundry Room Studios to capture a couple of demos in 1986. These demos found their way into the hands of A.O.C. drummer Reed Mullin who passed on the good word about Dain Bramage to Los Angeles independent label Fartblossom Records. This fantastically-named label agreed with Mullin's positivity and signed the band to record an album. Between July 20-24, 1986, the trio entered the twenty -four track RK-1 Recording Studios in Crofton, near Annapolis. The resulting album *I Scream Not Coming Down* was, according to Grohl, "a fine demonstration of our blend of rock, art punk, and hardcore. I still like it."

Thankfully, the songs contained on that album were a tad less contrived than the title itself. Grohl's ability to create simple but powerful patterns with dynamic yet understated fills came to the fore. However, the band relied more heavily on the interplay between guitar and bass. While such a dissonant approach may have worked for bands like Husker Du (whom they most often echoed), Dain Bramage were unable to combine the urgency of hardcore and the elasticity of jazz with quite such aplomb. In March 1987,

Dain Bramage was to call it a day less than a year after the release of *I Scream Not Coming Down.*

Despite Dain Bramage's growing audiences and critical acclaim, Grohl became tempted to change allegiances to Virginia hardcore band Scream. Grohl was still only seventeen when he saw a flyer of theirs hanging on a music store wall which he was immediately moved to act upon.

"Scream's first two records were among my all-time favourites, so this little flyer was more than just that. Originally, I'd just wanted to call (Scream guitarist) Franz, jam with them once or twice, then be able to tell my friends, 'I got to play with Scream!' So I called Franz a few times and finally got an answer. I explained that I was a huge fan, told him which bands I'd played in, and that I'd love to give it a shot… He never called back." [5]

A few months went by and Dave called Franz again, this time convincing him to schedule a proper audition. "After a few more practices, it was apparent they were serious about me joining." He continued, "This was something that never entered my mind, the possibility of actually joining Scream. I had to really weigh the options: 1) Leave my two greatest friends in the dust and travel the world with one of my favourite bands ever. Or 2) to stick with Dain Bramage and hope it all works out." [6]

Grohl initially decided to turn down the drummer's position in the band, despite his huge respect for Scream, largely due to a stronger allegiance to his friends in Dain Bramage. However, this all changed when he saw Scream play live again.

"I called Franz and told him 'no'. I explained my situation and apologised. I think he understood and invited me to their next show a few weeks later. It was one of the greatest Scream shows I'd ever seen. I changed my mind." [7]

Another reason for his decision to join Scream was that Dain Bramage's album tour had fallen through, so he felt he had less of a reason to stay. Eventually, Dave Grohl departed the Dain Bramage drum stool without any real warning to his friends. The Scream rehearsals had, they thought, been just for fun. Shocked by the decision, but nonetheless understanding, the remaining duo of Smith and Radding tried to form a new band. Their problem was, however, a simple one. Grohl was too hard to replace.

"After you've spent a couple years with Dave Grohl as your drummer it's easy to feel like no other drummer exists," stated Radding on the Dain Bramage fan site[8]. Radding started jamming with another band that included Samhain drummer, London May. Considered as a possible Grohl replacement, Radding, and Smith invited May to join them to record demos of Radding's new songs. They were never released and May moved to Los Angeles.

In late 1987, Smith moved to New York where he joined the bands Fun House and Carey's Problem, the latter of whom released one eponymous album. In 1991 he moved west to Eugene, to study environmental science at Oregon University. On completing his degree, Smith remained in Eugene and joined the ranks of an improvisational group of musicians called Sunday Brunch Breakdown. SBB became a regular at parties in their hometown but eventually came to an end when the various members moved on. Smith subsequently moved to Seattle, Washington, where he plays bass for numerous bands.

Raddan followed Smith to New York a year later in 1988. Here he developed a name for himself as a bass player of great creative versatility. Radding quickly immersed himself in the 'Downtown' music community. He performed in groups led by jazz and leftfield avant garde luminaries such as Elliott Sharp, Roy Campbell Jr., John Zorn and Marc Ribot, the latter of whom he toured Europe with as a member of Shrek. He also took the lead role in the Sun Ra repertory band Myth Science, that released a CD, *Love In Outer Space* on the legendary Knitting Factory Works label.

Radding relocated to Seattle in 1997, where he performed with an equally impressive array of avant garde jazz musicians. He returned to New York in 2002. Radding is a highly respected and in demand bassist whose own achievements have placed him on the international stage. He has featured on over thirty recordings, and has appeared at many major Festivals. Grohl, Smith and Radding

remain friends and still talk about a reunion of some kind.
Time permitting!

When Grohl first approached Scream, he lied about his age, telling
them he was twenty years old, rather than seventeen. He had
recently been expelled from High School thanks to his
all-embracing love of punk and the hardcore scene which perhaps
inevitably had been somewhat detrimental to his studies. He was,
he said in 1992, "so stoned that I had no idea what I was studying."

During those first rehearsals with Scream he found himself living
out a fantasy as he pounded at his kit along to a band he'd loved for
years, playing songs that had changed his life. Any thoughts of
continuing at school were filed away for good.

Rather than disown their son for dropping out, Grohl's parents
were actually very proud of him. "Yeah, (they were proud) 'cos
I was always a great drummer!" he said in *Metal Hammer* in August
2003). "And she (his mother) didn't even have to buy me a drum
kit. Both my parents were proud. They might not have put my
records on at night with a glass of Chardonnay, but they thought it
was a constructive application. And I'm forever indebted to both
of them." [9]

For Grohl, the decision to join Scream was more than just
a fantasy fulfilled. It also provided him with a direct route to the
core of the harDCore heartland. Until now, his band's had either
been adoring onlookers or interesting side attractions; with Scream
he was smack in the full glare of the hardcore spotlight. Yet it
wasn't this limelight that attracted Grohl – it was a music fan's
passion and a scorching desire to play in that actual band,
something which would resurface years later when he took to the
drums for rock band Queens of the Stone Age and later his
childhood heroes, Killing Joke.

"Seeing as how Scream records were among those I used to play
drums to on my bed when I was first learning, I knew all their
songs by heart," he stated in 1995. "I even had an advance copy of
their latest demo. So when Franz looked at me and asked, 'What do

you want to play? Some Sabbath? Or some Zep?' I said, 'Nah. Let's play...' and rattled off the names of all their songs. The next two hours were heaven for me, to be able to play Scream songs with the real deal."

Why was Grohl so hypnotised by the prospect of joining Scream? Well, their pre-Grohl history is both influential and fascinating. Scream had formed in 1981 with the line up of brothers Peter and Frantz Stahl on vocals and guitar respectively. Skeeter Thompson took on bass duties while Kent Staxx played drums. Hailing from the musical wasteland of Alexandria, Virginia, they quickly set their sights on playing further afield. In 1982, despite having no record deal, they set off on their own self-financed tour of the US. Their main aim was to be accepted into the Washington harDCore scene, an important step for any serious hardcore punk act. Quite simply DC was, as Frantz Stahl put it in an interview in the December 1982 edition of punk bible *Flipside*, "the big headquarters."

Initially, however, they found few friends among the DC hardcore elite. The scene was extremely small and largely revolved around the workings of Dischord. Scream's first gig in Washington was at the city's HB Woodlawn venue but unfortunately the crowd almost universally rejected the band's combination of hardcore guitars and Bad Brains–style reggae vibe. It didn't help that they did not look the part. They didn't spike their hair, they wore tennis shoes rather than boots. The punk rock fashionistas took immediate note and struck Scream's name from their little black books. In a 1982 interview with the *Touch And Go* fanzine, Skeeter and Pete gave their version of events.

"It took us a while to sort of get into the scene," explained Skeeter. "The first time people heard us they weren't sure what we were trying to do. We played the first Wilson Centre show (legendary regular shows that featured all of the hardcore and punk big guns of the time)" continued Pete, "...and the crowd naturally rejected us because we were outsiders."

When asked if the problem was that the band weren't cool enough for the DC scenesters, both Pete and Skeeter were unified in their brutally honest reply: no, it was because they simply weren't good enough. "I think we were good but we were pretty lackadaisical and Pete would be the only person really into it… I was pretty nervous if there was more than fifty people, because we were used to playing parties," recalled Skeeter. [10]

The Wilson Centre shows were integral to the creation of the early DC harDCore scene. Located in an area renowned for its high refugee population, the Wilson Centre housed a free clinic, social service facilities and an employment office. It rented out its basement venue in order to raise funds. HR, frontman with Bad Brains had long been on the lookout for a non-profit making venue at which to put punk shows on. The Wilson Centre was perfect – not only ideologically, but also architecturally. The first gig included a staggering array of bands including Bad Brains, Minor Threat, Black Market Baby, GI, SOA, Red C, Law and Order, Broken Cross, Mod Subbs, Prophecy, Scream and Void.

It was at a May gig at The Woodlawn High School, an alternative public school in Arlington, that the elitism of the DC scene became most apparent. Playing with DOA, Minor Threat, SOA and Youth Brigade, Scream was met with far more than just apathy from the audience. Most of them simply walked out, much to the dismay of Jello Biafra who had been performing with DOA. He immediately offered the band support and advice, encouraging them to stick to what they believed in.

Talking to US fanzine *Thrill Seeker2* in late 1982, Skeeter Thompson outlined how Biafra had encouraged them. "Yeah, (Biafra) is great, we've always been on sort of the same frequency. He was the only person who encouraged us. Because right after that (Woodlawn) show, I didn't want to play in front of any more DC crowds, because of the way they treated us. We go out there and we're being serious – I don't mean totally serious politically, I mean about our music, something that moves us – and they treat it like a joke." [11]

With Biafra on side, it wasn't long before Ian MacKaye also started to take notice of the hardcore newcomers. Despite initial reticence, he became more and more excited by the band's uncompromising style – ultimately he signed the band to his Dischord label and teamed up with Don Zientara to produce their debut album *Still Screaming*.

The resulting twenty song set was recorded in three days during October 1982. The album amply displayed the band's willingness to adopt diverse sounds while Pete Stahl's vocals employed melodies that separated the band from the more macho elements of the punk and hardcore scene. Melody was central to their songs, even at their most raucous. The album's production duo also gave the tracks an added fuzzy sheen, providing them with a punkier sound than they had shown in the live setting.

Lyrically too, the band stood out from the popular view of the East Coast hardcore set of the time. Quite simply they didn't obsess on straight edge philosophies and teen punk ideology. They were far more interested in the personal politics of a far wider worldview. This did not prove to be an altogether popular slant. Hardcore fanzine *Capitol Punishment* declared Scream to be "a bunch of jocks trying to be punk". Other fanzine writers were especially disappointed with the band's lack of an obvious political agenda. Of course Scream weren't alone in this, but they were singled out.

"People think that just because we're from DC that we're straight-edged and they think that we have to bring it up so we'll talk about it," the band explained to *Flipside* in December 1982. "A lot of people think it's a movement in DC and it's not. Some kids are into drinking and drugs and some aren't, that's all. Too many people make too much of a big deal about Straight Edge." [12]

Over the course of the next two years, Scream pushed their sound to ever wider extremes, exploring reggae as much as heavy metal. *This Side Up*, the band's self-financed second album, was recorded in two sessions during March and July 1984 and released in 1985.

In an attempt to push the band's diversity to its logical extreme, they opted to employ the different sessions as showcases for the seemingly duelling styles which sat at the heart of their hardcore attack: heavy metal and reggae,.

The two sessions were thus spilt in half over each side of the vinyl. The A-Side was produced with Dr Know of Bad Brains. The B-side found Scream employing the services of heavy metal guitar player Robert Lee "Harley" Davidson, from a local covers band, who gave this session a stronger, more beefed up rock sound.

While the Straight Edge obsessives in DC grew increasingly disenchanted with Scream's broader styles and influences, this approach succeeded in winning Grohl's latest band a growing national fan base as well as not inconsiderable support abroad. By the time of their third album, Scream became only the second hardcore band after Bad Brains to take their show to Europe, playing among other places the Bojangles Club in Nottingham, England. This East Midlands city was an important centre for the flourishing British hardcore scene thanks to acts like Heresy, and later Kings of Oblivion, Force Fed and Killing Floor.

What Scream discovered in Europe was a highly politicised scene with many of their gigs taking place in the punk squats of Holland and Germany. It was an experience that was to stoke a political fire in their bellies. Ironically, in light of their previous localised criticism for being apolitical, they would return to DC with a passionate sense of purpose that far outstripped many of their counterparts.

The band became far more politically involved, particularly with left-wing politics. However, their approach was far more humanistic than the dogmatic stance of many of their contemporaries – among the many blistering shows they played upon their return was a set for the 'Concert For a Free Chile'.

The dawn of 1985 found Scream booked to play with Black Market Baby and Reagan Youth at Georgetown's Key Theatre. The gig was being staged without the owner's knowledge or consent and ended in extreme violence. Although rumours of a dead fan proved to be unfounded, at least one person was stabbed and many were injured.

Violence of this kind was now a permanent feature at harDCore gigs and as a result many venues had closed their doors to the scene. When a show at the popular DC venue Woldon Centre ended in a similar level of violence, it closed its doors for good. It was clear that something had to be done or the DC scene would just implode.

Among the DC cognoscenti there were a number of people who wanted to shift the scene's focus away from clannish braggadocio and towards a wider political fight. One of these bands, Positive Force, urged people to instead use their energy to point out wrongs in US congress.

Positive Force vocalist Guy Picciotto announced a Punk Percussion Protest at the South African Embassy to be held in June, 1985. Inspired by an ongoing demonstration at this embassy and anti-capitalism events staged by Crass in the UK, several punks turned up at the Embassy and pounded drums, tin cans, anything that would make a sound. Thereafter, the so-called 'Punk Percussion Protest' became a regular activity for Positive Force over the coming years. Indeed during the 1990 Iraq war, a twenty-four-hour anti-war drum vigil outside The Whitehouse caused the then-President Bush to complain to the press, "those damned drums are keeping me up all night."

Scream's third album for Dischord, was suitably titled *Banging The Drum*, in honour of Positive Force's percussive protests. This even more diverse album was part recorded in the UK in the summer of 1996 by Southern Studios' John Loder. However it didn't get a release until the following year. With sounds ranging from full-blown punk rock to near-blues interludes, from reggae passages to percussive onslaughts, it found Scream developing a musical affinity with bands like Soulside, Beefeater (and much later Fidelity Jones), who embraced an eclectic approach to hardcore. Scream maintained that this musical fusion was a sonic manifestation of their political beliefs.

Throughout this period Scream became the chosen band for all

Positive Force benefits (taking over from previous favourites Beefeater). They also became increasingly involved in gigs for Amnesty International. That said, the main focus of Scream was still their live show and they also continued to tour with unbridled enthusiasm. In *Flipside*'s spring 1986 issue, they described themselves as road warriors whose need for each other was, according to Skeeter, "an obsession, almost like a drug. It's more like a habit." [13]

However, after a lengthy 1987 European tour with Fire Party in support, the Scream habit finally proved too much for founder member and drummer Kent Staxx. He quit the band to return home to his wife and child. He would become a carpenter based in northern Virginia and would also drum for the reformed Iron Cross.

For the first time since their inception some six years ago, the original line-up of Scream had been broken up. They decided to keep going, and made tentative steps towards finding a replacement. These included putting drummer wanted flyers in music stores around DC...

Enter Dave Grohl. He played his first gig with Scream at an Amnesty International benefit. Scream's set ended with part of the audience marching on the embassies of various countries known for human rights violations. It was, if nothing else, a powerful introduction into the world of Scream.

From here, Grohl became a part of the band with surprising ease. The endless touring provided them with the chance to bond and the opportunity for Pete Stahl to take on a fatherly role over the teenage Grohl.

"When Pete found out my real age and that he was ten years older than me, he became my father figure," explained Grohl to *unamass.com*. "We'd be on the road for months in a van, and he'd be teaching me how to behave on the road, how to survive without burning out, how to have fun, when to be serious. And he'd protect me from Skeeter!" [14]

Skeeter would openly tease the young Grohl, subjecting him to daily taunts and forcing Grohl to inhale the stench of his 'Road Warrior' feet. All a part of being in a family for sure, but Stahl made sure that Skeeter's antics didn't turn Grohl into an outsider.

Scream's first Grohl-related release came in the shape of 1988's *No More Censorship*. The album was released on Washington-based RAS (Real Authentic Sounds) Records, a label known for reggae but with ambitions to break into the rock market.

Grohl's inclusion on *No More Censorship* was instantly notable. The band's drum sound was suddenly much bigger and more direct while his trademark subtle fills came into their own. Also notable was the presence of his voice on backing vocals.

Despite gaining critical acclaim the album was in fact a huge disappointment to many Scream fans who felt the rock side was too traditional, claiming all of the band's hardcore allegiances were being stripped out. The record was a commercial failure and the band was forced to continue on their endless road trip to promote themselves.

"My first trip to Europe was amazing. In February of 1988, we flew into Amsterdam and spent the next two months playing in the Netherlands, France, Germany, Italy, Scandinavia, England and Spain. Most shows were in squats (buildings taken over by punks at war with the system, fighting the police for their right to a place to live) and youth centres, very few were in bars or night-clubs. It was awesome. Most shows were actually pretty crowded since Scream was one of the few American hardcore bands to visit Europe previously."

Scream toured the US five times and Europe three times during this period. However, their sound was never quite straightforward enough for the increasingly narrow palate of the international hardcore fraternity.

"We were a punk rock band who also played hard rock. Franz was playing all this great metal guitar stuff which would then go into these really fucking fast hardcore punk riffs. You know, people were like... they just couldn't figure it out," explained Grohl during an early Foo Fighters interview. "They had enough rabid fans to sell a few thousand records every year and stay steadily out on the road," he explained further to Eric Brace of *unomas.com*. "(A couple of major record labels) came sniffing around, but nothing ever happened." [(15)]

In 1989, Scream captured their frenzied live show for the first time on the album *Live At Van hall In Amsterdam* on Konkurrel Records. They also went into the studio in December of that year to record what was to be their final album, *Fumble*. The set failed to see the light of day until July 1993 when it was released to coincide with the Scream reunion tour, featuring Grohl back behind the kit, by then an international success as a part of Nirvana.

Fumble was a particularly interesting moment in the Grohl story, as it also displayed the beginnings of his songwriting ambitions. Furthermore, he also adopted a recording technique to work on his own stuff that would resurface in the early days of Foo Fighters – multi-tracking himself playing every instrument. Grohl had discovered the technique one day when he visited Barrett Jones in his Laundry Room Studios.

"In between Scream tours, I was hanging out with Barrett more and more, helping him out with his solo project in the studio. Since he had his own eight track in the basement, we would jam on his songs and record them pretty quickly. I sometimes played bass or guitar on some songs. That summer I realised that if I were to write a song, record the drums first, then come back over it with a few guitars, bass, and vocals, I could make it sound like a band. So I came up with a few riffs on the spot and recorded three songs in under fifteen minutes. Mind you, these were no epic masterpieces, just a test to see if I could do this sort of thing on my own. It was the beginning of a beautiful relationship."

No epic masterpiece perhaps, but Grohl's first effort turned out to be a highlight on Scream's final album *Fumble*. Called 'Gods Look Down', the Grohl demo displayed both the musician's power and a sense of vulnerability. It was this balance that would mark out his earliest demo recordings. Indeed, Jones himself is adamant that

Grohl's version of 'Gods Look Down' was far superior to the Scream version. "I knew Dave could play from working with him before," Jones told *unomas.com* from his studio in Seattle, "but that first song he did by himself was incredible, and is still one of my favourite things he's ever done. He walked in and started laying down tracks, and he was just so damn good at it from the very start that it drove me nuts." [16]

Despite having no label to release *Fumble*, Scream's popularity in Europe sustained them for another tour through the spring of 1990. It was, as Grohl has described it, "a real ballbuster, twenty three shows in twenty four days." So demanding was the schedule that bassist Skeeter Thompson quit three-quarters of the way through. His replacement came in the shape of J. Robbins of Jawbox. Thomson had suffered some personal problems but managed to sort himself out long enough to return to Scream after the European jaunt drew to an end.

Skeeter's mid-tour departure didn't stop the band from recording yet another live album as a part of the German *Your Choice Live* series. Recorded live at Oberhaus, Alzey, Germany on May 4, 1990, the album again captured the band at their live best with a set drawn from each period of Scream's existence.

Skeeter Thompson decided to return to the band when they got back to the States, but the homecoming was marred by the discovery of an eviction notice in Peter Stahl and Skeeter's mailbox. The notice demanded they vacate the premises the very next day. Faced with impending homelessness, they decided on the only logical course of action – they went out on the road again!

They hastily booked what was to be Scream's final tour. It was the summer of 1990 and the band found itself increasingly out of favour with the US punk scene. The dates were plagued with low attendances and cancellations. Then, halfway through the tour while they were in LA, Skeeter upped and walked again.

Word soon started to get back to harDCore headquarters of Scream's impending demise. With no thoughts to the adage 'flogging a dead horse', the remaining members vowed to search for a new bassist and carry on. Suddenly Scream and their roadie were stranded in LA with no money to get home and no way of playing live to earn any more cash.

"This was in September of 1990 and we were there for a month, staying with Sabrina - Pete and Franz's sister - who lived out there," recalled Grohl in 1997. "Our roadie, Barry, was from Canada, and he was getting these social welfare checks mailed to him in LA, so we lived off of that."

Scream's Pete Stahl also recalled this as a dark time in the band's life. Talking to Eric Brace of *unomas.com*, he explained: "Man, that was a really depressing time. We were all so broke, just sitting on my sister's couch, all of us wondering if that was it." [17]

For Dave Grohl, of course, it wasn't. In Seattle, a band called Nirvana had a debut album to promote but no drummer. A twist of fate had opened up an opportunity for Grohl that would eventually cement his place in rock history forever.

2

MTV MELTDOWN:
SELLING PUNK TO THE MASSES

ANOTHER DRUMMER JOKE
What's the final thing a drummer says before being kicked out of a band?
"Hey you guys, I've got a few songs we could try."

In 1986, just as the DC harDCore explosion was finding a truly international stage through the Dischord/Southern Studios partnership, the seeds of a band were being sown that would ultimately enjoy global domination and acquire historical cultural significance. That band was Nirvana and the scene they belonged to became known as grunge. Nirvana were themselves huge fans of the DC scene – in fact, they were fans of punk rock from *everywhere*.

The Nirvana story starts in the redneck town of Aberdeen, where a young Kurt Cobain had discovered a taste for punk and hardcore through a friendship with Matt Lukin and Buzz Osborne of local band The Melvins. Cobain and school friend Chris Novoselic would spend their free time hanging around the Melvins rehearsals. Inevitably, they both started to harbour dreams of forming a band.

"(Aberdeen) is a logging town," Cobain said in 1990. "That was all there was to do round there. Chop down trees and work in sawmills. I didn't want that sort of life. I was a real misfit. The place was full of jock, meatheads…" [1]

"We were branded Satanists back home," explained Novoselic a year earlier. "This girl came knocking on the door looking for a wallet and she goes, 'You know what the other kids told me in the neighbourhood? Don't go there, they worship the Devil.' That's why nobody ever bothered us in redneck country. We would neither confirm or deny Satanic affiliations."

"Maybe it was those desecrated cemetery pieces burned in our front yard," added Cobain. "But you don't have to do anything to be considered extreme back there. Just take a lot of acid." [2]

Cobain started recording his own songs as early as 1982. He would drive the short distance to his Aunt Mari Earl's house in Seattle - she was a musician with a number of instruments and recording equipment.

By 1985, Cobain had formed his first band Fecal Matter with the Melvins' drummer Dale Crover, who was to play bass in this latest outfit. Together the duo recorded a demo at Earl's house using a TEAC four-track. The session lasted for a few days with the duo recording the backing tracks at full volume before adding Cobain's vocals. The final tape consisted of seven songs showing early hints at the Nirvana sound, and a lyrical bent which focussed on the personal politics of an angry teenager. Much like his counterparts in DC, Cobain's targets were school, the education system, the attitudes of other kids in school and so on. Interestingly, the tapes included an early instrumental version of 'Downer' which would appear on *Bleach*, Nirvana's first album.

Over the next couple of years, Cobain would play in numerous bands. One such group, Brown Cow (their original name Brown Towel was retired off after being mispelt on a poster) featured Crover on drums and Osborne on bass. He also played in a number of bands with Novoselic: one with Cobain on guitar, Novoselic on bass, and Bob McFadden on drums; another with Novoselic; plus a short stint with the Stiff Woodies, a band which included Osborne, Crover, Lukin and Gary Cole in its line up.

It wasn't until 1987 that Cobain and Novoselic teamed up with the intention of forming a band that would last more than a few gigs. Joining the duo on drums was the first in a long line of drummers, Aaron Burckhard. Together the trio started gigging extensively and even recorded what is considered to be the first Nirvana demo, at KAOS, Olympia's Evergreen State College's radio station.

Nine months later, Cobain and Novoselic entered Seattle's

Reciprocal Recording studio to record a number of songs with engineer Jack Endino (ex-Skin Yard). Their drummer for this session was Dale Crover. Burckhard had been replaced because the duo claimed they were dissatisfied with his performance. Indeed, prior to the recording, in October 1987, they placed an advert in Seattle music paper *The Rocket*. It read: "SERIOUS DRUMMER WANTED. Underground attitude, Black Flag, the Melvins, Zeppelin, Scratch Acid, Ethel Merman. Versatile as heck."

In the next few months, Cobain and Novoselic would go through a series of drummers. Crover had rejoined the Melvins and they had all moved to San Francisco. He was replaced by Dave Foster who played in the newly-named Nirvana's debut gig in Seattle on April 24, 1988, as a part of the Sub Pop Sunday gigs at The Vogue. Foster would be forced to quit the band when he lost his driver's license and they subsequently reinstated Burckhard, but he was later dropped again.

Nirvana once again placed an advert in the next issue of *The Rocket*. This time it read: "DRUMMER WANTED. Play hard, sometimes light, underground, versatile, fast, medium slow, versatile, serious, heavy, versatile, dorky, nirvana, hungry."

Eventually Cobain and Novoselic enlisted the drumming skills of Chad Channing, whom they had first met when Nirvana had shared the bill with Channing's band Tick-Dolly-Row. Nirvana had finally settled on a line-up and could begin its complicated and ultimately tragic path to rock beatification.

Nirvana were unwittingly about to become the core part of a new rock scene evolving in Seattle. While New York and Washington obsessed on the harder, faster and tighter ideology of harDCore, this new and only-loosely associated batch of Seattle bands were using their punk roots to address a far wider sound. To them, 1976 punk rock did not represent Year Zero, or a sound paradigm, simply an attitude and approach through which rock music's history could be redressed.

Thus, these bands would explore the sub-metal riffing of Black

Sabbath, the melodies of Steppenwolf, the dynamics of Creedence Clearwater Revival, even the frailty of Neil Young. To them, the whole of the rock pantheon was up for grabs. It was an approach to the standard song that echoed much of Sonic Youth's experimentation but raged to the same intense volume as Black Flag.

At this stage the mainstream was dominated by bands that had stripped rock of its original anger and replaced it with a sanitised MTV compliance. The new bands coming out of Seattle were far more in tune with rock's original outsider ethos.

Soon, the burgeoning Seattle scene was awash with innovative and exciting bands. One of the originators – Green River – split into two factions, becoming known as Mudhoney and Mother Love Bone (later to be renamed Pearl Jam), each offering a pivotal take on the sounds of Seattle's underground. Mudhoney offered punk's take on 1960s garage rock, through hardcore's distortion. Their debut six track mini-album *Superfuzz Bigmuff* quickly came to be seen as the blueprint for the Seattle sound, thanks to the inspired trash pop of 'Touch Me I'm Sick'.

Other bands emerged with a similarly loud, brash and dirty approach. Swallow produced a rock sound that flirted with the punk pop aesthetic of Buzzcocks; Blood Circus produced minimalist rock that used Motörhead as its inspiration; Tad delivered a sound which was as huge and downright crushing as their main man's actual size - ball-breaking rock straight from The Stooges' back door; Soundgarden drew on the licks of Led Zeppelin; The Walkabouts injected folk-inspired songs with the dissonance of early Pixies; Girl Trouble were the sound of the Cramps after they'd been taken outside and beaten black and blue.

In 1989, *Melody Maker*'s Everett True, the journalist who is generally regarded as the man who discovered Nirvana, produced an article called 'Sub Pop: Rock City' (after the central record label of the scene and a Mudhoney track). In it, he described the Seattle scene as the "most vibrant, kicking music scene encompassed in one city for at least ten years."[3] He used the term 'grunge' on numerous occasions to describe the guitar sound throughout the piece. Grunge. The word stuck and the scene had found its name.

When Nirvana's ten track demo tape landed on the desk of local label Sub Pop, an association was agreed that ensured history in the making had begun. Like Reciprocal Studios, Sub Pop had formed to capture the energy of the nascent Seattle rock scene. Thus, with Channing settled on the drum stool, Nirvana returned to Reciprocal to record their first single for their new label. Once again working with Endino, they recorded a cover of Shocking Blue's 'Love Buzz', alongside their own tracks, 'Big Cheese' and 'Spank Thru', plus a never-released song 'Blandest'.

The debut Nirvana single, 'Love Buzz/Big Cheese' was released in November, 1988, although it didn't receive its first UK review until the following February. The record, which launched the mail-order only 'Sub Pop Singles Club' was limited to a run of only 1,000 copies, all of which were individually numbered.

"Nirvana are beauty incarnate," wrote Everett True in his review of the single. "A relentless two-chord garage beat which lays down some grievous foundations for a sheer monster of a guitar force to howl over. The volume control ain't been built yet which can do justice to this three-piece! ...a limited edition of 1,000; love songs for the psychotically disturbed." [4]

In an interview with *NME*'s Edwin Pouncey a few months later, Cobain was less than complimentary about their single. "I wish we could have recorded it a lot heavier," he said. "It was one of our very first recordings. We weren't sure just what we wanted to do, so it turned out kinda wimpy compared to our most recent recordings." [5]

Those most recent recordings eventually appeared on June 15, 1989, as Nirvana's debut album *Bleach*. "This is the biggest, baddest sound that Sub Pop have so far managed to unearth," wrote Pouncy in his *NME* review of the album. "So primitive that they manage to make label mates Mudhoney sound like Genesis. Nirvana turn up the volume and spit and claw their way to the top of the musical garbage heap." [6]

Bleach immediately marked out the world of difference between hardcore and grunge. Here the tracks were slowed down while guitars were piled up high. The effect was like a juggernaut rolling through open roads, unstoppably heavy and seemingly on the verge of losing control. Among the grunge blueprints however, one song stood out for its lightness of touch: 'About A Girl', which opened with a gently strummed guitar, offered the first real hint at the strength of Cobain's ability to conjure up timeless pop melodies. It also represented a breathing space from Cobain's howled vocal style, which often left him hoarse.

As a collection, *Bleach* suffered from the 'too samey' sound. Guitars and drums never benefited from varied EQ'ing, and because the album was recorded so quickly (the Sub Pop way) there were no chances to try different takes with alternative mike set ups for any instrument. Furthermore, the set occasionally veered into over looming experimental territory, especially on 'Sifting', where Cobain's tune-smithery had yet to acquire that ability to know when enough is enough.

"It's nice doing a record quickly, but then, it's nice to not be in a hurry," producer Jack Endino said in 1997. "To be able to step back and go, 'Wait a minute. Let's get a different drum sound on this song. Why don't we play with a different guitar amplifier?' That's the sort of thing you can't do when you've got a day to do an album. You just have to set up the mikes and go. Which is why *Bleach* pretty much has the same guitar sound from beginning to end 'cause we had one guitar amp, one day to record it. We recorded on eight track, but we didn't even use all of them – we used six or seven, usually. You basically just roll tape. And that's what's fun about indie rock, but that's also what limits it sometimes." [7]

Ultimately however, whatever the failings in its overall sound, *Bleach* was the album that introduced the world to the sound of grunge. This was the sound that everyone would try and emulate in order to get on the grunge gravy train in the coming months.

Bleach also highlighted a growing problem in the Nirvana camp. Kurt was increasingly unhappy with Channing's drumming. The tracks 'Paper Cuts' and 'Floyd' were lifted from the original sessions with Dale Crover on drums because it was rumoured that Cobain felt the new drummer couldn't improve on the originals.

Furthermore, although second guitarist Jason Everman featured in the band shots for the album, he didn't actually play on it. While Nirvana were on a US tour in support of *Bleach* however, Everman left the band. Cobain and Novoselic maintained that he was fired, while Everman himself insists the departure was his own decision. Whatever the reason, Everman eventually became the bassist for Soundgarden, while Nirvana retreated into the studio to record their next release, *Blew EP* as a three piece once again.

In April 1990, the band went in to Smart Studios in Madison, Wisconsin, with Butch Vig producing. The intention was to start work on the band's second Sub Pop album. It was a session that was once again to show up Cobain's dissatisfaction with Channing. Throughout the week-long session, the frontman frequently stepped behind the kit to show the drummer what he felt was required.

Things came to a head on the spring US tour with Cobain becoming openly hostile to Channing. After those dates, Channing was ousted from the drum seat, although he maintains he left of his own accord.

"All I can think is the reason they got rid of Chad was more personality-wise," explained Jack Endino in 1997. "I always thought Dale (Crover) was a brilliant drummer, and it was pretty hard for anybody to come up and fill his shoes. And when Chad first joined the band, he had to sweat it a little bit; it took Chad a while to get into the groove of it. When I recorded the 'Love Buzz' single, I didn't think he was very good. He wasn't hitting very hard; it was hard to record him. That's why the drum sound on 'Love Buzz' is really not that great, because I had to do horrible things with it to try and make it sound good at all. Because he was barely touching the drums. By the time they did *Bleach* he was playing much better and by the time they did those demos with Butch Vig, I thought he was playing very well indeed." [8]

Channing was gone and thus opened the vacancy that Grohl would fill with legendary results. Despondent about the precarious situation Scream found itself in, Grohl called his friend Buzz from the Melvins. "They were coming into town and I said, '(Scream) kinda broke up. We're stuck. So, when you come into town, if you can put us on the guest list, that would be great.' He said, 'What happened?' (and) I told him."

Buzz tipped Grohl off about the aforementioned Nirvana drummer vacancy and also suggested his chances of being enrolled were very good: "He told me, 'Nirvana came to Scream's show in San Francisco a couple of weeks earlier and said they thought you were awesome and if you were ever available that you should give them a call.'" [9]

'I had *Bleach* and I had heard it before," Grohl told *manateebound.com*, "so I'd thought about it for a couple of days and called Kurt up. He said, 'Well, actually we already have a drummer.' They were playing with Danny (Peters) from Mudhoney. I said, 'OK cool. Ya know, give me a call when you come into town – we aren't doing anything.'" Not prepared to be drummerless for long, Cobain and Novoselic had approached Mudhoney's Dan Peters to fill the role.

Grohl looked to have been left high and dry. Later that night, however, Kurt called him back and said to Grohl, "Maybe you should come up here." Grohl packed up his kit bag and headed off for Seattle. On September 22, 1990, with Peters apparently enrolled as the latest Nirvana drummer, the band played the Motor Sports International Garage in Seattle, sharing the bill with The Derelicts, The Dwarves, and The Melvins. Numbered among the audience was Dave Grohl.

Grohl stayed for a while with Novoselic in Tacoma, and then moved in with Cobain, who was living in Olympia. A week after the Motorsports Show, Cobain made an appearance on KAOS where he announced the arrival of Dave Grohl as Nirvana's latest drummer. According to rumour, Peters had not even been told he was out of the band.

Recalling his earliest meetings with Cobain and Novoselic, Grohl said that they were in awe of both his pedigree and the scene he had been a part of. The Nirvana boys were, it transpired, huge fans of the DC scene. Grohl on the other had was less than enamoured with the grunge revolution.

"When I went up there to meet with Kurt, the first thing he said to me was, 'Wow, you're from Washington!' Everybody out there worshipped Washington. It was weird after that to see what people made of Seattle and that scene. As far as I'm concerned, all that had already happened in DC." [10]

"I think one of the reasons they wanted me was that I sang backup vocals," Grohl said in 2001. "I don't remember them saying, 'You're in the band.'" [11] But Grohl was in the band and this signalled the final demise of Scream.

In the aftermath of Scream's demise, Pete and Franz Stahl went on to form Wool with Government Issue drummer Peter Moffett and bassist Al Bloch. The band made a name for themselves with a rough hybrid of melodic hardcore and hard rock and delivered a blistering introduction with the debut *Budspawn EP* on the independent External Records. Following the departure of Moffett, Wool signed to London Records with new drummer Chris Bratton in tow. Their subsequent album, 1994's *Box Set* took the basic tenet of that debut EP and expanded it into potentially chart friendly post-grunge rock directions. Sadly commercial success was never to be theirs.

Scream came back together again for a reunion tour in 1993 in support of the posthumously released *Fumble,* and then again in 1996 while Franz Stahl was also playing with Foo Fighters (as will be chronicled below). However, critics were less than positive about this latest reincarnation of these Washington DC old-timers. This release of *Fumble* was met with sharp criticism for its apparent cashing in on Grohl's success with Nirvana (a later live album was also unfairly accused of cashing in on the Foo's popularity).

Regardless of how Scream were later perceived by a somewhat uncharitable press, Grohl recalls his days in that band with genuine, unbridled relish. In 1995, he said, "The feeling of driving across the country in a van with five other guys, stopping in every city to play, sleeping on people's floors, watching the sun come up over the desert as I drove, it was all too much. This was definitely where I belonged."

In many ways, Scream was Dave Grohl's first love. This was the first band that he worked with intensively. He cut his teeth as a performer and studio musician with them, took on an increasingly large role in the songwriting and was able to play a significant part in their development. They were the yardstick he would measure everything by in the future. And that included Nirvana.

There are, however, many Scream fans who would argue that Grohl's' arrival with the band marked out the creative decline of the once triumphant hardcore ambassadors. His time coincided with a far more hard rock-orientated sound. The earlier hints of reggae, that all-pervading Bad Brains influence, quickly diminished and the straight-ahead driving rock sound soon dominated.

This was obviously partly due to the fact that Grohl's drumming pushed this kind of sound. His technical ability – though breathtaking – was often overpowered by the sheer volume of his drumming. The rest of the band could sometimes be seen to be following suit.

Furthermore throughout the Scream years, Grohl's oft-cited need to be in the driving seat came to the fore. His increased role in the band eschewed all of the accepted ideas of a drummer's place in a band. Here he quietly assumed a central creative position and gradually displayed an authority that underlined his position in the Scream legacy.

It would be wrong however to assume that this inability to remain a backroom boy while the others soak up the glory was driven by ego. In fact, the need to take care of things, to organise and continually push is something that is central to Grohl's psyche. It's the trademark of a hyperactive, the product of an inability to sit still for one minute.

Perhaps one of the most touching examples of this came when Grohl's parents split up when he was only seven. He took it upon himself to become the man about the house, taking care of everyone in the process. "I could look after myself pretty easy so I just focused on making sure the family was happy. I've been doing it ever since," he told Q's Michael Odell in February, 2003.

Whether or not Scream benefited from Grohl's paternalism is open to debate. He certainly gained invaluable experience and exposure in his time in that band. It was a truly worthy experience of which he never talks in a negative fashion. One fact about this era in Grohl's life certainly remains true - Scream leave behind a legacy of great moments, both with and without Dave Grohl.

Just as the Washington harDCore scene had become synonymous with Straight Edge ideology and, in the shape of Positive Force, political activism, the Seattle grunge scene became associated with its own, somewhat questionable ethos. In this case, the ideology was the so-called slacker generation. Grunge was its soundtrack and Nirvana the reluctant heroes.

Slacker was a derisory term given to an aspect of what had been coined Generation X, a media-invented demographic created to attempt to pigeonhole disaffected American youth. This was the generation born between 1961 and 1981 – the children of the baby boom generation – who became viewed as a generation of underachievers.

The term Generation X was adopted from the Douglas Coupland novel of the same name, in which three intellectuals wonder aimlessly through life, never fulfilling, or even attempting to fulfil, any of their natural potential. Its movie counterpart, Richard Linklater's *Slacker* gave the Gen X concept an even more heavily -focussed look and sound (it used Seattle grunge for its soundtrack) and provided the greater media with the hook it needed to approach, and ultimately condemn the so-called 'generation without conscience'.

The need for the creation of this new demographic came from the older generation's desire to set itself up as the lofty standard from which everything had fallen. Where post-WW2 veterans viewed the birth of rock 'n' roll with disdain, so too the children of the 1960s, the baby boomers, looked down their noses at this generation who were politically inactive and would rather consume that protest. Much was made of the growth in the video games market; the onslaught of buddy shows on TV which seemed to carry no message beyond consumerism; and the increasingly non -oppositional music. The slackers, it was thought, were losers and proud of it. And further more, they certainly weren't going to do anything about changing things.

This slacker attitude was apparently born out in the need among Generation X'ers to look back with nostalgic warmth rather than push forward into the unknown. Thus, unlike the generation before them, these artists, musicians, actors, painters etc merely appropriated the surface level attributes of their medium. When applied to grunge it was argued that bands like Nirvana and Mudhoney were merely lifting the sheen from the surface of the greats and never aspiring to the creation of anything of a lasting resonant depth.

The generation was supposedly "numb and dumb," lazy apathetic under-achievers who would return home to their parents after graduating from college. X-ers (as they were called) were thus identified as white, upper-middle class and college-educated, with no ambition beyond hanging out, and getting a MacJob to pay for their lifestyle (a MacJob was Coupland's term for a dead-end occupation). Slacker was a million miles removed from the Yuppies of the 1980s. Indeed, where the 'me' generation of that decade had valued the ability to make it alone, the X-ers were seen as a generation that truly valued relationships. They were, after all the first "latch key" children. Those who lost their family community to the dollar.

Of course, the Generation X (or Generalization X as *Village Voice* critic Mike Rubin called it) argument was fundamentally flawed. First and foremost in the fact that the thing which marked this generation out was its desire *not* to be tagged with a marketing demographic. No sooner had the term slacker been invented than the people it was aimed at rejected it wholesale. To adopt the term as a way of describing yourself meant victory to the media and the marketing people. Fierce individualism has always been a basic tenet of this generation.

One of the most argued points of the Generation X debate was that it was a catch-all phrase intended to cover a hugely diverse range of people. It was, however, the slacker tag that *really* upset people. Here was a generation that was being pigeonholed as lacking real ambition or vision, and yet these same people were actively altering world perspectives. Furthermore, on a personal level, people weren't just sitting back and letting things happen. Voting figures may have been in decline, but it would have been wrong to assume that this meant a politically apathetic generation were being unleashed upon the world. People remained politically active, but addressing things that they faced on a day-to-day level.

Nirvana, quite simply, were not slackers. They were neither middle-class graduate under-achievers, nor were they apathetic MacJobbers. In fact, they had a work rate which would put most people to shame and ambitions that looked towards global domination. Musically they were bungee jumping without a safety harness. Yet their songs was accused of pandering to the Generation X need for enhanced emotional responses in their music. They wanted sounds that reinforced their dark and sad side. Quite simply music was the language through which the slacker generation expressed its feelings.

Unwittingly, Nirvana and their contemporaries were being adopted as the epitome of Generation X and, in the chaotic months that followed, their powerful beauty and questioning lyricism would be used as a soundtrack for a global marketing ploy – through Nirvana, corporate materialism would be sold to this most cynical generation.

Dave Grohl joined Nirvana just a few short weeks before the release of their next single 'Sliver'. Clocking in at just over two minutes, the single not only displayed the band at their most pop, echoing REM at their most frivolous, but in some cruel twist of fate it also featured departing drummer Dan Peters.

Sub Pop had wanted another record out of the band as quickly as possible and even went as far as to interrupt a Tad session at Reciprocal on July 11, so that Nirvana could lay down a new track. So, while Tad were on their lunch break, Nirvana came in, borrowed Tad's gear and knocked out their next single. As a result, Peters may have been the band's shortest-lived drummer, but he did manage to stake his claim to drumming on one record.

"It wasn't that we were unhappy with Dan's drumming, it was just that Dave has qualities which match our needs a little closer," recalled Cobain. "He takes care of backing vocals for a start. We were blown away by him when we saw him playing with this band Scream a few months ago and Chris and I agreed we'd ask him to join Nirvana if we ever had the chance. Ironically that chance came just weeks after we got Danny in." [12]

Following a burst of intense rehearsal in which he learned the entire Nirvana back catalogue and jammed on numerous covers, Dave Grohl made his debut appearance with Nirvana on October 11 at the Northshore Surf Club in Olympia, WA.

A mere nine days later, he was on a Transatlantic flight – in which all of the band would film themselves for footage to be included on the official Nirvana video, *Nirvana: Live Tonight! Sold Out!* – to play a short UK tour and take part in talks with major record labels. To say that Grohl had been thrown in at the deep end was something of an understatement.

Immediately prior to the first date of the UK tour, the band went into London's Maida Vale Studios to record a session for Radio 1's *John Peel Show*. In what was to be Grohl's first recording session with his new band, the trio ran through 'D7', 'Molly's Lips', 'Son Of A Gun' and 'Turnaround'. Even at this point, Grohl was still learning the band's songs with Kurt taking to the drum kit regularly to advise the new sticksman.

The UK tour kicked off at Birmingham's Goldwyn's Suite on October 23. The following night found them in London at The Astoria. Support came from Godflesh and L7. In his review of the gig, *Melody Maker*'s Jonathan Selzer was less than complimentary, complaining that, "there's none of the clenched, drawn-out tension of the *Bleach* LP, and in fact they sound almost sincere, as if everything's too geared towards gaining our sympathy… Nirvana only seem to have one song. This generally consists of the finely ground drawl of Kurt Cobain repeating a phrase over and over again until it sounds trite and then everybody shakes their hair for a bit. Yowsa. Good bits are few and far between, the slow-burn and anthracitic undercurrent of 'Blew'. The Prong-like incisiveness of 'Big Cheese', and that's about it. But tonight The Astoria is seething, a sea of moshers bubbling over, people swimming over heads and tangled stage divers being subsumed back into the froth. The mythology of remoteness comes round again, but no one is willing to come around to the fact that Nirvana simply don't live up to it."

It was a rare moment of opposition to the Nirvana frenzy from *Melody Maker*. Indeed, only that afternoon they had been interviewed in their hotel by that magazine's journalist Push, who was far more positive about the band. Following the interview, all three members of Nirvana ventured to leafy south west London for a meeting with Island Records.

With all of the hype surrounding the grunge explosion, it was inevitable that the majors would come sniffing around for their piece of the action. Soundgarden and Mudhoney had already signed major deals and Nirvana looked certain to follow. "There are six or seven labels interested in us now, but we're keeping our options open," explained Cobain. "It's mainly a question of who understands us best."

"But we have to remember that a major wants you to make money for them, and if you don't do that, they can fuck you and they fuck you hard," added Grohl (who had already suggested that the best thing about being in Nirvana was being taken out for meals by the record companies!) "Oh, sure," Novoselic confirmed, "but also bear in mind that we've got a lawyer. We have the same lawyer as the Rolling Stones, Poison, Kiss and the Bangles!" [13]

The fight by the major labels to secure Nirvana continued throughout the rest of their stay in the UK. Leeds Polytechnic on October 25, revealed a guest list stuffed to the gills with A&R people, while the following night in Edinburgh, Island even went as far as to supply free drinks for all of the bands playing on the bill!

The final night of the tour found the band pulling into Nottingham to play at Trent Polytechnic. Nottingham had long been a stronghold for rock music (the city's Rock City nightclub being a huge national draw at the time) and hardcore. It was of little surprise that the grunge aesthetic spread like a rash on that Saturday night.

The Nirvana gig that night was startling. The band ran through their set like a blitzkrieg, seemingly punishing their equipment as each new song unfolded. As with the London gig, the audience was a sea of moshers and stagedivers. However, unlike that night the band themselves were absolutely on fire. Cobain delivered his melodies with an executioner's gusto, Novoselic attacked the air with his bass with a passion that verged on anger, while Grohl attacked his skins, hair flailing everywhere, with bombastic glee. The energy of his pounding was matched only by the size of his grin.

Backstage after the show, the band were in jubilant mood. They had been joined by Everett True (who had also played on the encore – he had once recorded for Creation Records as The Legend) and were keen to party. Grohl joked along while continually pulling the sweat soaked hair from his face. I was there too, reporting for local fanzine *Overall There's A Smell Of Fried Onions*. We talked for a while. He seemed good-humoured but slightly stunned by the size of Nirvana's UK following.

"It seems weird that a few months ago I was stuck in LA, in

a band without a bass player, not knowing what to do next… and now this," he enthused to me. "It's all happened so fast. But I can't wait to get into the studio to start recording the band's next record. Kurt and Chris are great guys. They create a really special, huge sound. And there just like me… from Nowheresville."

For a few weeks it appeared that Charisma Records had secured Nirvana, but lengthy negotiations with Geffen (DGC) put the band on down time for the remainder of the year. Novoselic took the chance to enjoy a holiday while Cobain's break was interrupted by being admitted to hospital and diagnosed as having irritable bowel syndrome.

Grohl on the other hand decided to use the time pursuing his favourite goal – making music! Since those first multi-track recordings of his own music back in the pre- *Fumble* sessions for Scream, Grohl had continued to lay down his tracks with his friend Barrett Jones. He had subsequently amassed quite a collection of music.

On December 23, Grohl went into Jones' Laundry Room studio and embarked on a session which would produce six new songs: 'Pokey The Little Puppy', 'Petrol CB', 'Friend Of A Friend', 'Throwing Needles', 'Just Another Story About Skeeter Thompson' and 'Colour Pictures Of A Marigold'. Many of the songs themselves owed a huge debt to the influence of Cobain's songwriting. Strangely however, it wasn't so much the grunge sound, but the use of lilting, understated melody.

'Pokey The Little Puppy' was a four minute, three chord hardcore instrumental run-through, which echoed Ian MacKaye's Fugazi with its bass-led dissonance and edgy dynamics. Only a slow-grinding, chugging guitar middle-eight, complete with guitar hooks following the bass line offered any hint as to Grohl's latest day job with Nirvana. 'Petrol CB' owed a huge debt to Cobain. The melody scorched between distorted howl and Neil Young-esque chorus, while guitars were cranked up and swinging between heavy fuzz and almost acoustic strum. 'Friend Of A Friend', a confessional dark acoustic strum along the song found

Grohl singing about his friend's friend, the guitar. An instrument which is presented as being a replacement for human love. "When he plays, no one speaks," laments Grohl. A touching moment in which Grohl displayed his rarely seen softer side, and one of the highlights of the session.

'Throwing Needles' offered both a peak into Grohl's future and a quick look into his past. With its pounding drums, thrashing guitars and pop melody, it could have come direct from the debut Foo Fighters album. However, the rock dynamics also echoed the final recordings of Scream.

Scream make another return on 'Just Another Song About Skeeter Thompson" in which Grohl eulogised his one-time bassist over a hardcore assault. The spoken words told of Skeeter's new -found relationship with a Dutch girl on the band's second European tour. She was wealthy and Skeeter started turning up in nice clothes, so the story goes. Eventually he moves in with her.

"She was really good looking, really cool, you know," Grohl explains as guitars, drums and bass fly through a breakneck groove. This quite bizarre track would turn up as a B-side to The Melvins *King Buzzo EP* in 1993 that featured Grohl on drums. King Buzzo was otherwise known as Buzz Osborne.

The final track recorded during these experimental sessions was 'Colour Pictures Of A Marigold', which once again found Grohl strumming an acoustic guitar while he delivered a near-falsetto vocal performance, complete with harmonies. Perhaps the least interesting song from the session, it did however display a touching frailty in his delivery.

With these exploratory sessions completed, Grohl went to Music Source Studios, Seattle, for a session with Nirvana on New Year's Day, 1991. They recorded 'Aneurysm' and a new version of 'Even In His Youth'.

Technically Nirvana was still signed to Sub Pop, although a deal had been agreed with Geffen. Reports suggested they would sign that deal on March 30 for a $287,000 advance and a buy-out from Sub Pop for $75,000. Furthermore the band would have to contribute half of this sum. Sub Pop also received a 2% royalty on the next two albums (extended to three with the release of *Incesticide* in 1992).

"It was unbelievable," explained Grohl in 2001 of the band's sudden high income. "We went from selling amp heads and 'Love Buzz' singles for food, to having millions of dollars. Coming from Springfield, Virginia, I went from having no money at all and working at Tower Records to being set up for the rest of my life. I remember the first time we got a thousand–dollar check. We were so excited. I went out and bought a BB gun and a Nintendo – the things that I always wanted as a kid." [14]

Ironically it wasn't the biggest advance on offer for Nirvana, who had also been offered $1m by Capitol. Nevertheless, at a Seattle show, Cobain introduced the band as "major corporate rock sell–outs" before launching into their first performance of their soon–to–be–epochal single, 'Smells Like Teen Spirit'.

In May, Nirvana started work on their follow up to *Bleach*. Tentatively titled *Sheep* the set was to be recorded at Sound City Studios, Van Nuys in California. Butch Vig, who had already worked on the demos earlier in the year, was installed as producer.

Talking about the recording in 1997, Vig recalled how impressed he was by the Grohl's drumming. "Kurt had called me up and said, 'I have the best drummer in the world now. He plays louder and harder than anybody I've ever met.' And I'm like, 'Yeah, right.' But they were totally right. Kurt's guitar was super–loud and the bass was super–loud, but the drums... there were no mics on them in this room and they were just as loud acoustically as the amps! And also Dave turned out to be so cool; really easy to work with, and full of energy, and really brought a lot of life and fun to the sessions. He kept it real light." [15]

Previous Nirvana producer, Jack Endino threw a different light on Grohl's actual creative input on the songs on what would eventually become the watershed album, *Nevermind*. "You'll notice if you play the Chad (Channing) demos for the *Nevermind* stuff and compare them to *Nevermind,* they're exactly the same drum part.

The guy was getting pretty good when they got rid of him. But Dave is obviously an amazing drummer himself, so what are you going to do? He was a much harder hitter than almost anybody." [16]

The drum parts, it would seem, were set in stone within Cobain's own imagination. He had written the songs, and he knew what the drums needed to be like. It is one of the ironies of Grohl's post-Nirvana career that he has been accused of megalomaniacal tendencies when it comes to the drum parts, but this was never levelled at Cobain whose genius seems rarely to have been questioned.

Grohl himself had another take on Cobain's need to dictate the beats. "Kurt was kind of a drummer himself," he said in 2001. "When he would play guitar or write songs, if you ever looked at his jaw, he would be moving his jaw back and forth, like he was playing the drums with his teeth. He heard in his head what he wanted from a rhythm, and that's a hard thing to articulate." [17]

Following the recording of *Nevermind*, the band headed out on a tour of the west coast of America, taking in Denver, Salt Lake City, San Francisco, Hollywood, Tijuana, Santa Cruz, Sacramento and Portland. It was in the middle of these dates that the band went to see Butthole Surfers and Kurt Cobain first met a woman by the name of Courtney Love. Journalist Everett True already knew Love through her band Hole. He subsequently introduced Cobain to her, although it also transpired that Grohl had previously known of Love.

With a short break before their August tour of Europe, Grohl once again went into the studio to record some more of his own tracks on June 27. This time, however, he didn't use The Laundry Room, but instead opted for WGNS Studios in Arlington. The engineer for these sessions was Geoff Turner, although Barrett Jones did assist.

Jones's Laundry Rooms had in fact temporarily closed down. Jones subsequently followed Grohl to Seattle in June 1991 ("Dave had just moved out here and joined some band I'd never heard of called Nirvana!"), where he would eventually set up a studio in his west Seattle home and eventually record the first post-*Nevermind* Nirvana material, plus a session with King Buzzo on which Grohl played drums (this eventually became a King Buzzo single in 1993).

Grohl recorded four songs at the WGNS session: 'Hell's Garden', 'Winnebego', 'Bruce' and 'Milk'. It was immediately apparent how much the *Nevermind* sessions had effected him. Song arrangements, melodies, guitar style and even drum and vocal balance had grown in a similar direction as his band's recent recordings.

'Hell's Garden' featured a quiet melodic verse which erupted into a straight ahead power chord punk guitar hook, which echoed 'White Riot' by The Clash, complete with screamed vocals. 'Winnebego' was reminiscent of Green River with its neo-country melody, guitars picking out octaves at breakneck speed and drums seemingly tumbling over themselves, before highlighting the dynamics with razor sharp precision. 'Bruce' offered a slower Led Zeppelin-esque groove over which a multi-tracked guitar feedback soup rocked like Metallica while 'Milk' presented the most obviously Cobain-inspired moment, thanks to its combination of grunged-up country and western verse, one word chorus and melodies that echoed 1960s act Love.

Although these were solo recordings, it is possible that Grohl had written them with Nirvana in mind, perhaps seeking an increased involvement in the songwriting, as had happened with Scream. Indeed, 'Marigold' was eventually recorded with the band and included during the *In Utero* sessions and later released as a B-side to the 'Heart Shaped Box' single in 1993. Grohl supplied the vocals. According to the book, *Nirvana*, by Jeremy Dean, 'Winnebego' was also recorded by Nirvana and placed on a B-side, however the track has never surfaced as a Nirvana recording either on an official or bootleg release.

Another interesting aspect of this second Grohl session is that it shows how calm things were for Nirvana at this stage. That he could even consider solo material (whether for release or not) reveals how unexpected the band's success was for everyone. Certainly the rollercoaster ride they were about to embark upon would make it increasingly difficult for Grohl to record his own material for quite some time.

The first single to be lifted from *Nevermind* appeared on September 9. 'Smells Like Teen Spirit'. So much has been written about this one pivotal track, but as a deliberately simplistic review, it was a monstrous record. Wave after wave of quiet-to-a-storm crescendos built around Kurt's increasingly melodic guitar licks and a vocal line that was about as hooky as a pop record could get. The video for the song subverted the cheerleader popularity hierarchy in high school into a punk rock revolt. However, it was still polished enough to be MTV-friendly and the music station jumped on the record.

Stunning as the song was, the speed with which it captured the airwaves was nothing short of unbelievable. Almost immediately '...Teen Spirit' became the soundtrack to a generation, with its lyrics becoming instant catch phrases for the so-called slacker kids.

However, there was also a crucial point about the timing of this track. Nirvana's major label debut arrived at a point when rock music was in decline. Alternative rock bands like The Pixies, Sonic Youth and REM were past their best. Even more recent indie bands like Dinosaur Jnr and Lemonheads had failed to live up to their original promise. There was simply a huge gap in the market. With maximum marketing and promotional exposure through Geffen's well-oiled machine, Nirvana quickly filled that void. However, it was their talent, and Cobain's increasing iconic status, that helped them sustain this position.

In the UK, 'Smells Like Teen Spirit' peaked at #6. It also went Top 10 in the US *Billboard* charts. Despite the success of the single, Geffen only pressed 50,000 copies of *Nevermind*, shipping a modest 46,251 of these. Indeed, neither band nor label expected the album to do that well.

In 2001, Grohl talked about the band's lack of confidence in the album's commercial potential. "It didn't seem possible," he admitted. "The charts were filled with fucking Mariah Carey and Michael Bolton. It seemed like we were about to make another pass through the underground. One of the first people to say they thought the album was going to be huge was Donita Sparks of L7. And I didn't believe her. I was going, 'There's absolutely no way.'

It was playing the Reading Festival in England in August, 1991 - we were maybe fourth on the bill - watching the audience respond to 'Smells Like Teen Spirit'. It was something about the song. People just bounced to it. Basically, it's a dance beat - the verses are like Cameo-disco drumming and the choruses are heavy -metal 60s go-go." [18]

Nevermind was eventually released on September 24, three weeks after that Reading Festival appearance. Critics were united in their praise for the album. "Forget all the prejudices you may or may not have about Seattle's Sup Pop scene of three years back," wrote *Melody Maker*'s Everett True. "There will not be a better straight -ahead rock album than *Nevermind* released all year... When Nirvana released *Bleach* all those years ago, the more sussed among us figured they had the potential to make an album that would blow every other contender away. My God, have they proved us right." [19]

Steve Lamacq wrote in the *NME*: "*Nevermind* is an album for people who would like to like Metallica, but can't stomach their lack of melody; while on the other hand it takes some of the Pixies' *nous* with tunes, and gives the idea new muscle. A shock to the system." [20]

In the US, *Rolling Stone*'s Ira Robbins was perhaps more guarded, but nonetheless positive: "...the thrashing *Nevermind* boasts an adrenalised pop heart and incomparably superior material, captured with roaring clarity by co-producer Butch Vig... Too often, underground bands squander their spunk on records they're not ready to make, then burn out their energy and inspiration with uphill touring. *Nevermind* finds Nirvana at the crossroads – scrappy garage land warriors setting their sights on a land of giants." [21]

In 2001 Grohl talked about his feelings upon hearing the finished album. "Hearing your music played on the big speakers for the first time after the track's been completed – that's the payoff, like when 'Smells Like Teen Spirit' first came through the speakers. The only demos we'd done of that song were on a boombox – we were used to hearing it sound like a shitty bootleg. All of a sudden, you have Butch Vig making it sound like Led Zeppelin's *IV*. And as we were mixing the album, Krist and Kurt and I would take a tape of the songs and just drive around the Hollywood Hills, listening to it. That was something else." [22]

The band had already embarked on a coast-to-coast tour of the US when *Nevermind* was released. By October 12, the album had already gone gold. Their audience started to change accordingly. Alongside the hardcore grunge kids that had supported the Sub Pop Nirvana, there appeared a new breed of fan. The MTV college kids. For the band whose hearts still lay firmly in punk's underground, this change of audience was alarming.

Indeed, both Grohl and Novoselic would regularly talk in interview about these new fans as being jocks and meatheads. When asked a couple of years later if he regretted the things his drummer and bassist had said, Cobain admitted, "Yeah, I do, I do, but the point we were trying to get across was never stated in the right way. I was upset at finding myself having to play in front of really rude, sexist jerks, I'd never had any desire to play to people like that and never expected to have to.

You know, a person can say a lot of stupid things when they're going through stressful times in their life. I don't regret the majority of things I was trying to convey, but they didn't translate right. And there were a handful of things I can remember that I really regret us saying.

Like when Chris said, 'For the most part, heavy metal kids are just stupid.' I couldn't say that. I was a heavy metal kid at one time. That's just too insulting, it's too extreme a thing to say. You have to elaborate on things like that or not say them at all." [23]

While Grohl and Novoselic often busied themselves with verbally attacking their new audience in interviews, Cobain's already notorious mood swings became increasingly extreme. By the time Jack Endino's Skin Yard supported them in Amsterdam, he sensed the band, and especially Cobain, might be buckling under the pressure of new found fame.

"In Amsterdam, he [Kurt] wasn't doing too good. It was a really weird show. Kurt was really pissed off; there were all these people with cameras and movie cameras on the stage, and he was a little out of tune and he was very angry at these cameras: 'Get the hell off my stage!' And backstage he was really uneasy, he looked really pale. Everybody seemed to be really uneasy and very unhappy. Like suddenly the success was starting to bother them because people were starting to come at them. Suddenly people wouldn't leave them alone." [24]

Grohl put the band's frailty down to the their inability to deal emotionally with such a huge change in their lives after so many years of slumming it in the punk tradition. "There was that punk -rock guilt," he admitted. "Kurt felt, in some way, guilty that he had done something that so many people had latched onto. The bigger the shows got, the farther we got from our ideal. We were all in such a weird state. It was such a whirlwind that no one really had any time to feel comfortable with it." [25]

Following the US tour, the band returned to Europe for another string of dates. This time they opened at Bristol's Bierkeller on November 4 before travelling to London's Astoria the next day, which was followed by Wulfrun Hall in Wolverhampton. The following day found them recording their first ever live TV appearance for *The Word* on Channel 4. Cobain introduced their rendition of 'Smells Like Teen Spirit' with the immortal words "I'd just like to say that Courtney Love, of the pop group 'Hole', is the best fuck in the world".

The tour continued through Europe before returning in November for yet more dates. No one could ever accuse Nirvana of resting on their laurels. On December 7, at Rennes, Transmusicales Festival in France, the band opened with a cover of The Who's 'Baba O'Riley', with Grohl on lead vocals. Cobain's voice was packing up due to the intensive touring. Soon after, the band decided to cancel the rest of the European tour the press statement explained, "Kurt Cobain was rendered virtually mute with a viral throat infection."

In the middle of that UK tour, *Nevermind* went platinum. On January 11, 1992, however, the album did the unthinkable for a band that had grown out of the US alternative punk scene – it went to #1 on the *Billboard* Album chart. Furthermore, it would return to the top spot again on February 1 and by 1996 would sell almost fourteen million copies worldwide. Seven million of those in the US alone.

With the band's huge success came new frictions. Cobain started to become uncertain about the royalties. Cobain's argument was quite clear as to why he deserved more money. They were his songs. "At the time, when we were signing contracts and stuff like that it was always divided equally and that was fine," he explained in 1993. "But I never realised that I would become a millionaire and then all of a sudden, need money. It's a ridiculous situation really... Well, we (the members of the band) didn't agree on it right way. It took a bit of convincing on my part. I still believe in all-for-one, one-for-all y'know. We're a group, we're a three piece. Chris and Dave are equally as important as I am, as far as persona of the band goes, in the way we're perceived. We're [perceived as a band]. But I had written 99 per cent of the songs and many were the times when I've taken Chris' bass away from him and shown him what to play, and sat behind Dave's drum kit and shown him what to play, stuff like that. I don't enjoy being in that sort of dictatorship position, but I came up with the songs at home, and introduced the songs to the band and I could be asking for a lot more." [26]

But the potential for arguments over money wasn't the only factor gnawing away at the band's status quo. They were also increasingly aware of the unhappy effect touring was having on the camaraderie they'd once cherished. For Grohl, this was especially difficult. Having toured extensively with Scream, he had far more experience of the bond that exists between members of a band. When any one person loses that feeling of belonging, it is easy for them to suddenly feel isolated.

Dave Grohl was becoming increasingly isolated. Partly due to the fact that Cobain and Novoselic had a very tight friendship, but also because the stresses of touring in the spotlight meant that he could never enjoy the relaxed intimacy of friends just hanging out together.

"Franz and Pete (Stahl) are like my brothers," he said of his previous band cohorts in comparison to relationships within Nirvana. "We spent all our time together, in the van going to gigs, sleeping on friend's floors. In Nirvana, we didn't hang out. We'd pull into town on the tour bus, do interviews, play in front of thousands of people, do more interviews, go to the hotel, and watch TV until you fell asleep." [27]

There were two more relationships within the band dynamic that were beginning to cause problems. Both were a part of Cobain's life, and both caused Cobain to become subject to even more extreme mood swings; they were Courtney Love and his drug use. With both taking a stronger role in the frontman's life, Grohl especially, started to feel like staying with Nirvana might not be worth the hassle.

"There would be times when we would really connect – smile and laugh and feel like a band. And there were times when you felt lost and questioned what you were doing there," he has said. "There were times when I had to back off completely and think, 'I'm just the drummer in this band.' And there were other times when we'd all share something really beautiful, like a show or recording or just a vocal harmony. That's when you really felt like you were part of something great." [28]

Whatever the positive aspects to life in Nirvana, the fact remained that a huge separation was opening up between Cobain and the rest of the band. "Being in a band is like being in a relationship," he explained. "Whether it's a love relationship or just a friend [thing], there's people that you just connect with for no real reason at all, but you feel the same [about a lot of things].

When Kurt was into doing drugs, Krist and I didn't do that stuff, and Kurt did, so there was just this line drawn," Grohl said. "People who do drugs and people who don't. And we would hear about it the next day. Like when we played at Roseland at the New Music Seminar [in New York], Kurt died the night before [and had to be resuscitated], and I didn't find out about that until after the show. So I was totally oblivious to what was going on." [29] Cobain's problems with drugs have been extensively chronicled elsewhere, but suffice to say, it was becoming a debilitating factor for the band.

Although Nirvana were riding on the crest of a commercial wave (and Kurt and Courtney celebrated the birth of their first child, Frances Bean Cobain, on August 18), the cracks within the band were starting to appear. Dave Grohl was faced with the challenge of trying to remain focussed on the band or simply moving to greener pastures. He chose to block events out.

"People have tantrums, people's tempers flare," he philosophically explained. "But I can block everything out. I'm not really an emotional person at all. Just because I'd rather ignore emotion than confront it, so when it comes down to really heavy shit, it kinda breezes right past me. I don't really want to get involved in anyone else's problems and I don't want to be the cause of anyone else's, so I just lay low. I think maybe that's what'll keep me sane through this whole trip." [30]

But the trip was about to go completely insane.

3

RECLAIMING PUNK FROM THE MTV MASSES

ANOTHER DRUMMER JOKE
What do you say to the drummer in a successful band?
What's your name again?

Dave Grohl started 1992 on both a euphoric high and at the point of near-exhaustion from the previous few months. The success of Nirvana had been a shock to the system and he dealt with it in the only way he knew how - by playing live. With Cobain on an enforced sabbatical, Grohl and Novoselic joined forces with Buzz Osborne of the Melvins for what was to be the first of two Osborne-related projects that year.

Performing as Melvana, the trio played on January 15 at Crocodile Cafe, Seattle. The show featured covers of many of the trio's favourite punk songs, including two by Flipper, Sacrifice and Way Of The World that were bootlegged as a 7" single on Teen Sensation Records.

The second instalment in the Osborne recording came with the July 1992 release of the aforementioned *King Buzzo* by Buzz Osborne on Boner Records. This was a part of The Melvins' pastiche of the Kiss solo albums, in which head shots of each member of the band were shown in full make-up on otherwise identical sleeves. The Melvins presented the same concept with a punkier look.

King Buzzo featured four tracks – 'Isabella', 'Porg', 'Annum' and 'Skeeter Dave'. Grohl played drums and provided vocals for the last, a version of his own 'Another Story About Skeeter Thompson', which would turn up later that year on his *Pocketwatch* cassette album (more of which later). For the *King Buzzo* release, however, Grohl hid behind the *nom de plume* of Dale Nixon.

The friction over royalties with Cobain festered beneath the surface for quite some time following an initial spat in March, 1992. However, when Cobain suggested that the new arrangement be backdated to include *Nevermind*, the band came close to splitting.

Grohl explained how, "everybody was saying, 'Let him have this one because the band will break up. You guys could make fifteen million dollars next year. Just let him have this one.'" [1]

Fortunately, the situation – a common problem for bands who have enjoyed major success - was eventually reconciled. However, it still offered the first signs of the increased division that had started to appear between Cobain and the rest of the band. Nirvana went triple-platinum with an album that, oddly enough, many were now complaining was far too glossy and spiritually removed from their punk roots. How fickle the music-loving public can be sometimes.

To add to these apparent internal band divisions, the media had started to focus increasingly on Cobain. Given this solo platform, he chose to bring up the subject of money on numerous occasions. In one interview with journalist and personal friend Everett True, (in which short individual interviews with Grohl and Novoselic appear, seemingly as an after-thought) Cobain would complain that outsiders were making money out of the Nirvana name.

"The corporate side of our image is so exploitative, it's one of the only ways we can retain our dignity." He argued, "One of the main things I regret about the success of this band is… (he brandishes a copy of a Nirvana comic book and a Nirvana poster booklet). We're being totally raped by these [people], we have no control over that stuff. They sell hundreds of thousands of those magazines and we don't get a dime out of it, we don't even have a say-so in what pictures are used and what quotes are re-written." [2]

It's an outburst that shows what unhappy bedfellows success and artistic integrity are. Especially so for Cobain. Yet, some observers argued that Cobain's suggestion he should have control over quotes and images used also showed the difficult and fine line he was walking between creative integrity and egotism. The Nirvana history was not, they suggested, only there for the band to rewrite. A few years later, artists like Jennifer Lopez and Mariah Carey would be publicly lambasted for suggesting such a defined control over the information generated around them. But for Nirvana, these critics complained, it was being attributed to a sense of creative integrity.

To be fair, however, many major acts did subsequently insist on closer controls and veto of articles about them and images of them. For pop artists, it is often put down to being a diva and, indeed, some punters love them even more for it. Cobain was in that odd position of coming from a punk background, an ethos that sometimes stifles an artist's licence to defend what he sees are his rights, at the risk of being called "a sell-out". Although it is unrealistic for a public figure to control every word or photograph about themselves – take biographies such as this one as an example – it is also understandable that they might become concerned when they do not even respect the material being produced about them. He was in a no-win situation. Unfortunately, with Nirvana being the biggest band on the planet, it was inevitable.

Cobain's increased dominance of the media spotlight seemed out of keeping with the original ethos of the band. To further highlight his growing distance from the other two band members, Courtney Love was taking a featuring role in his life. Indeed, the couple were now referred to in some media circles as 'Kurtney'. Publicly, at least, Novoselic and Grohl were becoming seen as just the bassist and drummer respectively.

Speculation surrounding Cobain's apparent drug dependence was also placing him in an unwanted spotlight away from the concerns of the band. On June 23, the morning after the band's performance at Northern Ireland's King's Hall, Cobain collapsed. Despite claims that he was suffering from a stomach ulcer exacerbated by a love of junk food, it later transpired that the collapse was a result of methadone withdrawal. Cobain had apparently forgotten to take his methadone on the previous evening and had been too sick that morning to take it. Matters were not helped by his severe stomach ailment, which many close to the singer said plagued his entire life. Rumours about his health and well-being were rife.

Nirvana seemed to be publicly falling apart, but no one was prepared to confront the situation in print until Keith Cameron hit the controversy full on in an August issue of *NME*. Drawn from an interview which had taken place in Madrid, Spain, Cameron accused the band of going from "...nobodies to superstars to fuck-ups in the space of six months! That had to be a record." [3]

In the feature he asked Cobain directly if he was using heroin. The singer flatly denied it, even going to somewhat bizarre extremes to back up his claim. He even asked Cameron to feel his arms. Cobain considered a lack of track-marks to be proof positive that heroin wasn't his drug of choice.

The journalist then attacked the band for supposedly turning into the very creatures they had always claimed to despise: self-indulgent rock stars, with Cobain arriving late for interviews, refusing to do photos and generally forcing band and crew to accept his partner, Courtney Love into the fold. Again, this was not new territory for any major rock band, nor was Cobain's eagerness to be around Love essentially anything to be chided, but because the Nirvana frontman was now being held up as a modern day punk icon, his every move and comment was being scrutinised.

This feature understandably caused angry reactions with the entire band. One of the most ironic statements in the feature actually came from Grohl. Despite Nirvana being accused of embracing rock star arrogance, he used the platform to criticise such attitudes. Perhaps in an attempt to detract from the destructive goings-on within his band, he slammed U2's Bono, whom he had met on the Irish band's US tour earlier that year.

"It was such a bummer (meeting Bono) because when I was thirteen I thought *War* was a great album! He reeks of rock-star-ness; he was not a human being. He wanted us to open up for them on tour, and I said 'No, that's not what we're into.' And he was saying 'You owe it to the audience, you've got to take the next step! He was desperately trying to make that connection. 'Do you like the blues?' 'No'. Do you like gospel?' 'Er, no, not really.' 'So what kind of music do you listen to?' 'Punk fuckin' rock man!' And then, of course, he tells me about punk rock and he was there and he was the meaning of punk rock. After meeting that guy it made me want to give up being in a rock 'n' roll band." [4]

So Nirvana were too punk rock to support either Guns N' Roses or U2, but not punk rock enough to avoid the pit falls of stardom. Grohl and Novoselic may have maintained some level of integrity, but Cobain simply dug an even bigger hole for himself in the interview. He had never made any claims to be a punk rocker, he insisted. He wasn't anything to do with the underground. He even describes Nirvana as "a commercial rock band." With *Nevermind* turning out to be the zeitgeist album of the time, Nirvana almost appeared to be separating themselves from their past.

The increasingly unstable band atmosphere was exacerbated by complicating external factors. For a start, the past seemed intent on suing Nirvana! First of all, a 1960s band also called Nirvana attempted to stop Cobain *et al* from using their name. A delay in bringing the case meant it was dropped, despite the fact that the original Nirvana had even enjoyed some chart success in their day.

Also displeased with Nirvana was Killing Joke, who filed a motion against them for intellectual theft. Killing Joke bassist Paul Raven maintained that Nirvana's 'Come As You Are' borrowed liberally from their 1985 hit 'Eighties'. Novoselic went to court in Los Angeles to represent the band, however Killing Joke decided to drop the lawsuit for their own reasons. In his 2000 book, *Eyewitness Nirvana: The Day-By-Day Chronicle,* by Carrie Borzillo-Vrenna, Nirvana's manager of the time, Danny Goldberg, admitted the band and management's acknowledgement of the similarities. Goldberg said: "We met to discuss what (*Nevermind's*) second single would be. We couldn't decide between 'Come as You Are' and 'In Bloom.' Kurt was nervous about 'Come As You Are' because it was too similar to a Killing Joke song, but we all thought it was still the better song to go with. And, he was right, Killing Joke later did complain about it." [5]

The accusation from Killing Joke came as a huge disappointment to Grohl who had been a fan of the band – especially in their earliest incarnation. Ironically however, as will be detailed, Grohl would later play drums on Killing Joke's 2003 album, *The Death and Resurrection Show.*

"Dave and I had a few laughs about that (the court case) over the past year or so," admitted Raven. "He mentioned it to me when I met him backstage at Pantera a couple of years back." [6]

Following the aforementioned birth of Frances Bean Cobain at Los Angeles Cedars Sina Hospital, the tabloids and music press were all offering their opinions on the Nirvana/Hole celebrity couple. Both Grohl and Novoselic became increasingly frustrated by the media's obsession with Cobain's private life and attempted to rescue the situation. While he was in Cedars Sina Hospital himself to detox, the drummer and bassist went to visit Cobain. They talked about getting down to recording the next album, and the possibility of doing some benefit gigs.

The Nirvana story had become far too much about personalities and not enough about music and the only people that could rectify the situation were the band themselves. If their plan was some kind of counter attack, then it came on August 30 when Nirvana headlined the Reading Festival in the UK. Both before the actual weekend and on the day of the show, there had been much speculation about whether or not the band would appear due to Cobain's drug use. There had also been numerous stories about the band's impending demise, most recently in the shape of Cameron's damning *NME* article.

"... it was the classic, typical English journalism," Cobain was quoted as saying. "Sensationalism. I have absolutely no respect for the English people. They make me sick. I thought I'd never say anything racist in my life, but those people are the most snooty, cocksure, anal people and they have absolutely no regard for people's emotions. They don't think of other humans at all. They're the coldest people I've ever met." [7]

Perhaps as a reaction to what he saw as the British press' invasive attitude towards his private life, Cobain came out fighting at the show. Dressed in a blonde 'Courtney' wig and a surgical smock, he entered the stage on a wheelchair before he stood up, shuffled to the mic, sang the opening line of 'The Rose' and pretended to collapse. It was a theatrical send-up of the recent stories, a very public debunk of the mythology that was growing around him.

If such histrionics had seemed somewhere between Spinal Tap and an amateur dramatics troupe to some onlookers, then what followed was little short of breath-taking. Fired up with anger-fuelled passion, the band stormed through a triumphant set, Grohl's drumming in particular driving the band to new extremes.

Cobain's earlier anti-media comments were carried on during the between-song banter as the band joked about their reported "demise." "This isn't our last show!" exclaimed Novoselic. "Yes, it is," came Cobain's reply. "I would like to officially and publicly announce that this is our last show." "Today!" replied Novoselic. "Until we play on our November tour," added Cobain. "Or do you want to record a record in November?" It was, as might be expected, a crowd-pleasing moment.

This performance has now gone down in the annals of music history as one of the greatest festival gigs of all-time. The following week, the press had to agree: "Lethal and punishing between the bitter 'Polly' pill, and absolute 'Teen Spirit' abandon. And hell – heroin or no heroin – Nirvana can still kick out devastating rock 'n' roll harder than any American band in a decade," wrote Mary Anne Hobbs in the *NME*. Nobody present could argue with her.

Unfortunately, aside from this magnificent gig, progress with Nirvana was slow and despite any hopes for a new album before the end of the year, nothing was forthcoming. The band had been recording demos with Jack Endino at Word of Mouth Studios, Seattle (formerly Reciprocal Studios), but they were a long way short of any kind of finished material. According to Endino, the sessions were very tense and at one time were even interrupted by the arrival of the police, due to a noise complaint! Dave Grohl, it transpired, was playing his drums too loud.

"His drumming was so loud, it was going right through the walls of the building," recalled Endino. "It was only the second noise complaint we'd ever had! It was kind of embarrassing. But they were almost done at that point." [8]

Geffen opted instead to release an album of "Rare B-Sides, BBC Sessions, Original Demo Recordings, Out-takes, Stuff Never Before Available"; called *Incesticide*, the set was culled from a number of their early sessions. Grohl only performed on six of the tracks included: 'Turnaround', 'Molly's Lips' and 'Son of a Gun' from the BBC Radio 1 *John Peel Sessions* and 'Been a Son', 'Aneurysm' and the only track credited to Cobain, Novoselic and Grohl. '(New Wave) Polly' from the BBC Radio 1 *Mark Goodier Show* sessions. Released in December 1992, *Incesticide* proved to be something of a chore for the band's newer fans, selling disastrously compared to *Nevermind*.

While all eyes were on the release of *Incesticide* and Nirvana's demos for their next album, Grohl sneaked out his own debut solo album. Called *Pocketwatch*, it appeared with surprisingly little fanfare. In fact, despite the fact that it was a solo album from the drummer in the biggest rock band of the decade, very few people picked up on it at all. Thus was partly because it was a cassette only release (in the punk rock tradition) and because he went by the unlikely moniker of Late!

Pocketwatch was in fact the two aforementioned sessions he'd recorded while in Nirvana. He had opted to call himself Late! because he didn't want to be seen as using his position in Nirvana to launch a solo career. It is also likely that Grohl didn't have the confidence to put out a high profile record. Despite his ability to take care of things for other people, and also to block things out, Grohl was extremely insecure when it came to aspects of himself. Up until this point, with the exception of Dain Bramage, he had never actually instigated his own band.

With Nirvana, any attempts to move his songwriting forward had been thwarted, a fact that must have left him feeling unsure of the songs he'd demo-ed. What's more, it can't have helped that his main band featured the talents of Cobain who was, in many people's eyes, the finest songwriter of his generation.

The *Pocketwatch* tape came out on the Simple Machines label, as part of their Tool Cassette series. The Arlington-based Simple Machines imprint was set up by Jenny Toomey and Kristin Thompson in 1990 in order to put out music by themselves and their friends. They pushed the DIY punk ethic by attempting to find creative ways to avoid the established music industry methods.

The Tool Cassette Series was launched in 1991 as a way of keeping records in print without having the costly pressing process. They would quite literally dub copies from a master tape as orders came in.

Talking about how she came to release the Late! tape, Jenny Toomey explained that she had been visiting the Laundry Room when she first heard it. "I thought it was great," she explained, "and I hassled him for a tape. About six months later, he gave me one when I was visiting in Olympia. My label was releasing a series of cassettes that focused on music that was either unfinished, imperfect or finished and perfect by bands that no longer played out, like Geek, My New Boyfriend and Saturnine. It made perfect sense to ask Dave to add his solo tape to the list, and he said yes." [9]

The track listing for *Pocketwatch* was true to the chronology of the recording. 'Pokey The Little Puppy', 'Petrol CB', 'Friend Of A Friend', 'Throwing Needles', 'Just Another Story About Skeeter Thompson' and 'Color Pictures Of A Marigold' from the initial session, with 'Hell's Garden', 'Winnebago', 'Bruce' and 'Milk' from the second session.

The copy of *Pocketwatch* that Grohl gave to Toomey was second generation; this was what they used as a master! It would also eventually cause Simple Machines huge problems as news leaked out about the tape. Very quickly the master started to wear out. This wasn't such a problem during the Nirvana times when Grohl remained tight-lipped about the project. But with the launch of Foo Fighters in 1995, orders for the tape went through the roof.

"It's sort of been a thorn in our side," said Toomey in 1997. "Each mention of the cassette in *Rolling Stone* or wherever translates to piles of mail, and for the most part, these kids have never bought anything through the mail from an independent record company, so when they haven't received their tape in two weeks they write us nasty notes about how we've stolen their $5 and their mothers are going to sue us. The *Late!* tape has broken many an intern! But the one strange redeeming quality of the tape is the tape itself. Almost every time I listen to it – even now at this point of definite saturation – I still have to think it's a great record. It has a depth and vulnerability and crunch that you don't find on the Foo Fighters' record." [10]

With the master tape now degenerated beyond repair, *Pocketwatch* has gone out of print forever. However there had been talks about remastering onto CD. Eventually Grohl decided that it wasn't faithful to the original ethos behind the collection.

"He went back and forth with the idea and then it fell off the face of the earth," she said, "I think he's worried about the quality. Which I can understand and appreciate, but his modesty is killing us! I know he also thinks it's cooler to have it this way. Which it definitely is." [11]

Pocketwatch was a small statement of Grohl's independence in the face of overwhelming corporate manoeuvring. It represented the side of him that intended to remain true to the original DIY underground beliefs of punk rock, as all around him became increasingly alien. It was his final anti-ego, DC hardcore project – despite being musically removed from those far off Washington days.

"I always tried to keep them sort of a secret," he told David Daley of *Alternative Press* in 1996. "I wouldn't give people tapes. I always freaked out about that. I have the stupidest voice. I was totally embarrassed and scared that anyone would hear them," he said. "I just wanted to see how poppy or how noisy a song I could write.

It was always just for fun. You could do anything you wanted."

In January, 1993, a Nirvana performance found Grohl stepping from behind the drum kit to sing and play bass. It was at Morumbi Stadium in Sao Paulo, Brazil for an impromptu version of 'Rio' (by 80s stars Duran Duran). Cobain played drums, Novoselic played guitar and Grohl stood centre stage with mic in his face and bass in his hands. Despite being a nerve-racking moment for Grohl, he evidently enjoyed the experience. The track has never surfaced on bootleg however, so its quality remains a mystery to all but those who were present.

While in South America, the band recorded some more demo material for their forthcoming album. What was beginning to come clear was that if Geffen were hoping for a *Nevermind* part 2, they were going to be disappointed. These songs were far more confrontational.

Given Cobain's comments about the band's none-punk status, such a reversion to a more underground sound came as a welcome surprise. Cobain struggled to personally adapt to mainstream success. His heart still lay with abrasive rock 'n' roll. Indeed, he even started saying how much he hated *Nevermind*. One thing was for certain, the next album wasn't going to be for the "meat head jocks" or "the kids in Skid Row T-shirts". This album was going to be for the band alone. And if people got it, then fine. If not, it would be their loss.

As if to underline the band's desire to kick back against the mainstream sound of *Nevermind* and embrace their punk roots, they enlisted US punk legend Steve Albini in the role of producer. Albini was perhaps best known for Chicago band Big Black. This was initially a solo venture with Albini plying his guitar shards over a Roland drum machine for the debut *Lungs* in 1982. The following *Bulldozer EP* found him working alongside Jeff Pezzai on bass and Santiago Durango on drums. The resulting sound was far more muscular than before. The mini album, *Racer-X*, took the pile-driving, industrial hardcore sonics to an even deeper extreme.

With the introduction of a new bassist, Dave Riley, in 1985 the trio set to work on their debut full-length album *Atomizer*. It proved to be a full-on, abrasive assault on the senses as guitars and vocals twisted around the relentless jackhammer of the drum programming.

The *Headache* EP that followed in1987 was even more out on a chaotic extreme, thanks to the freeform psychosis that inhabited the records darkened grooves. Later that year, the band's final album, *Songs About Fucking,* was released to critical acclaim. It remains one of the most belligerently confrontational albums to have emerged from the US punk scene. A fusion of genuflected chaos and adrenalised beats, like muscle and sinew tense to the point of near-destruction, the Big Black finale would go on to influence bands as diverse as Ministry/Revolting Cocks, Nine Inch Nails and, of course, Nirvana.

Upon their demise, Albini formed the short-lived Rapeman, followed by the understated Shellac. He also forged a career as a producer working with, among others The Pixies, The Breeders and, much later, PJ Harvey.

Even though Jack Endino had recorded some of the demos for the next Nirvana album, he has claimed that he hadn't set his sights on doing the album sessions. He instinctively knew that it would be a tense affair, with the band taking the almost perverse step into the non-commercial slipstream. When he heard that Albini had been approached, he was amazed.

"While they were recording the demos with me they happened to mention, 'Yeah, we were thinking of having Steve Albini do the record.' And I was just like, wheeew! 'Steve, huh, yeah? That's a cool idea.'" That's going to be amazing! But there's going to be some fireworks. Because all the major label people and a lot of fans were going to want to hear *Nevermind* Version 2. And Steve, of course, would have no interest in making *Nevermind* Version 2. And I thought this could be a really cool Nirvana record, but I didn't envy Steve at all. Steve is gonna get blamed, and shit is gonna fly, and that's exactly what happened. Fortunately, Steve dealt with it the way he usually does; by telling everybody to fuck off." [12]

Recording of what would become Nirvana's third album, *In Utero* took place in fourteen days over the end of February and the beginning of March. The sessions took place at Pachyderm Studios in Cannon Falls, Minneapolis, where the band booked in as 'The Simon Ritchie Bluegrass Ensemble'. It was to prove to be a relatively relaxed session, with the band completely focussed on the task at hand. Among the seventeen tracks recorded was a brand new version of Grohl's 'Marigold', which although turning up on an early promo of the album, didn't make it to the final cut.

Rumours abounded that their record company didn't like it; that they pressurised Nirvana to make the mixes more palatable (Geffen staunchly denied this, so did Nirvana); suggestions the band were in disagreement with Albini and so on.

The furore surrounding *In Utero* refused to go away and more headlines about Kurt and Courtney's relationship only served to heighten the frenzy around the band. And all this at a time when Nirvana were not even on the road or in the charts – they were taking a break from touring for an enforced holiday.

Where most people would use the free time to catch up on some rest and relaxation - Grohl, who was increasingly turning into the hardest working drummer in rock - rejoined Scream for an eleven-date reunion tour. Even Skeeter Thompson was in the line up.

The tour was in support of the aforementioned posthumous release of *Fumble,* which Dischord had released with hardly any fanfare. Once again here was a Grohl-related project in which he refused to use his connections with Nirvana. Interestingly, Grohl's lone royalty cheque from his time at Dischord with Scream is framed and still on the wall of his home studio. It is made out for $30!

"When Pete said all this (Scream material) was going to come out on CD, first he just asked me some questions about remixing the stuff. Then it turned into, 'Why not do a show at the 9:30? Then it turned into a whole tour!" Grohl explained. [13]

It may have looked to the observer to be something of a busman's holiday for Grohl, but it gave him a necessary reminder that touring could be fun; that it needn't involve a feeling that you are simply a part of the rolling machinery. Pete and Franz were, as he often mentioned, his brothers and working once more with them gave him a desire to regain that sense of togetherness within Nirvana. To ensure the reunion tour captured the same excitement that had helped them through those endless jaunts around Europe and the US, they even used their trusty old van, a Dodge Ram.

"I'm so glad that we're doing this." Grohl said at the time. "I think it will throw everything back into perspective. So we'll play these clubs and maybe sleep on people's floors like we always did, then in the Fall I go out with Nirvana and fly into cities and play in front of ten or fifteen thousand people, go to a nice hotel, watch TV until I fall asleep. It's not the same as playing on a small stage with guys who are basically my brothers." [14]

Among the Scream dates were three nights in Washington, two of which took place at the legendary 9:30 Club, which had been the first reliable venue in the city to book punk and new wave bands. It was subsequently where much of the early DC punk scene flourished.

However, by the early 1990s, the venue had turned into one of the least popular places for the local music scene to play. Subsequently drummer Dante Ferrando started to explore the idea of opening a live music venue with an emphasis on nurturing raw talent and embracing the cutting edge. He put the word out among the DC music cognoscenti that he was looking for investors in the project. A group of business people and musicians subsequently put money into the venture. Among them was Dave Grohl who bought a 20% stake.

"I knew when I was starting the club that I'd need investors who were in it for the right reasons," explained Ferrando. "People who knew that a rock club is not a great investment and want to do it anyway so that the music gets heard. Dave was an obvious person to approach, of all the people I knew who might have money to invest and who might be interested in Washington having another good live music club." [15] "…it's something I wanted to do," [16] explained Grohl, some four years later.

With Scream's reunion tour over, Grohl returned to the Nirvana camp to prepare for the forthcoming *In Utero* tour. For this, they enlisted the services of Pat Smear from US punk legends The Germs on second guitar and Lori Goldston (a member of Seattle's Black Cat Orchestra) on cello. It was the start of a musical union between Grohl and Smear that would continue into Foo Fighters.

On September 14, *In Utero* was released in the UK, reaching a disappointing #8 in the charts. The album had its US release on September 21 entering the *Billboard* chart at #1. However, the sales were much less than had been anticipated, with US sales of 180,000 and worldwide figures of only 500,000 in first week of release. In contrast to the multi–platinum album *Nevermind* this was a very poor performance. *In Utero* would eventually go triple platinum, although its predecessor hit six–times platinum by 1994.

It has been said that *In Utero* was the sound of the band hitting the self-destruct button. But in reality, this was the sound of the band wide open and at their most brilliantly honest. An album where self-expression was everything and, as such, it was, almost ironically, their most alive, energised and razor sharp set. It was almost as if each member of Nirvana sensed that this was their final statement, and they had nothing to lose. Sales were irrelevant, *In Utero* had to be the definitive Nirvana beast.

Inevitably however, given the confusion that surrounded the band at the time, *In Utero* came across as incredibly confused. A collection of fractured tomes to Cobain's increasing confusion at life. Which could in fact be brought down to three things: the intensity of his relationship with Love, the disappointment at his relationship with an ill–informed yet obsessively invasive press and utter disgust at the whole idea of grunge.

Although the former two subjects would dominate the lyrics, the latter obsession cane to the fore in the breathtaking diversity captured in the music. Here the trio could be heard leaping from the safety net of both the formulaic *Bleach* and the mainstream -rock-dressed-up-as-punk ambiguity of *Nevermind* into an unknown universe. At once hard, but unnervingly gentle, brittle yet muscular, the songs offered an almost childlike wonder at the concept of extremism. But laced with that almost adolescent petulance, manifested in the increasingly pantomime-like gear trashing.

Witness here the disgruntled temper tantrums, the snarling one-liners, the snide put downs and above all, the defiant gestures; *In Utero* was the ultimate reaction to the disappointment Nirvana found at the door of global fame. Furthermore, it was their answer to the self-loathing they felt at creating *Nevermind* the album that had started a revolution, which would ultimately see punk rock tamed at the hands of MTV. It may not have been the sell-out album in its creation, but it was the vehicle upon which their own generation of garage bands and angry punks would jump aboard to grab a piece of the corporate pie. Middle-of-the-road rock bands would listen to *Nevermind* then grunge up their sound and start wearing lumberjack shirts to appeal to a new audience.

Indeed, with punk now tuned into a soundtrack to adverts, punk icons used for branding exercises and both grunge and heroin chic dominating the cat walks, it seemed as if the entire punk dream had been sold to the highest, and the lowest, bidders. *1991 – The Year Punk Broke* was the claim of Sonic Youth's documentary film of the time; however by 1993 its spirit was broken. *In Utero* was the sound of three men living with the knowledge that they had to take some of the blame.

Yet, there was an irony in the whole punk sell-out debate. *Nevermind* was always going to be a mainstream album, from the minute they started recording to the point they mastered it. There was no attempt to leave any edges that might snag the mainstream listener. There was no intention of playing the underground game.

Not that *In Utero* was the underground champion that it had been rumoured to be. The press reaction to the album was somewhat muted. *NME*'s John Mulvey concluded: "As a document of a mind in flux – dithering, dissatisfied, unable to come to term with sanity – Kurt should be proud of it. As a follow-up to one of the best records of the past ten years, it just isn't quite there. Perhaps it was dumb to expect anything more."

Elsewhere *Melody Maker*'s Sharon O'Connell suggested that Nirvana was the prefect example of Jean Baudrillard's theory of *simulacrum* in action. She suggested that anything of sufficient cultural significance can become obliterated by the mountain of media coverage it inspires. "If the images of that thing are reproduced ad-infinitum, if the text it generated piles up high enough around it, they will resonate so powerfully as to obliterate the original. That thing will be devoured by its own ghosts.

The endlessly parroted rumour, half-truths and innuendoes (you've heard 'em all) have built steadily up like layers of an onion around Kurt Cobain, who, shell-shocked by success, is literally shrinking from the world. Nirvana's hungrily awaited third album," she concluded, "is not quite the rubbed-raw confrontational, fan-alienating catharsis it's been talked up to be." [17]

It is true that the final version of the album was not the abrasive force originally envisaged. Indeed, producer Albini argued that the finished version actually suppressed the extreme edginess of the original recordings.

In the months that followed the album's release, Nirvana toured the US. However, in the days - and sometimes weeks - between gigging, Grohl continued his own sessions at The Laundry Room. He had by now put together a large catalogue of self-penned and self-played tunes. Although he has never stated that they were ever intended for release, or even for Nirvana, when surrounded by so much uncertainty in Cobain's band, Grohl must have inevitably – perhaps even subconsciously – been looking for the possible next step.

Grohl is, as has already been noted, almost a workaholic, whose energies and temperament would dictate that he would have to become involved with something else very quickly if his band split. He simply wouldn't be able to tolerate being idle. Doing his own thing, even at this stage, would have been a possible, and indeed logical, option.

Towards the end of 1993, Grohl would once again supply his drumming skills to another band. However, this time around the band was being touted as an alternative-rock supergroup which was being put together to record the soundtrack to a forthcoming film about the Beatles' Hamburg era, *Backbeat*. So, for Grohl it was a case of from the biggest band on the decade, to the biggest band of all time!

The Backbeat Band consisted of Thurston Moore (Sonic Youth), Greg Dulli (Afghan Whigs), Mike Mills (REM), Dave Pirner (Soul Asylum) and Dave Grohl. The songs recorded were rock 'n' roll standards like 'Money', 'Long Tall Sally', 'Twist And Shout', 'Please Mr Postman', 'C'mon Everybody' and 'Good Golly Miss Molly'. However they were delivered in a contemporary style, with vocals even echoing Cobain's own strained, growling tones.

Both the film and soundtrack album would see the light of day in 1994 (the soundtrack album in March and the movie in August), however they would be almost universally panned in the press. However, far from being the karaoke session that *Backbeat* threatened, the soundtrack actually allowed the combined forces of the players in the Backbeat Band to bring out fresh dimensions to these well-known and endlessly covered classics. Grohl's drumming especially produced a forceful energy that was completely lacking in either the Beatles' versions or the originals. The combination of his heavy hitting style and those trademark fills helping to bring out extraordinary performances from musicians who were often better known for their self-indulgence.

The Backbeat experience gave Grohl a taste for soundtracks that would resurface a few years later. It also gave him the impetus to get back to the studio with Nirvana when, in January 1994, the band went into Bob Lang Studios in North Seattle. Whilst there they recorded the song 'You Know You're Right' which would eventually surface in 2002 on the *Nirvana* retrospective compilation.

The band also messed around on a few other Nirvana tracks that would remain uncompleted. Cobain hadn't turned up at the studio until the last day of the session which gave both Grohl and Novoselic two days to sit around and wait. Unused to wasting time in this way, Grohl used the session to lay down some more of his own songs with Novoselic on bass. These were 'Exhausted' and 'Big Me'. He also recorded a cover of Angry Samoans' track, 'Gas Chamber, plus an untitled track which featured him on drums and Earnie Bailey playing a theramin which was treated through an Echoplex tape-loop echo machine (a theramin is a musical instrument – in the past used by Jon Spencer Blues Explosion and the Beastie Boys among others - that works by passing a hand over sound waves – it sounds like a violin bow on a saw and stars in the soundtrack to hundreds of horror films).

That they used Nirvana time to record songs not written by Cobain highlights the increased tension within the band. Both Novoselic and Grohl were growing tired of Kurt's ongoing 'health problems'. And the fact that he had chosen to squander the little time pencilled in to record new tracks was a matter of great concern to them.

On February 2, the band flew to Europe, to embark on their lengthiest tour yet. The opening dates in France, Portugal, Spain, Switzerland and Italy went without hitch with the band giving what is considered among fans as being their finest TV performance in Paris' Canal Studios.

However, with the start of the German leg, things started to go very wrong. The opening night at Munich's Terminal 1 went ahead as planned, but the following night's show was cancelled due to Cobain losing his voice. A specialist diagnosed severe laryngitis and bronchitis and told him to take two to four weeks rest.

Grohl remained in Germany to record the 'Please Mr Postman' promo for the UK single from the Backbeat soundtrack, while

Cobain and Smear headed for Rome. Novoselic returned to the US. On his first evening in Rome, Cobain sent a bellboy from the hotel to get a prescription for Rohypnol. He ordered two bottles of champagne.

The following morning, Courtney Love awoke to discover Cobain in a coma. He had overdosed, reported as accidental following the combination of the drug and the alcohol.

Following five hours emergency treatment at Umberto i Polyclinic Hospital in Rome, Cobain came out of his coma on March 5 and returned to the US three days later. Dates in Czechoslovakia and Germany were subsequently cancelled.

Cobain's state of mind and volatile private life continued to take precedence over the band's music throughout the coming weeks as more European dates in Germany, Holland, Sweden and Belgium fell under the axe. Further media reports of police being called to Cobain's Seattle home amidst fears for his own safety (from himself) fuelled the growing sense of chaos around Nirvana.

The situation was becoming increasingly difficult for Grohl and Novoselic who were in effect being stopped in their tracks by their singer's actions. Grohl continued to record material at Barrett Jones' Laundry Rooms Studio but became more and more frustrated at the enforced sabbatical.

Novoselic's concern for his friend, and anger at the situation, encouraged him to take Love's lead to make Cobain undergo "tough love" treatment. Approximately ten people, including Novoselic, but excluding Grohl, spent five hours solid attempting to force Cobain to face up to his problems. He subsequently agreed to enter a detox centre.

Following this treatment, a series of revised British dates were announced. They were to take in Manchester, Glasgow, Birmingham, Cardiff, London and Dublin. But they would never take place.

On April 8, 1994, Cobain's body was discovered in a room above the garage of his Washington Boulevard home. He had shot himself.

Grohl was reported to be "devastated" by the news. He even considered giving up playing all together. "I think about his smile a lot," Grohl recalled some years later. "And his laugh. He had a funny laugh, this fucking cackle. I remember him being happy. It's easy to remember him being sad… He really, really loved creating music. Every night, when we were living together, he used to go into his bedroom, I was sleeping on the couch, and he would go in and write for hours in his journals… He was a gentle, sweet, caring person. He was always so nice to my mom [*laughs*]. A lot of people imagine him as this terror, when, honestly, he was one of the nicest people you ever met. And I like to think about the shape of his hands, and the way he moved his mouth when he played the guitar. Those are the kinds of things I remember. I definitely feel lucky to have known him. He changed my life forever in so many ways. And I miss him. I think about him a lot." [18]

Any actual self-imposed retirement by Grohl proved to be short lived. On June 4, 1994, he played a one off gig with The Backbeat Band at the MTV Awards in New York. The band performed 'Money', 'Long Tall Sally' and 'Helter Skelter'.

Grohl's need to get back playing again underlined the fundamental difference between him and Cobain. Beyond all the weirdness that had enveloped Nirvana, the simple fact was that Grohl still loved playing and making music. He loved performing – why else would he have agreed to reunite with Scream, or play live with Buzz Osborne, or even perform Beatles covers with the Backbeat Band? Indeed, music remained beating at the heart of Grohl's waking day and probably featured heavily in his dreams too.

By contrast, Cobain had began to despair at the lack of excitement he felt with music. In his suicide note Cobain admitted: "I haven't felt the excitement of listening to as well as creating music… for many years now," he famously wrote. "I feel guilty beyond words about these things. For example, when we're back stage and the lights go out and the manic roar of the crowd begins, it doesn't effect me the way in which it did for Freddie

Mercury who seemed to love, relish in the love and adoration from the audience. Which is something I totally admire and envy… sometimes I feel as if I should punch in a time clock before I walk on stage." He continued "I've tried everything in my power to appreciate it."

On July 12, Novoselic and Grohl played live together for the first time since Cobain's death. The performance was as a part of the Stink Puffs; a band led by ten-year-old Simon Timony. This came about through Timony's friendship with Cobain. The young musician had sent a copy of his own EP to Cobain as a present, a fact that Cobain acknowledged in the liner notes of *Incesticide*. Timony had then met Nirvana during the band's Fall 1993 tour and even joined them onstage for one of the gigs.

The Stinky Puffs gig was on the opening night of the Yo Yo A Go Go Festival, held in Olympia. Talking in 1997, Sheenah Fair, Timony's mother explained that she had initially approached Novoselic to join the band on stage. But then Grohl also joined in, unannounced.

"I saw Dave checking out Krist (Novoselic) just about to go on," Fair said. "And I said, 'Dude, get a drum set. Come on, come on with us. This'll be good, it'll be good for you.' He's like, 'I'm gonna fuck it up - I don't even know your music!'" Eventually, Grohl did agree to go on, and though their appearance was unannounced, the media on hand for the opening night of the festival insured instant coverage of the event. "One journalist said that Simon had performed a mass healing," says Fair. "And that's really how it felt." [19] The set was recorded and gained a full release the following year.

The first post-Cobain Nirvana release came in the shape of the *MTV Unplugged In New York* set which had been recorded on November 18 at Sony Music Studios. Initially it had been intended as a double album entitled *Verse Chorus Verse* whereby one set was to be culled from that *MTV* performance, while the other was to be a career-spanning compilation of the band's live show. It was a plan that was aimed at meeting the demand for live recordings of the band that had spurned a huge global bootlegging operation. Indeed, the *MTV* set was already widely available on bootleg.

Soon after the announcement of the live double, Geffen were forced to issue a retraction. The *MTV* show would now be issued alone. The reason was simple, both Grohl and Novoselic had found the process of going through the old tapes too emotionally draining. Although they had decided on which songs were to be used, and the performances they were to be taken from, the duo decided that it was simply too soon after Cobain's death to mix the album properly.

MTV Unplugged was released on November 1, entering the US *Billboard* charts at #1 while hitting #2 in the UK charts. Even before Cobain's death the acoustic performance was charged with a strangely chilling undercurrent. However, post-suicide, it became drenched in poignancy. Everything from the choice of covers, to Cobain's own lyrics (again) were carefully picked over by fans and critics looking for clues about his death. "As things are," wrote Andrew Mueller in *Melody Maker*, "*Unplugged...* is at best gut-twistingly poignant, and often nigh unbearable."

Perhaps the most telling cover version on the set was David Bowie's 'Man Who Sold The World'. Once a sub-metal world domination fantasy for Bowie, before turning pantomime pop song for Lulu, Nirvana's version came over like a confessional. Here was Cobain, wracked with guilt for being undeserving of the attention heaped upon him post-*Nevermind*, holding a mirror to himself. Unlike Bowie however, Cobain was unable to hide his feelings behind a series of personas. It was impossible to listen to the set without thinking of what could have been.

Interestingly, Grohl played bass on the band's version of The Vaselines' 'Jesus Doesn't Want Me For a Sunbeam' – another song choice that seemed to offer some kind of hint at Cobain's state of mind. Later in November the long awaited full-length video, *Live! Tonight! Sold Out!* was finally released to almost predictable rave reviews. A week later Grohl once again took up his drumsticks, this time to drum for Tom Petty on *Saturday Night Live*. He subsequently considered joining Petty's band full time.

"Right after Kurt died, I was getting all these offers from other bands to come and play drums for them, and frankly I was a little offended," he said in 1997. "So I lay low for a while, but after you've been in the dance for so long, it just doesn't make sense to stop." [20]

Grohl didn't stop. He was starting to formulate ideas for his very own band, to be called Foo Fighters. Also refusing to stop, however, was the Nirvana machine. Certainly posthumous releases were a part of the healing process for both Grohl and Novoselic. However, in the years that followed Cobain's death, these records would turn into battle grounds between the remaining members of Nirvana and Courtney Love. Furthermore, with the exception of the live set *From The Muddy Banks of the Wishkah* (which came out in September 1996), future Nirvana activity attracted as much publicity for these disputes as for the actual music itself.

The protracted legal wrangles – during which Grohl was once described as "the group's sixth drummer" – centred around who ultimately controlled Nirvana and the band's back catalogue. Details of the disputes – in the form of court papers pored over by the world's media (particularly that surrounding a box-set to commemorate the tenth anniversary of *Nevermind*) – highlighted the severity of the internal band arguments. Some observers suggested that Nirvana must have been on the verge of splitting up just before Cobain's death anyway. Other reports claimed Cobain was recording with members of other bands, including REM – although this is not a concrete precursor to a Nirvana split, as Grohl's own solo recordings and extra-curricular gigging proved. After months of very public and acrimonious disputes, Grohl, Novoselic and Love settled out of court.

"At the end of the day, it's just not worth all the pain and the anguish," Grohl told *MTV News*. "God, I had to get up at 9am to do a deposition today, and it's just not worth that to me because my contribution has been made. The band is over and forever that music will be there. There are times when I honestly don't give a shit who's running the cash register. I'll always be the guy who played drums in that band, and to me that's more important than control or power or money or whatever." Finally, in October 2002, Geffen issued a retrospective compilation, a career-spanning set simply called *Nirvana*.

There is no doubting Nirvana's legacy. They introduced a breath-taking new spin on the rock lexicon and created a collection of era-defining songs. However, Grohl's own input has often been underplayed. There was surely more to Grohl's role than simply hitting the skins according to Cobain's instructions.

His precise, hard-hitting drumming gave the band a hitherto unknown rhythmical clarity that complemented Cobain's songs. His well-tuned ear for a catchy melody and haunting harmony plus his own backing vocals all added invaluably to the mix.

Some have argued that Grohl was the necessary final piece in the creative jigsaw, without which Nirvana might never have attained the level of success they did. That is open to debate of course. At the same time, it is all too easy to put down the group's greatness to just one individual. That Grohl is regarded as just another drummer is perhaps one of the cruellest drummer jokes of all.

4

ALONE AND AN EASY TARGET

ANOTHER DRUMMER JOKE
How do you know if the drum riser is level?
The drummer drools from both corners of his mouth.

In the chaos that followed Cobain's death, Grohl contributed to a recording session that was to inadvertently shape his next move. It was May 29, a week before Grohl's *MTV* performance with the Backbeat Band, and both he and Pat Smear had agreed to contribute to an album by long-time friend Mike Watt.

Watt had been bassist with legendary hardcore act Minutemen, who regrouped as fIREHOSE after the death of singer–guitarist D Boon in a 1985 van accident. In the early 1980s, Minutemen were considered to be the peers of Husker Du and Meat Puppets, doing much to subvert the traditional rock music structure and push the alternative scene. Just as the band were verging on mass popularity (they regularly played with REM and were expected to join the Georgia band's rise to international fame) the band's singer/ songwriter (and Watt's best friend) was killed.

Following a brief period in which Watt considered giving up music altogether, he formed the band fIREHOSE from the ashes of Minutemen. The debut album picked up where the previous band had left off and pretty soon numerous major labels were courting them. They eventually signed to Columbia, releasing a total of seven albums before their eventual break up in 1994.

Both Grohl and Smear had been huge fans of Watt's bands. Such was his repute among the underground community that he even guested on the Sonic Youth side project Ciccone Youth and with bass duo DOS. He would also briefly join Perry Farrell's first post-Jane's Addiction project, Porno for Pyros.

Watt's debut solo album was in fact a huge collaboration with musicians he had worked with, or become associated with over the years. The fifty strong line-up of guests read like a who's who of alt-rock, ranging from Eddie Vedder (Pearl Jam), Henry Rollins and Sonic Youth to Flea, Perry Farrell and Dave Pirner (Soul Asylum). Grohl and Smear were the icing on the all-star cake.

Of course, the similarities between Watt's and Grohl's situation were remarkably similar. Both had experienced the loss of their band's singer and songwriter, both had been forced to face up to the idea of quitting music altogether and both had finally found solace in music. However, there was another factor that brought added poignancy to the collaborations; Pat Smear had also suffered the loss of a friend who happened to be an irreplaceable member of his band The Germs; singer Darby Crash (aka Paul Beahm).

Punk band The Germs had formed in Los Angeles in1977 with a line up that included Belinda Carlisle on drums! Their debut single, 'Forming' is often cited as being the first example of US punk's metamorphosis into hardcore. Following the band's one and only album *GI*, The Germs disbanded, only to reform a few months later in 1980. A week after their first reunion concert, however, Crash died from a heroin overdose. He'd just recorded the song 'Suicide Madness'.

If the line up for Watt's album, *Ball-Hog or Tug Boat?*, had seemed a little like a post-tragedy self-help group, then the inclusion of Flea, whose friend and original guitarist of the Red Hot Chili Peppers, Hillel Slovak, had also died of a heroin overdose, only added to this.

In fact, this project was an important part of Grohl's grieving process. Despite the fact that Watt was actually accused by cynics of being insensitive to the recent loss of Cobain, the sessions for *Ball-Hog or Tug Boat?* were extremely helpful to Grohl who realised that his life would remain in music after collaborating with so many musicians he admired.

Talking about the tragic common ground that existed between himself and Grohl (and Novoselic), Watt noted: "Krist grew up with [Kurt], so it was like me and D Boon in a way. When you lose your guy, it's fucked. And some English paper accused me of not dealing with Kurt's death. It was a really weird thing. But we did get talking about it after we'd recorded a little bit. The big difference was, me and D Boon were not famous, and Krist and Kurt are. I guess it was the first time [Grohl and Krist] played together on a record since [Nirvana], and it got blown all out of proportion. Whereas me and D Boon were little enough for it to be a private thing for us. It never has gotten to be private for Krist or Dave. Dave's going to come out with his new band, and he's going to have to deal with this thing, over and over again, where, man, I was turning people *on* to D Boon. A lot of the dudes didn't know about us - we were little. Punk was little, so I got to turn people onto D Boon." [1]

Ironically, Watts received a huge amount of criticism from the press for employing so many well-known artists. He was, the media harshly claimed, simply hitching a ride on their coat-tails to launch his own solo career. It is unlikely that any single member of his line-up of guests would have agreed with this sentiment. Put simply, Watt was, and still is, a legend.

For the album, which was released in February 1995, Grohl played drums on 'Big Train' and 'Against The 70s' while Smear supplied vocals to 'Forever' and 'One Reporter's Opinion'. During the session, however, Grohl gave Pearl Jam's Eddie Vedder a copy of the two-track demo he had made at Robert Lang's Studio at the same time as Nirvana's 'You Know You're Right' was recorded.

However, this didn't necessarily mark the beginning of Grohl's solo career. Even at this stage he wasn't sure whether he wanted to make music anymore. Drumming for other people in one-off projects was one thing, but pouring the emotional energy required for making music with a band was another thing entirely. Indeed, he even contemplated joining Tom Petty's Heartbreakers band as a full-time member.

"I was this close to joining," he says. "It was so much fun. I was really scared. I was most afraid that they had watched (MTV's)

Unplugged and decided to get me from seeing that. But when we rehearsed, they treated me like I was in the band. It was such an honour. But I figured that I was twenty-six-years-old and didn't want to become a drummer for hire at that age." [2]

The final boost his spirit needed came from an unlikely source. Seattle band 7 Year Bitch had also lost a member of their band. In a postcard to Grohl, they urged him not to give up. "After Kurt's death, I was about as confused as I've ever been. To continue almost seemed in vain. I was always going to be 'that guy from Kurt Cobain's band' and I knew that. I wasn't even sure if I had the desire to make music anymore. That fucking letter [from 7 Year Bitch] saved my life, because as much as I missed Kurt, and as much as I felt so lost, I knew that there was only one thing that I was truly cut out to do and that was music. I know that sounds so incredibly corny, but I honestly felt that. I decided to do what I had always wanted to do since the first time I'd recorded a song all by myself. I was going to book a week in a twenty four track studio, choose the best stuff I'd ever written out of the thirty-to-forty songs that had piled up, and really concentrate on them in a real studio." [3]

So Grohl and Jones started to trawl through the tapes he'd demo-ed over the last few years and came up with a final list of fifteen. The next step was to book time in Robert Lang's Studio. The sessions took place between October 17 and 23, 1994. By this stage Grohl was so used to the recording process whereby he played everything, that he was able to work extremely quickly, recording them in the same order that they would eventually appear on the finished album. The first track 'This Is A Call' took a mere forty-five minutes to record.

"It became this little game," he said at the time. "I was running from room to room, still sweating and shaking from playing drums and I'd pick up the guitar and put down a track, do the bass, maybe do another guitar part, have a sip of coffee and then go in and do the next song. We were done with the music in the first two days." [4]

Tracks recorded during this session were 'Alone + Easy Target', 'Good Grief', 'Exhausted', 'Podunk' and 'Floaty', originally recorded at Barrett's studios in 1992. From 1993 he recorded 'Big Me', 'Weenie Beenie', 'For All The Cows', 'X-Static', 'Wattershed' and 'Butterflies'. While 'This Is A Call', 'I'll Stick Around' and 'Oh, George' were all demo-ed in 1994. Grohl also recorded a new version of Winnebego from the *Pocketwatch* tape. Grohl played all instruments, except for 'X-Static', which featured guitar by Afghan Whigs' Greg Dulli (whom Grohl had worked with in the Backbeat Band).

"He'd do a whole song in about forty minutes," said Dulli. "I was completely fascinated by it. He could do it because he has perfect time. He'd lay down a perfect drumbeat and work off that. He'd play drums, run out and play bass, and then put two guitar layers over the top and sing it. I was just watching him record, and he asked me if I wanted to play. I didn't even get out of my chair. He just handed me a guitar." [5]

"The first four hours was spent getting sounds," wrote Grohl in 1995. This was a cinch for Barrett, whom I'd asked to produce since he was the one person in the world I felt comfortable singing in front of. By five o'clock we were ready to record. Over the past six years, Barrett and I had perfected our own method of recording. Start with drums, listen to playback while humming tune in head to make sure arrangement is correct, put down two or three guitar tracks - mind you, all amplifiers and everything are ready to go before recording begins - do bass track and move on to next songs, saving vocals for last."

Interestingly, of the songs recorded, three had actually been written in period since Cobain's death. These were 'This Is A Call', 'Oh George' and 'I'll Stick Around'. 'This Is A Call' had actually been written on a mini-electric guitar while Grohl was on his honeymoon in Dublin. He'd married long time girlfriend, photographer Jennifer Youngblood in 1993.

With the recording and a rough mix done, Grohl duped up one hundred copies of the completed demo and started circulating them among friends and industry people. The demo went under the name

Very early Nirvana press shot.

Cobain and Grohl at Novoselic's Seattle house, 1990.

Drumming for Nirvana at the Seattle Center Coliseum,
September 11, 1992.

The shy former drummer has grown into his role as Foo frontman.

On-stage with Pat Smear, Foo Fighters, 1997.

Two fans spot Grohl out and about in Leicester Square, London, 1999.

Drumming for QOTSA at the Coachella festival, April 2002; wondering why he didn't get that new drum stool after all.

Taylor with his wife at the *Kerrang!* Awards, 2002.

Queens of the Stone Age, "who rock ten times harder
than anything I've ever done."

2002 line-up of Foo Fighters at MTV Europe Awards, Barcelona.

Killing Joke.

Grohl with wife, Jordyn Blum, 2002.

Foo Fighters. This was the only information apart from song titles.

"I just wanted to release this tape that I had done on my label, with no names on it, and then get an independent distributor and send it out to the world, maybe 10,000 or 20,000 copies so people would think, 'God, who is this band Foo Fighters? I've never heard of them before.' I just wanted it to be this real anonymous release." [6]

Grohl's ambitions for this collection of songs may have been minimal but the demos quickly became the industry's worst kept secret. Bootlegs started to appear on the market and major labels started sniffing around to sign the drummer up. Says Grohl: "… my first mistake: my trip to the duplication lab downtown for one hundred copies. My next mistake was my blind generosity. That fucking tape spread like the Ebola virus, leaving me with an answering machine tape full of record company jive."

However, Grohl was still not happy to launch himself onto the world with a full-blown solo career. He decided to put a band together for the project. He had also made a decision that would help him to put the past in its place. He vacated the drummer's seat for the first time since those Freak Baby days. Grohl was to be singer and guitarist in the new band.

Thanks to Novoselic's involvement in the initial Nirvana-era Bob Lang recordings, rumours started to circulate that the two would be reunited on this project. Both had remained close since their Nirvana days when their friendship had been cemented on that last Nirvana tour when Grohl and Novoselic had opted to travel on one tour bus while Cobain and Love travelled in a separate tour bus with Pat Smear.

To add to the rumour of Novoselic and Grohl working together, the duo had actually recorded some material at The Laundry Room. "He (Novoselic) was like, 'Man, d'you wanna jam?' It seemed to really spark something in me. So we got together in Barrett's studio and wrote maybe four of five of these jams, no vocals, just bass and drums. It was really cool, we wanted to get in the van and go on tour, doing this bass and drums thing. But Krist was really busy with things like Bosnian Relief Organisation and he has a farm now, out in the middle of nowhere in Washington. So he's actually really busy."[7]

The first person Grohl approached to join the band was Seattle local Nate Mendel, who's band Sunny Day Real Estate had recently split following one album on Sub Pop. Grohl had first met Mendel at a Thanksgiving Party held at the former's house. Mendel's girlfriend was a good friend of Grohl's wife and the two hit it off immediately. Interestingly, it was at this party that Grohl confirmed his suspicions that his house was haunted. After the party, the remaining friends (Mendel included) used a Ouija board to contact the spirits. Grohl's ghost expressed its displeasure by rocking the table violently and spelling out answers to their questions. Everyone freaked.

Said Grohl: "Jennifer asked if there were spirits in the house. The glass on the Ouija board spelled out 'Y-E-S'. I was just looking at Jennifer and she wasn't moving at all. The glass was travelling without her pushing it. Jennifer then asked, 'What happened here?' The glass spelled out 'M-U-R-D-E-R-E-D'. I asked who was murdered, and got the reply 'M-Y- B-A-B-Y'."[8]

Grohl subsequently discovered that, according to local legend, in the late nineteenth century, a Native American baby *was* murdered by its mother and buried in a well. The mother's ghost supposedly haunts the area, waiting for her child to be given a proper burial.

The next piece in the Foo Fighters band jigsaw slotted into place with the arrival of Pat Smear. Such was Grohl's admiration for Smear - and insecurity at his own recordings – that it had taken him ages to give Smear a copy of the demo. Indeed, Grohl had been such a fan of Smear's guitar playing that he had memorised almost every word spoken by the guitarist in the early 1980s LA punk documentary, *The Decline Of The Western Civilisation* – and this was long before he'd become the fourth member of Nirvana.

"I called Pat up a couple weeks after I gave him the tape," Grohl said in 1996, "way before we had a tour booked, probably before we had even played with each other. I asked him what he was doing. He said he was working on his guitars." [9]

The conversation, according to Grohl had gone: "(Working on guitars) For what?" "For a tour." "Whose?" "Ours." [10] Smear was on board. "After you've been in the coolest band ever," Smear explained, "what do you do? I sat on the couch with the remote control in my hand for a year. I didn't know if I ever wanted to be in a band again. I was just working on solo stuff. Dave and I had kept in touch and I had heard about his tape, but I didn't know what to expect. When I heard the tape, I flipped. Dave gave it to me at a club and I went home. After I listened to it, I went back to the club. But I didn't want to ask to join the band. I waited for him to ask me."

Now all Grohl needed was someone to take the unenviable position of sitting in the drummer's seat. Enter William Goldsmith, Mendel's band mate from Sunny Real Estate. Grohl subsequently got his wife to pass two copies of Foo Fighters' tape on to Goldsmith and Mendel. It wasn't made clear what Grohl was intending. There was some mention of recording, or simply working together, but no suggestion of becoming members of a band.

"We listened to the tape and we liked it a lot, but we didn't know what would happen next," Goldsmith explained. "Then I was in DC that week after our last tour and he called. It was a great phone call. He was like, 'Oh, so your band's in the shitter.' I told him 'yes'. He said, 'All right. Let's play.'" [11]

Grohl had seen the bassist and drummer in action twice with Sunny Day Real Estate and had been impressed by their energy as much as their ability. This energy was important to Grohl's game plan, as he explained in 1996: "My main concern wasn't finding someone who could do everything exactly as it was on the tape, but someone who had really good energy. There's not very many of them. When I saw Will play, I was really amazed. So I called Nate and Will and... we started playing. After the second or third time in William (Goldsmith)'s basement, we had the songs down." [12]

With the final addition of the Sunny Real Estate rhythm section, Grohl felt he had the right band to publicly launch Foo Fighters. The band decided to perform for the first time at a private keg party in a friend's house. The band even provided the kegs of beer.

Despite the band's activities, rumours still circulated that Novoselic would be joining as well. Eventually Grohl put paid to these rumours: "For Krist and I, it would have felt really natural and really great, but for everyone else, it would have been weird and it would have left me in a really bad position. Then it really would have been under the microscope." [13]

On January 8, 1995, Foo Fighters received their first public airing, although they were announced under Grohl's name. It was on Eddie Vedder's *Self-Pollution Radio Show*. Vedder introduced the songs as being by his friend Dave Grohl. The tracks he actually played were the demos Grohl had handed to Vedder during the Mike Watt sessions. 'Gas Chamber (No Action)' led the broadcast, with 'Exhausted' following. The track which followed Grohl's segment was Babes In Toyland's 'Pain in My Heart'.

A month later the entire band flew to The Shop Studio in LA to do a final mix on the demo tracks. The session was booked in for the beginning of March, however the band called ahead and blagged a support slot at the Jambalaya Club in Arcata, CA on February 23. It was to be the first time the public would get to see Foo Fighters live; a show that Grohl has fond memories of.

"We cut out stencils and sprayed them on top of shirts we bought at a thrift store," recalled Grohl. "There'd be, like, Hooters T-shirts with our stencil over it, and we sold them for three bucks. We opened for a band called The Unseen. We thought they'd be some wicked punk-rock band, but they turned out to be a cover band made up of seventeen-year-old kids who dressed like The Jam and could play any song you asked for. We just drank, and danced. It was such fun, and there were no rules and no expectations." [14]

Of course, this show wasn't exactly the most widely-advertised performance imaginable, and as far as the wider world was concerned, Grohl was still contemplating his future. The demo tape had become common knowledge, along with Grohl's constant claims that he wasn't intending to do much with them. Even at this stage, the public opinion of the drummer was that he would probably join another high profile band.

Adding fuel to this idea was Grohl's appearance in the drum seat for Pearl Jam on three of their Australian dates in March 1995. On March 16 he played along to 'Sonic Reducer', March 17 'Keep On Rocking In The Free World' and on March 22, 'Sonic Reducer' again and 'Against the 70s', one of the songs he'd recorded with Mike Watt.

"That was kind of a fluke. We had Foo Fighters just about ready to go on our first tour opening for Mike Watt and we were to be gone for a little over a month," explained Grohl of how the Pearl Jam shows came about. "I had all these frequent flier miles so I thought I might as well have a little vacation before the tour. Pearl Jam was on tour down there and we have a good friend doing the tour accounting for them and another friend of ours is their tour masseuse or witchdoctor or whatever. So we thought we would just fly down, book ourselves into the same hotel and surprise them.

I thought it was so great because we got to go and see some of the Pearl Jam shows and I was so excited just to be a spectator and have all the fun of someone who doesn't have to go up onstage and play. Because I get so incredibly nervous before I play. Whether it's drums or guitar, I get really, really nervous. And so I was looking forward to going down and hanging out and seeing friends and having something to drink and watching the show. The first night I got there, we went to the show and they asked me if I would play a song with them... and then it was like – vacation was over." [15]

Joining forces with another band full-time was no longer an option, however, as by this stage Foo Fighters had not only put together their first tour, but also inked a deal with Capitol Records. So much for only putting out a few thousand records on his own label!

The deal was a production and distribution (P&D) deal for

Grohl's label *Roswell Records Inc.*, through which all Foo Fighter records would be released. As a result, Grohl retained his intention of being on an independent label; however by signing this label to a large major, he was also showing signs that he had greater confidence in the material than he'd previously stated. Grohl wanted his new venture to be successful on a commercial level, just as his previous band had been.

Grohl was, of course, perfectly in tune with the changing face of the music industry. By this time it was becoming increasingly difficult for small independents to finance videos, tours and other means of promotion. It was obvious that Grohl wanted his venture to succeed on a large scale, so signing a P&D deal was the obvious way forward. Through the deal he gained the funding required to push the band forward, without losing control.

So, Foo Fighters started their career in the strange position of being on an independent label, but through a major. They wanted to be small enough to gain credibility despite featuring two members of the biggest rock band of the 1990s. And last but not least, they had a frontman who used to be a drummer, but still claimed to want the anonymity of the drum seat. Finally he wanted the band to be seen as just that, a band, despite the fact that it was common knowledge that Grohl had written and recorded all of the songs on the demo, and that these tracks were now re-mixed and ready to be released as a Foo Fighter album. It was all a long way from the second-generation copied *Pocketwatch* set.

In the few days preceding the album mix down, Foo Fighters played two low profile shows at *Satyricon* in Portland, (March 3) and Seattle's *Velvet Elvis* (March 4). This latter date found five hundred people queuing around the block to gain entry to the one hundred and fifty capacity venue. On completion of the album mix, they played another two equally low key dates at *Pan* at Silverlake on March 10 and then on the last day of the month, at Albuquerque's *Dingo's Bar*.

These opening Foo Fighters shows were important in that they gave the band time to iron out any problems in lesser known venues. Furthermore, they provided the band with a good chance to enjoy life on the road away from the media glare. Following Nirvana's last tour, in which the camaraderie that Grohl had loved so much all but disappeared, it was important for him to rediscover the same feeling with his new band.

These few dates were extremely successful on all counts. The crowds who witnessed the performances were very vocal in their support. The band gelled enormously as a unit, with Smear becoming something of an enigmatic figurehead for the rest of the band, while Grohl himself was able to counter some of the nerves he suffered playing live. He had become extremely susceptible to stage fright in the latter days of Nirvana.

On April 12, Grohl was able to test his nerves further as the band headed out on a twenty–date tour of the US in support of Mike Watt. Hovercraft supplied the second support. Opening in Phoenix on April 24 and coming to a close on May 20 in San Diego, the tour would wind round the US, taking in Denver, St. Louis, Nashville and Atlanta before eventually hitting the higher profile locations of New York, Philadelphia, and on April 25, Grohl's own club, the Black Car in Washington DC. Perhaps the most noteworthy gig on the tour came on the Chicago date at Cabaret Metro on May 6, at which Foo Fighters joined forces with Eddie Vedder and Mike Watt to perform songs from the latter's album.

Reaction to the band was positive throughout the tour, although some members of the audience insisted on calling out for Nirvana songs, much to Grohl's annoyance. "When we first started playing people would come to shows and shout for us to play 'Heart Shaped Box' and I thought they were joking. But they were serious. I was afraid I was never gonna be able to shake it off," Grohl explained a few months later. [16]

With anticipation growing for the release of the debut Foo Fighters single and album, rumours started to circulate that Grohl had agreed to join Nailbomb as well. Nailbomb was the side project for

Sepultura's Max Cavalera. It later transpired however that nothing had been agreed.

"What really happened," says Cavalera, "is, I met Dave a couple of times, he's into Sepultura, so I gave him a Nailbomb CD and he liked it. I called him and asked him of he wanted to play at the Dynamo. He was really into it, but he was on tour with Foo Fighters. Otherwise, he said he'd have definitely done it."

On June 3, Foo Fighters played their debut UK gig as unannounced support for Teenage Fan Club at London's King's College. The set list for the show ran: 'This Is A Call', 'I'll Stick Around', 'Winnebago', 'Watershed', 'For All The Cows', 'Weenie Beenie', 'Butterflies', 'Big Me', 'Podunk', 'Good Grief', 'X-Static', 'Alone + Easy Target' and 'Exhausted'.

Interestingly, despite the band's stated desire to remain out of the spotlight, the contract that the photographers were requested to sign allowed only three songs during which to shoot the band, which certainly showed that Grohl had his sights set firmly on global success.

It has already been noted that Cobain had stated his desire to control all of the content that was generated around Nirvana, but Grohl already seemed to be seizing the horns of this particular issue. He was learning from Nirvana's mistakes and putting a solid foundation into place from day one.

Of the level of paranoia that surrounded Nirvana when it came to unofficial merchandise, Grohl claimed to be ambivalent. "Having been in Nirvana, I can see both sides," he said. "I'm not worried. You can't be paranoid for the rest of your life – so I'm not totally paranoid. And in that sense I still am relatively naïve. I think that's a good thing, because I can't stand distrust; I hate feeling like everyone is out to get me and that everyone wants a piece of me.

Life's too short to sit around worrying about whether someone's going to bootleg your T-shirt. It's like, fuck man, if a kid's going to bootleg a Foo Fighters T-shirt, all right. I don't endorse mass bootlegging, but the bottom line of it is that some kid's going to be walking around wearing a Foo Fighters T-shirt." [17]

Despite the fantastic audience response to the debut London gig, press reactions were less than ecstatic. Nirvana champion Everett True was particularly negative in his review for the *Melody Maker*. Discussing this later with Grohl, True admitted that a part of his problem with the band was that too much sympathy was being extended towards the new band.

"That's true," Grohl agreed. "Well, it's hard. It's hard for me... (clicks teeth)...I don't know. I don't take a lot of the sympathy because...I read somewhere recently that you should never ask a man if he's OK. It's true. It's so belittling. It makes you feel like nothing, pee'd on. But it's hard, because a lot of the times when people write about the band, there's always some personal interjection, and people do feel really sorry for Krist and I. And I don't feel sorry for myself," he continued. "I'm sorry that a lot of things happened that did, but I'll never ask for anyone's sympathy. I know it's there though..." [18]

True's initial reaction to Foo Fighters was fairly typical of a media who viewed Grohl's latest venture through cynical eyes. He would variously be accused of succeeding through default, launching a sound-alike band off the back of a legend and, perhaps most bizarrely of all, abusing Cobain's legacy. Grohl was in a no-win situation from the start.

Nine days after the London show, a promo 12" of 'Exhausted' hit the streets featuring the new version of the track he'd recorded at Bob Lang's studio sessions, coupled with a new version of 'Winnebego' from *Pocketwatch*. The debut single 'This Is A Call' arrived a week later on June 19, backed by 'Winnebago' and 'Podunk'.

'Winnebego' had barely changed from its earlier incarnation, while 'Podunk' gave little insight into the nature of the album that would follow. Both tracks were to be omitted from the final album tracklisting. While the former was a match for any of the tracks on the album, 'Podunk' was a dull and rambling grunge-by-numbers rocker, complete with screamed verse and melodic chorus.

'This Is A Call' on the other hand was a joyous celebration of distorted guitars, machine gun drum fills and melodies straight from the Beach Boys songbook. The perfect introduction to the self -titled debut album. 'This Is A Call' reached #5 in the UK chart.

Foo Fighters fittingly appeared on Independence Day, July 4, 1995. Opening track 'This Is A Call' clearly laid out the Foo Fighters' manifesto. Solid, up front drums, grinding distorted guitars playing counterpoint to occasional simple jangly guitar refrains, strong sing -a-long vocal melodies and an arrangement that was as simple as it was effective.

Perhaps tellingly, the vocals on 'This Is A Call', as with the rest of album, remained low in the mix, Grohl's thin voice occasionally being beefed up with double tracking. "I just have an amazing insecurity about my voice... I think Michael Stipe once said that his sinuses were a God-given gift and that's why his voice is so nasally and bizarre as it is. To me, it's more of a curse. I'd rather have them repaired so I can sing like Luciano Pavarotti..." [19]

Not surprisingly, drums were to the fore throughout, guitars were occasionally so distorted as to sound distant, although the bass frequently lacked any real punch. Despite such potential failings, the overall effect was of a garage band. For a major label debut (albeit through an independent label) *Foo Fighters* was surprisingly raw and under-produced. Indeed, it had more of a demo quality than any album Grohl had previously been involved with.

The band's sound was clearly centred around the grunge axis; however to suggest that the Seattle sound was the only influence at play undermined the huge part that Grohl's DC roots played on the songwriting. Throughout, flashes of Bad Brains, Minutemen and even Scream pulled songs in an altogether more energised punk rock direction than the slow-paced rockers that had marked out Tad, Nirvana, Mudhoney et al. Furthermore, *Foo Fighters* displayed an obvious debt to 1977-era punk bands from the US and the UK and British artists like Led Zeppelin and early David Bowie.

Perhaps the most obviously Nirvana-esque songs came with the second track, 'I'll Stick Around' which combined furious guitar riffs with mellow, lilting vocals before erupting into a screamed chorus, evoking the vocal interplay between Cobain and Grohl. This may have been a trick that had become associated with Nirvana's biggest hits, but they certainly weren't the first band to do this.

'Big Me' found Grohl in more contemplative mood with country-esque twang delivering a love song to his wife, Jennifer, before 'Alone + Easy Target' reintroduced the distorted guitars for another anthemic rocker. Again, vocal melody was understated, while guitars and drums delivered a masterclass on power punk. A trick reproduced on the melodic hardcore groove of 'Good Grief'.

With 'Floaty', Grohl could be found deep in Mudhoney territory, combining the rawness of punk with sub-heavy metal riffing and a steady rock beat *a la* Led Zeppelin. The British rock legends had been a huge influence on the entire Seattle scene – with Soundgarden taking the admiration to the level of near-imitation.

'Weenie Beanie' found Grohl in full-blown hardcore mode, complete with distorted vocals and rock dynamics. A close cousin to the B-side track 'Podunk', it proved to be the least effective track on the album. Sounding too much like pastiche to hold much weight - in fact it was comic book thrashcore.

'Weenie Beanie' represented one of the greatest problems faced by Grohl on this album. Realising that people would be scouring the tracks for any reference to Nirvana - be it sonic or lyrical - he seemed to be intent on showing how much he wasn't messed up and how much fun he was having. While Nirvana's final days were surrendered to overbearing unhappiness, Grohl seemingly threw in this throw away song to underline his new found joy. Nirvana this certainly wasn't.

In contrast to the comedy value of 'Weenie Beenie', 'Oh, George', one of the most recently penned songs on the album, was laced with a sombre mood, Grohl's voice at its most emotional, displaying the kind of vulnerability that made the *Pocketwatch* tape work so well.

'For All The Cows' found Grohl stripping Husker Du of their punk flavour, reducing them to their country and western roots, while the Greg Dulli track 'X-Static' offered slow-grinding rock, with drums rumbling like a juggernaut. Vocally the song featured an almost apologetic melody, so understated was Grohl's voice.

Back on the hardcore trail, 'Wattershed' was Grohl's gloriously thunderous tribute to Minuteman and fIREHOSE. Indeed the 'tt' in the mispelt title was a direct reference to Mike Watt. Final track 'Exhausted' was perhaps the least commercial of the album's songs. Despite the poppy melody, the song meandered through a pea soup of distorted guitars, feedback and sub-metal dynamics before reaching its power chord climax. Its minor chord sequence and extended feedback was reminiscent of Joy Division's debut album.

Of the songs recorded during October 1994's Bob Lang session, only 'Butterflies' remains unreleased. A slow-paced strum along which erupted into a full-blown assault; complete with heavy metal dynamic in the bridge. The song may not have represented Grohl's finest hour, but its country and western-style chorus harmonies, and verse melody was reminiscent of the unlikely source of Sly and the Family Stone's 'Stand!' which, along with the song's Clash-like two-note guitar solo wouldn't have sounded out of place on the album. The sheer driven, hardcore edge of the track may even have sat well on a Scream record.

The media's reaction to the album was, in the main, positive. Inevitably perhaps, common reservations were expressed, among them the opinion that Grohl's new venture was far too over-shadowed by the legacy of his previous band.

Metal Hammer's Pippa Lang gave the album the maximum five stars, noting that "Grohl has transferred from drum stool to mike and guitar with astounding ease... Leaping to the fore with relish, his vocals have the same winsome quality as Cobain, but, and here's the crux, Grohl's achieve a far wider range, never grating, always stretching deliciously to those higher pitches."

She also declared *Foo Fighters* to be, "an album of great personal triumph, dripping with easily likeable melodies, and a sort of 'clean grunge' vibe. Tidier and, dare I say, better played than anything any of the four have done before. Like a collaboration waiting to happen, the chemistry between Grohl, Smear, Goldsmith and Mandel positively crackles."

Less ecstatic but nonetheless positive was the UK's *Sunday Telegraph* whose James Delingpole said, "This month's biggest surprise is the remarkable debut by Seattle's Foo Fighters. Knowing their pedigree, I had feared the worst... somehow, the band have passed through both minefields unscathed. It helps that their leader, Dave Grohl, is just as good on vocals as guitar as he was with his ticks."

One of the more cynical responses came in John Aizlewood's Q magazine review. "Grohl has taken the wise man's approach: he's stopped drumming and recruited men who know their way around the block, but won't eclipse the leader. Foo Fighters sound wise too, sufficiently like Nirvana to serve as a reminder where they came from, but not so blatant that they'll be pinned down as copyists. Foo Fighters are grunge-quite-lite... Grohl (was) never regarded as a songwriter or vocalist (so) these expectations may prove to be his undoing, but just as likely right now, they may yet be his making. He's done what he can."

That *Foo Fighters* was endlessly compared to Nirvana was perhaps a little unfair on Grohl. One of the reasons he had wanted to launch his latest venture with near-anonymity was so that people would listen to the songs without prejudice. However, to criticise him for making music that was reminiscent of Nirvana was ridiculous. Both he and his previous band had come from the same punk tradition. They had been into the same bands, enjoyed the same influences, talked the same language. This was exactly why Grohl fitted in to Nirvana so quickly. And yet the media could not resist making the link. To some, Nirvana, or rather Cobain, had somehow been attributed with owning the copyright of the sound.

Style magazine *i-D* typified this angle: "Dave Grohl *has* managed to bring some of that Nirvana spirit to his new band: fierce bass, pounding drums, soulful vocals, and always, always, a guitar melody underpinning the whole shebang. *HE* would have approved."

The undercurrent to such references was that for Grohl to even consider playing this kind of music could be seen as a form of intellectual and emotional theft. A strange position for the man who told U2's Bono that his main music was punk rock – and it had been this way since he was a teenager.

"They don't understand that when I was fifteen and had *Zen Arcade* [Husker Du], that's when I decided that I loved this music," he argued. "For me to do anything else for the sole reason of doing something different would be so contrived. For me to put out a free-form jazz record to be as far away as possible from Nirvana would just be ridiculous.

I knew that when I was recording the album, people would say 'OK, that song has some distorted guitars and heavy drumming and a strong melody to it, it must be like Nirvana.' The instant I realised that, I thought 'Fuck it, I don't give a shit!' What else am I going to do? It's just what I love to do." [20]

Given the circumstances surrounding Nirvana's demise, it was inevitable that people would pore over Grohl's lyrics looking for clues to his feelings about his previous band, and more importantly, Cobain. These tunnel-visioned critics seemed to ignore – or be ignorant of the fact – that many of the songs actually pre-dated the singer's death.

Grohl was adamant that his lyrics had no real meaning, they were just a jumble of words that fitted with the melody. This claim led to one journalist accusing him of being skilled at 'psychic hoovering', namely to be able to remove himself and his subconscious from his own past. Grohl would admit that even he could see real life situations that had subconsciously influenced his own lyrics, albeit, he explained, only after the event.

"Often, I'll sit around and try to deny all the personal influences, like 'Oh yeah, these songs, a lot of the lyrics are just nonsense.' When I write them, it's usually just before stepping into the vocal booth and Barrett [sound engineer] will be going, 'C'mon, we've got five minutes, you've got to write something.' So I write some stupid words and the syllables fit and it rhymes, so I go in and sing them. Then, three years later, I'll look at them and think, 'Oh my God, I think I actually meant something.' It's frightening. And it's not like the album is some bleeding heart for twelve quid, either. But it's helped. It really has helped." [21]

One song in particular was focussed upon, 'I'll Stick Around', which seemed to allude to Cobain's departure through the repeated lines "I don't owe you anything" and "I'll stick around." When people first started asking me these questions I was like, 'piss off, you fucking sod.' I would totally deny if, but I wasn't lying when I denied it. I just didn't realise it… ('I'll Stick Around') is just a very negative song about feeling you were violated or deprived." [22]

Talking to the *NME* he argued, "… even the last interview I did for another English publication leaves people under the impression that 'I'll Stick Around' is about Kurt. And I'm so fucking sensitive to that, but there's nothing I can do. There's absolutely nothing I can do. I can sit down and I can say totally with all my heart, I'll swear on a stack of Bibles, whatever, that that song is not about Kurt.

And I hate sounding so defensive but Jesus Christ, it kills me to think that people would think that I have no respect for the guy, that I have no respect for Nirvana, that I have no respect for the past five years of my life… that's fucking ridiculous. I just don't want people to think that I would be so disrespectful as to trivialise this shit in my songs, just belittle it by writing a song." [23]

Not content with just analysing the lyrics, critics also pored over the cover artwork. The sleeve featured a picture of a gun (the photograph was by Grohl's wife Jennifer). Many people wrongly claimed the image was a sick reference to Kurt Cobain's death. Closer inspection revealed that the weapon was in fact a ray gun called a *XZ38 Disintegrator Pistol* – a toy from the 1950s which was in perfect keeping with the band's kitsch UFO imagery. Grohl told *Rolling Stone* magazine: "To me, it's a toy. It has nothing to do with anything. I love kitschy 1940s and 1950s space toys. I thought it would be a nice, plain cover – nothing fancy.

Then I thought I'd catch so much flak, but everybody said it would be okay if I made sure everyone knew it was just a toy.

People have read so much into it. Give me a fucking break." [24]

Grohl's UFO obsession had already manifested itself in his choice of band and label names. Foo Fighters was the name given by the US Airforce pilots who had witnessed strange sights in the sky towards the end of the Second World War. These sightings had taken place over Japan and France and the crews of the B-29 bombers reported "balls of fire" which followed them, occasionally came up and almost sat on their tails, changed colour from orange to red to white and back again, and yet never closed in.

Of the many reports, one B-29 claimed to have made evasive manoeuvres inside a cloud, only to discover that after emerging from it, the ball of fire was following in the same relative position. It was, they reported, five hundred yards off, three feet in diameter, and had a phosphorescent orange glow. The ball of fire followed the plane for several miles before disappearing just over Fujiyama.

Many crews believed these "Foo Fighters" ("Foo" was slang for the French for fire 'feu') were a new German weapon, which they referred to as "Kraut Balls." However the pilot's reports were met with scepticism and the subject of "Foo Fighters" quashed once and for all. It was probably for the best that Grohl chose not to name his new band Kraut Balls.

This silence was broken when a crew from the 415th Squadron reported a pursuit by two "Foo Fighters" only to be attacked by a glowing red object two nights later. They were flying over The Rhine.

With reports of these "Foo Fighters" becoming more frequent, authorities attempted to dismiss them as a naturally occurring by-product of mutual electrostatic induction called St Elmo's Fire. However, reports continued to be filed until, in May 1945, five orange balls were sighted flying in a triangular formation near the eastern edge of Pfazerwald.

With the end of the war, "foo fighters" would pass into air force folklore, until, in the 1950s UFO sightings brought the subject back into the public domain.

Dave Grohl's label name, Roswell, had a similar extraterrestrial inspiration. On July 4, 1947, a UFO was reported to have crashed near the small town of Roswell, a farming and ranching community in south-eastern New Mexico. According to some reports, the bodies of four aliens were found near the ship. In other reports, one or more of the aliens survived for a period of time.

In the years since, the Roswell incident provoked rumours and countless conspiracy theories about government suppression of the truth of extraterrestrial life. However, in July, 1994, the Office of the Secretary of the Air Force concluded that the predecessor to the US Air Force, the US Army Air Forces, recovered debris from an Army Air Forces balloon-borne research project code-named MOGUL. Furthermore the report stated that many of the accounts appeared to be descriptions of unclassified and widely publicised Air Force scientific achievements. Of the widely reported alien bodies retrieved from the Roswell site, they concluded that they were actually anthropomorphic test dummies that were transported by US Air Force high altitude balloons for scientific research.

Of course, this report didn't satisfy the Roswell obsessives who continue to argue the existence of UFO materials and alien bodies. For Grohl however, the use of the names "foo fighter" and "Roswell" would only enhance his reputation for being a sci-fi nut. The subject would become a regular feature of his interviews. He would also go on to have a walk on part in the hit TV show, *X-Files*. However, his appearance was so brief that even Mulder and Scully would be hard pressed to notice his existence on film. Makers of the programme insist that "he is out there", somewhere. The Foo Fighter would also submit a track for inclusion on the *X-Files* movie soundtrack.

On July 20, Foo Fighters headed off on a US tour with Shudder to Think and Wool (featuring the Stahl Brothers from Scream). In the middle of the tour they made their television debut, appearing on *The David Letterman Show*, to play 'This Is A Call'.

The US tour subsequently made way for a European Festival tour taking in Lowlands Festival, Holland on August 22, Pukkelpop Festival, Belgium on August 29 and in between these two dates on August 27, Reading Festival in the UK, where Nirvana had made that historic appearance only three years earlier.

The Reading Festival show proved to be a huge success. Foo Fighters headlined the *Melody Maker* stage to a euphoric response from fans, many of whom tried on numerous occasions to reach the stage. The band were subsequently forced to interrupt their set a number of times to stop those at the front from being crushed. Some even scaled the huge poles inside the tent to get away from the crowds and to obtain a better view.

After four numbers, they were asked to stop playing. "OK, we're being kicked off the stage now," said Grohl to the annoyance of the crowd. "Er, I mean, we're taking a break," he added to calm things down a bit. Fortunately, there were no injuries, but a number of fans were treated for heat exhaustion.

"Why aren't this band playing the main stage?" asked the *Melody Maker* in their review. It transpired that the band had been asked many times to upgrade to the main stage as the promoters were predicting an overwhelming demand for them. Foo Fighters insisted on headlining the second stage instead. Again, admirable modesty from Grohl. However, even a down-to-earth rock-legend-in-the-making could not deny the frenzied response and so Foo Fighters subsequently accepted an invitation to headline the main stage the following year.

The following Monday saw the release of the second single from *Foo Fighters*, the controversial 'I'll Stick Around'. Backing the lead track were previously unreleased songs, 'How I Miss You' and 'Ozone'. The former was notable for the appearance of Grohl's sister Lisa on bass. The song itself echoed Velvet Underground with its discordant acoustic strum and audible fret rattle for the first few verses, before erupting in a distorted ascending power chord finale. 'Ozone' on the other hand was a cover version of a track by Kiss' Ace Frehley, thus reviving Grohl's connections with the Kiss solo ventures that started with the *King Buzzo EP*.

'I'll Stick Around' was met with generally favourable reviews, however *Kerrang!* slated it. "It doesn't. Stick around, that is. In fact, it goes through you like milk of magnesia. Neither as noisy nor as melodic as the fine first single." Nonetheless, 'I'll Stick Around' was their second Top 20 UK hit, reaching #18.

In October 16, Foo Fighters headed out on a European tour, opening at Circus in Stockholm, Sweden, where they introduced new track 'Enough Space' and a version of 'Down In The Park' by Gary Numan's 1980s electro outfit, Tubeway Army. They chose the tour to introduce a number of new songs, the first they'd written as a band as opposed to Grohl solo. At Parkhus, Copenhagen on October 18 they played 'My Hero', while on November 1 they debuted 'Up In Arms' at Madrid's Aqualung.

The Fall 1995 tour pulled in to the UK on November 10 at Wolverhampton's Civic Hall. The following night took in Glasgow's Barrowlands, which was followed by Leeds Town and Country. November 14 and 15 found the band playing two shows at London's Brixton Academy, the second of which was special set filmed for MTV's *I'm OK Eur OK* series.

A week later they delivered the third single to be taken from *Foo Fighters*, 'For All The Cows'. The B-sides were live versions of the title track and 'Wattershed', lifted from the notable debut Reading Festival performance. The single reached #28 in the UK charts. In support of the release, Foo Fighters also recorded a live session for Radio 1 at the Maida Vale Studio, where they played 'Winnebago' and 'Wattershed'.

Bringing the year to a close, Foo Fighters embarked on their first visit to Australia and the Pacific Rim. The tour coincided with a special release of *Foo Fighters* which boasted additional tracks culled from all of the B-sides to singles released so far. Immediately prior to this however the band performed on *Saturday Night Live* in New York City. Dave dedicated 'For All The Cows' to Mendel. It was his birthday.

December 1995 found the band in triumphant mood delivering stunning shows in Japan and Hawaii. Then following two dates in

Los Angeles and a brief Christmas break, Foo Fighters headed off to Australia. Their first date was at Melbourne Showgrounds on December 29 followed by a New Year's Eve gig in Sydney at the Macquarie University. This was clearly not a band about to rest on its laurels and Grohl's reputation as a near-workaholic was, it seemed, well deserved.

1995 drew to an end with the band riding on the crest of a wave. Their debut album had been well received, while the live shows were being met with ecstatic responses. Large sections of the media all over the world seemed to love the band, not only because they were immediately radio friendly but also because they were prepared to do interviews and anything they deemed worthwhile to promote the records. In an era when so many rock stars shunned the press and/or treated journalists with disdain, Foo Fighters amenable stance was welcomed across the media almost universally.

Grohl was quickly becoming known for his approachable manner and workmanlike dedication to putting in the hours. Not only had he earned himself the tag of 'nicest man in rock', he was also now being called 'the hardest working musician on the planet.'

Despite all this blossoming goodwill, the press still seemed unable to mention Grohl without referencing his previous band. Seemingly regardless of their own successes, Foo Fighters would regularly be likened to Nirvana, often in the most unfair ways. In their end of year round up *Melody Maker* rather uncharitably argued: "There remained the uneasy feeling about Foo Fighters that they were essentially Nirvana minus the angst, minus Kurt's creative distortion, cranked up but not fucked up, bouncy, meaty beaty grunge for crowd surfers and moshers who never really cared for the vertiginous trauma of Nirvana at their troubling best."

Regardless of such mean-spirit coverage, with the debut album *Foo Fighters*, Grohl had successfully managed to lay to rest many of the ghosts of his previous band. Only certain elements of the media still clung to the past. To many, it appeared as if he might have achieved the impossible and successfully thrown off what could have proved to be a terminally suffocating history. However, the journey still ahead of Grohl was to be littered with troubles...

5

WHAT HAVE WE DONE WITH INNOCENCE?

ANOTHER DRUMMER JOKE
Where can you find a drummer with ambitions to do movie scores?
Working behind the counter at Blockbusters.

The Australasia dates went ahead without any problems save for the Singapore gig on January 16 at The Harbour Pavilion when William Goldsmith was taken ill for the show. Grohl opened the set with a solo version of 'This Is A Call'. The tour came to a close on January 22 at Queen Elizabeth Stadium in Kowloon, Hong Kong.

Upon their return to the US, the band went directly to the Bob Lang's Studios, where they recorded a new version of the as-yet-unreleased *Foo Fighters* out-take 'Butterflies', and new tracks 'I'm Alone Again', 'Enough Space' and 'My Hero'. They also recorded a version of live favourite 'Down In The Park'. It was the second cover version they were to record, although it would definitely not be the last, as the process had lit up a fascination for cover versions within Grohl. In the years that followed, he would regularly include his interpretations of other people's songs into Foo Fighters sets.

Of this session 'Down In The Park' would turn up later that year on the *X-Files* soundtrack album *Songs In The Key of X*, 'Enough Space' would appear on the band's forthcoming second album, *The Colour And The Shape*. 'Butterflies' would again remain unreleased but would become a regular addition to the live sets while 'I'm Alone Again' would never be released or played live.

'I'm Alone Again' built on sub-metal riffing and a verse that echoed the angular dynamics of UK punk bands like Wire, revolving around guitar and bass picking out octaves over which Grohl delivered his trademark melodic vocals. Lyrically the song was perhaps Grohl's most transparent song yet, referring to his

118

recent marriage break up. A long way from the love song, 'Big Me' which had been pencilled in as the next single from *Foo Fighters*.

Prior to this recording session, Grohl appeared on the cult Seattle comedy-sketch show *Almost Live TV*. In the sketch that featured the Foo Fighters' frontman, comedienne Nancy Guppy would smash up the guitar that had been given to Grohl by Tom Petty. Grohl acted sufficiently alarmed by the act of wanton destruction, but the reality was that the guitar was only a cheap instrument bought from the Trading Musician store on Roosevelt!

March 1996 found Foo Fighters once again out on the road. To promote the shows, the band played an acoustic set for Rockline Radio. The set included an exclusive version of 'Wattershed' featuring Grohl's remarkably accurate imitation of Fred Schneider of B-52's fame. The song was renamed 'Watter-Fred' for the session. That the band had decided to do an acoustic version of one of the debut album's most hardcore moments was strange enough, but to hear Grohl delivering a story over the top in his best 'Rock Lobster' voice was almost surreal!

"Oh man, that was perfection!" exclaimed the DJ after the song had finished. If not perfection, exactly, it did provide an insight into Grohl's comedy talents. Even as a child he had used his ability to make people laugh as a way of becoming the centre of attention during family gatherings.

The first date of the band's spring 1996 tour with The Amps and That Dog opened in Denver with two nights at the Ogden Theatre on March 22 and 23. Following these shows the band would travel throughout the USA on a tour which took in thirty two dates, culminating with a free show at Whiskey A Go Go in Los Angeles.

The tour was in support of the release of 'Big Me' as a single, which arrived on March 3. Backing the lead song were three tracks recorded live for a Radio 1 Session in November 1995; 'Floaty', 'Gas Chamber' and 'Alone + Easy Target'.

On 15 June, Foo Fighters would play at the Beastie Boys' Tibetan Freedom Festival in San Francisco. Among the acts scheduled to play the festival were The Beastie Boys themselves, Red Hot Chili Peppers, Yoko Ono, Smashing Pumpkins, Fugees, Rage Against The Machine, Beck, Pavement and Sonic Youth among many others. The two-day concert, at the Polo Fields in San Francisco's Golden Gate Park, had the aim of highlighting China's human rights abuses in Tibet. Proceeds from the event went to the Milarepa Fund, a San Francisco-based non-profit organisation co-founded by the Beastie Boys in1994. Milarepa organized the concert along with Bill Graham Presents.

Adam Yauch of the Beastie Boys had become aware of the Tibetans' plight in 1992 during a trip to Nepal. Grohl, along with a litany of superstars on the bill, was drawn to support the cause almost without hesitation.

"The main point of the concert," explained Yauch, "really is to not just educate people about what's happening in Tibet, but to also let people feel more aware of how much we affect what goes on in the rest of the world. When you go into (a store) and buy a pair of pants, you don't really think about the fact that you might be putting on a pair of pants that some seven-year-old kid just made in a forced-labour camp." Statements such as this made Grohl's decision to play all the more understandable.

Foo Fighters played a short set comprising of mainly singles and live favourites. They proved to be one of the highlights of the festival's two days with their no-nonsense, straight-to-the-point songs proving to be the perfect boost to the afternoon malaise that at one point had threatened to set in.

Throughout July the band would take their live show on another tour of Europe's festival circuit. The tour would take in Poland's Sopot Rock & Pop Festival, Quart Festival in Kristiansand, Norway, Torhout Festival and Werchter Festival in Belgium (the former being a rain-soaked affair with a dismally disinterested crowd who seemed more intent on fighting than watching Foo Fighters), Eurokennes Festival in France, Ireland's Feile Festival and Scotland's T In The Park Festival. They also played club shows in France, Spain and Holland.

The tour came to an end with a triumphant set at The Phoenix Festival in Stratford, England. The festival that year had faced huge problems because people were unable to get to the site due to huge traffic delays. At some points, the jams would be greeted by the sight of an overhead helicopter flying a band in, or worse, bands speeding up the hard shoulder in their tour busses, accompanied by the police. Among the latter was the Prodigy, who would play twice that year. They would also strike up a lasting friendship with Grohl and Foo Fighters.

On many of the festivals the Foos had played that year, two acts were frequent headliners: David Bowie, doing the rounds in support of his *Earthling* album, and the rejuvenated and reformed Sex Pistols, out on their 'Filthy Lucre' tour. Both must have represented a dream come true for Grohl, especially the latter as he had been a Pistols fan since he first discovered punk. He had been into Bowie's music even longer. During the Festival tour, Grohl struck up a friendship with Bowie which would culminate in the two musicians working together, both live and in the studio.

The Phoenix Festival show found Foo Fighters at their very best, with Grohl's huge grinning antics playing counterpoint to Smear's lounging angst. Goldsmith's energy infused the set with a vibrancy that was unusual for a festival show, while Mendel sloped around the stage, occasionally bouncing on the spot, but lost in concentration.

The band may have played an amazing tally of over forty shows in two months, but they seemed like they could have gone on to do another forty. However they decided that the time was right to take a break from the relentless live schedule.

The routine of gigging brought out an interesting aspect of Grohl's personality: that he is less interested in the rock 'n' roll lifestyle than the actual physical process of touring. He enjoys the sense of the well-oiled machine moving through city after city. Not for him the rock star excesses of life on tour as a way of alleviating the boredom. He finds his pleasure from getting into the rhythm of the machine.

"I have fun. But I'm boring on the road," he told *Kerrang!* "I don't fucking do shit man. To me, getting on the bus and going for a ride is my favourite thing. I love being on the bus! I love getting in my bunk and closing my curtain. And I hear people laughing in the front lounge, or I smell the popcorn in the microwave, and I get all excited. I jump out and I'm like, 'Hey! What are you guys doing?" [1]

As for aftershow parties or tour bus antics, Grohl insists there is very little of this too. "If we're on a two month tour, then there'd be probably two or three nights on the whole tour where I'll get fucking obliterated. I don't smoke pot, I don't do coke, I don't do anything." [2]

Foo Fighters had two very important reasons for taking a break from touring. On the one hand, the band were itching to get into the studio to record their second album, and on the other, they were very much in need of a well-earned holiday.

Grohl however, doesn't take holidays. He hates them. His hyperactive nature means he finds it impossible to rest for too long. It had been the same way when he was at school. "I once went back to my mom's and looked through loads of old photos and shit. So, I started finding my old report cards! They were concerned with my hyperactivity. They all said: 'David could be a very good student if he could just fucking stay in one place and sit still.' There were lots of requests for my mom to come in and talk about it. But I did OK in school though, got good grades. Until I discovered pot and then I kinda just stopped going to lessons."

So rather than take a holiday like the rest of the band, Grohl instead decided he would get to work recording yet another solo album. Not for Foo Fighters this time, but a soundtrack to the movie *Touch*.

Touch was Paul Scrader's adaptation of Elmore *Get Shorty*, Leonard's bizarre satire about faith-healers in which an ex-monk uses his new found position as a faith-healer to explore all manner of un-Godly situations. The movie starred Bridget Fonda (who the one-time monk gets to seduce), Skeet Ulrich and Christopher Walken.

Next up, Grohl teamed up once more with old sparring partner Barrett Jones and went into Bob Lang's studios and, in only three weeks in October 1996, he delivered a series of musical vignettes to support the short film rushes he had been provided with. He didn't get to see the completed film until long after he had delivered his tracks.

The crossover from manic rock frontman to sensitive soundtrack composer was an important step for Grohl. In this album he could be seen to be finally leaving the ghosts of his past behind. Far from the creative straightjacket of grunge and all of the baggage that came with the style, and miles away from the dysfunctional trauma of those final days in Nirvana, he was now taking his music in any way that he fancied. He had graduated from the Seattle school and was now ready to move into a far wider market.

There was another aspect to the almost cathartic process of recording by himself again (with Jones at the controls). Laying down his own music had long been a valued pressure valve for Grohl. During his days with Scream he was able to explore new ideas and with Nirvana he could let off the frustration he was feeling. And now, with Foo Fighters, he was able to use these sessions to unburden himself of the weight of being the band's leader. He may have argued constantly that he was just another member of the band, but he was the singer, songwriter, arranger, guitarist (and everything else on *Foo Fighters*). He chose the name of the band and the label. He decided on the image for the album cover and his (now-former) wife took the photos. To all intents and purposes, Grohl was still Foo Fighters. The main pressure he felt came from the constant need to state that he was only one of four band members. Now back in the studio alone with no band, no one could accuse him of being coy in his denial of the band leader position he took, no one could accuse him of being egotistic in the way that he put together a band to play his songs, but refused to take responsibility for being the band leader.

So recording a soundtrack represented a fantastic form of escape for Grohl. There were no expectations, no rulebooks and no illusions. Just him, his instruments and his imagination. He would succeed or fail on his abilities, and no one else's.

There was another aspect of this recording that underlined Grohl's personality. Where many people talk about doing things, he just does them. So, while musicians whine constantly about wanting to record movie soundtracks, he went ahead and did one. This is very much the pragmatic ethos that drives Grohl in all that he does.

Music From The Motion Picture Touch finally emerged in July 1998 under the name of David Grohl. It proved to be a great album. 'Bill Hill Theme' contrasted a staccato guitar riff with chugging rock refrains that built to a huge crescendo motored by Grohl's powerhouse drumming. On 'How Do You Do?' he delivered the finest Foo Fighters track never attributed to the band. A beautifully crafted post-grunge pop masterpiece that, married a distorted riffing guitar with pounding drums and a melody that was totally and insanely infectious. 'Saints in Love' was a ballad between Grohl and Veruca Salt's Louise Post, which found honey dipped vocals cooing over swathes of melodic feedback and echoed distortion. Much like the Cocteau Twins playing footsie with Slowdive. It was emotional as it was mesmerising.

Elsewhere, 'This Loving Thing' featured John Doe of seminal LA punk outfit X on bass. X had long since turned to country and that was the genre that lay at the heart of this camp-fire classic. Doe also supplied vocals to the gorgeous 'Lynn's Theme'. 'Making Popcorn' and 'Remission My Ass' also wondered through country and western terrain with their picked guitars and tender hearts, while 'Spinning Newspapers' offered a surf guitar on the over mellow chords. On 'Richie Baker's Miracle', Grohl explored out-rock through *Twin Peaks* style ambience.

"Ennio Moricone has little to fear, it's true, but *Touch* is strong enough to hammer another nail in the 'drummer jokes' coffin," wrote *Guitar* magazine. "Hang out with the pop savant at his searing best, while you discover that there's always been a human being at the heart of your favourite rock beast," added *Melody Maker*, while *The Sunday Times* commented, "Who would have thought that a drummer would turn out to be grunge's Renaissance man? Grohl's talents are too diverse for him to establish a *Touch* sound *per se*; this is a bitty album, But some of the bits are very good."

Although reviews of the soundtrack album still referenced Nirvana and were frequently lukewarm, Grohl remained undeterred. Besides, there was a growing sense that the public's perception of himself and his band was increasingly at odds with the more negative slant many in the media persisted with.

In September 1996, immediately prior to recording *Touch*, Foo Fighters were given an MTV award for 'Best Group Video' for 'Big Me' – the first in a long line of famously comic yet revered promo clips. The video had been filmed in Australia at the beginning of the year and was directed by Jesse Peretz who had come up with the concept of using *Mentos* (the candy sweets) throughout the clip. Fans of the band would subsequently start throwing the hard sweets at the band when they were onstage!

In November 1996, only a couple of weeks after recording *Touch*, a piece of Grohl's distant past was released – an album by the strangely monikered Harlingtox Angel Divine. The eponymous album recorded in 1990 featured Grohl on bass, drums and guitar, with contributions from ex-Dischord singer Bruce Merkle on vocals. Barrett Jones played drums and Tos Nieuwenhuizen, from Dutch act God was on guitar. This was the same Tos that had featured along with Skeeter Thompson on the *Pocketwatch* tape track, 'Just Another Song About Seeker Thompson'.

Harlingtox Angel Divine was the first release from The Laundry Room record label, formed by Jones and former Sony A&R exec, Justin Goldberg (and of which Grohl is a major shareholder).

"Harlingtox was just me, Dave and Tos recording some music in one day, literally," Jones told *NME*. "Then we had a vocalist come in who took some time writing lyrics. This really is the band that never was! This is a scathing, mental voyage of an album," explained Jones. "The reason these tapes sat on the shelf for six years was because I didn't want someone else putting them out." [3]

Just as this skeleton was emerging from the cupboard, however, Foo Fighters started on a project that was to have huge repercussions within the band. They embarked on the process of recording their second album, the first as a band unit. On paper this exercise should have seen a near-cathartic rush as the four band members explored everything they had learned while intensively gigging. Unfortunately, it turned out to be something of a traumatic time.

Producer for the album was Gil Norton, who had been chosen for his work with The Pixies (among others). Barrett Jones had decided to devote his energies to his own recordings. The band also opted to use neither The Laundry Room for demos, nor Bob Lang's for the main session. The recordings subsequently took place at Bear Creek Studios, Woodinville, Washington. Recording started on November 18.

The circumstances surrounding the recording weren't very positive. The band had been almost constantly on the road or promoting records since they first formed. For Grohl, there had been the build up of recording the album, getting Roswell signed and even putting together the rest of the band. But for the others it had been a case of straight in at the deep end of mixing an album that had already been recorded.

The all-consuming nature of Foo Fighters started to take its toll on personal relationships. Grohl had split from his wife and was later rumoured to be dating Louise Post from Veruca Salt. They had also recorded together late in 1995 for the *Touch Soundtrack*.

Another problem that surfaced surrounded Grohl's apparent dictatorial qualities. Despite his admiration for each member of the band, reports started to surface that he had become quite dogmatic in his approach to arranging the songs. He would, allegedly, tell people what parts he envisaged and so on.

If this was the case, for a guitarist like Pat Smear this would have come as quite a shock. In fact he would often improve upon the ideas supplied to him simply by adapting them to his swashbuckling guitar style.

Much in the same way that Cobain had dictated some drum parts to Grohl in his early days with Nirvana, so Grohl became insistent on how he wanted the drums for each Foo Fighters track. The process caused huge problems for William Goldsmith who, naturally, had his own ideas.

The final problem lay in the band's choice of producer. Gil Norton had a reputation for working bands hard to get the right performance. This would mean numerous takes just to get one section sorted. It was a process which flew in the face of the way Grohl had always recorded in the past (nothing was completed in only forty five minutes as with the previous album) but it also brought with it feelings of frustration from the entire band.

As Christmas loomed, the band abandoned the recording sessions completely. The tracks that had been recorded so far were, 'Monkey Wrench', 'Hey, Johnny Park', 'Chicken Derby', 'Wind Up', 'Up In Arms', 'See You', 'February Stars', 'Everlong', 'Walking After You' and 'New Way Home'.

1997 opened with Foo Fighters playing live at Madison Square Garden with David Bowie for his fiftieth birthday Party. Grohl joined Bowie onstage for a run through of 'Hallo Spaceboy' and 'Seven Years In Tibet'. He would later appear on Bowie's acclaimed *Heathen* album, playing guitar on the Neil Young cover, 'I've Been Waiting For You'.

Any jubilation at playing the Bowie birthday bash was short-lived however. No one in the band had been happy with the end results from the November album sessions, so they decided to rearrange and re-record some of the songs in a different studio. They subsequently booked time in the renowned Hollywood studio, Grand Master Recordings. The reasons for using these studios – as opposed to one in Seattle or Washington DC – was simple. Grohl had moved to Los Angeles during 1996 following his split from

Jennifer Youngblood.

The band started work on the new versions of tracks for the second album in February. However, there was one notable omission from the sessions – William Goldsmith. He had, apparently, opted to remain at home in Seattle with his family, but would be joining the band to record his drum parts when required. That call never came however. Grohl had played drums on every track on the LA sessions.

The events that occurred around the recording of the album would lead to some observers making accusations that Grohl had cynically manoeuvred Goldsmith out of the drum seat for the recording sessions. Grohl himself has said that he doesn't like confrontation and will try to avoid it wherever possible.

There was another problem at the heart of the recording of this second Foo Fighters album. Grohl had to justify his choice of musicians. He was well aware that this album would be analysed in the same way that *Foo Fighters* was. However, the lo-fi, under-produced nature of that recording was in direct contrast to the effect he was now aiming for That album had been almost apologetic in its lack of sheen and as a result the drummer's musical prowess was never called into question. This time round though, each and every musician would be under the magnifying glass. If the drums weren't to Grohl's liking, the resulting drum track would have been glaringly obvious. Not something you would expect from the band fronted by the man who was once hailed as the finest drummer of his generation.

It is possible that Grohl had intended for Goldsmith to overdub drums on the Hollywood session. The intention was that he would absolutely still be a part of the band's live show. Perhaps not surprisingly, Goldsmith left Foo Fighters on March 4. An official statement read: "We are all very sad that William is leaving. It's like losing a family member. Plus he's such an amazing drummer. It is my sincerest hope that he will continue to rock the universe in all his future endeavours."

"We started recording in November," explained Grohl when

asked directly about Goldsmith's departure by *Melody Maker*. "We got into the studio, and it was really tough. William, Nate and Pat had never worked with a producer like Gil before. He really works you hard to get the best performance, and that's why he's such an amazing fuckin' producer.

It didn't really work out as we wished. So we decided to come down to Los Angeles and do it differently. We re-arranged the songs, I played drums on things, and we went at it from another direction.

At the end, we immediately started doing promotion and got ready for touring. It's another two years of your life, and I think that was why William decided that he wanted to stay at home and play with other people, and the other three of us should keep moving and find another drummer." [4]

Whatever the reasons for Goldsmith leaving Foo Fighters, the fall out from the affair would see Grohl being tarnished with accusations by outsiders of him being a dictator within the band – a fact that he would strenuously deny.

Fortunately, Goldsmith's replacement was only a tentative phone call away. Grohl had met Taylor Hawkins while he was drumming for Alanis Morrisette's band. When Goldsmith left, Grohl phoned the drummer to find out if he knew of anyone available to sit on the Foo Fighters' drum seat. Hawkins, it turned out, was up for the job. "(I) called him up in LA to ask if he knew any drummers, thinking he wouldn't want to join my band in a million years. When he said, 'Yeah, me', I jumped at it!"

That Hawkins had come from Alanis Morrisette's band wasn't as strange as it sounded. Morrisette's live show revolved around heavy rock versions of her poppier hits, many of which were transformed into Led Zeppelin-esque epics. Furthermore, a huge amount of emphasis was placed on the drumming, Hawkins' powerful style pushed the band even in the dreariest moments. With Hawkins, Grohl had found a drummer who could match him for power and volume, and surpass him with technique. "He's fuckin' incredible, totally capable of doing anything under the sun," enthused Grohl.

It was often argued that drumming for Grohl's band was the most unenviable position for any drummer to accept. Grohl had gained the reputation for being a hard taskmaster, so alongside claims that he was - and is - one of the best drummers in the world, it was a daunting job. Both these complimentary aspects of his reputation are strongly disputed by Grohl, who sees himself as a simple drummer, rather than a technical one. Modesty again, surely.

"I've taken one drumming lesson in my life, and quit because I had to relearn everything I knew," he said. "I had really stupid bad habits. I don't know... I'm just not the drummer that everyone seems to think I am and I do not understand a lot of what's said about me for one minute. Taylor's just unbelievable – he knows how to do fancy rolls and shit! It's weird, if Taylor does an interview, and whenever William did an interview, everyone's first question is always, 'What's it like being drummer with Dave Grohl?' – as if I'm some fucking drumming institution or something! It makes no sense 'cos Taylor is a way better drummer than I will ever be. I'm a completely minimalistic drummer." [5]

With Hawkins in the band and a new album eventually finished to the satisfaction of the entire group, morale within the Foo Fighters' camp was at an all-time high. The experience of recording the second album had been a draining one, but now they were ready to move on.

Following an acoustic set for Japanese radio on which they played 'For All The Cows', 'Big Me' and 'Up In Arms', the band played a one-off 'secret' show at the Alligator Lounge in Santa Monica on April 4. The show was intended as a run-through of the recently recorded tracks and also a debut run out for Hawkins. The set was mainly made up of new songs, with a few favourites from the previous album.

On April 28, 'Monkey Wrench' the first single from the forthcoming album was released as a two CD set. The single was exclusive to the UK. 'Monkey Wrench' had all of the hallmarks of the best tracks from *Foo Fighters,* but with two major differences –

the recording quality was about a million times better and any association with the grunge sound had been wiped away. This was a shiny new rock beast that boasted a classic Grohl sing-a-long chorus and chugging guitar dynamics that could have come straight from Metallica.

The overall atmosphere was less 1990s alt-rocker, more 1980s power punk. The opening guitar riff could have come from bands like The Dickies (or worse The Cars) while the verse had all of the ambience of Joan Jett and the Blackhearts (or worse Kim Wilde's 'Kids of America'). If the band were after a 1980s Brat Pack rock pastiche then they had succeeded. 'Monkey Wrench' wouldn't have sounded out of place on movies like *The Breakfast Club*, or *Pretty In Pink*. Indeed, if one band's sound echoed through the new recordings, it was the Psychedelic Furs in their US-dominating *Pretty In Pink*-era.

Yet, this was no bad thing, as 'Monkey Wrench' retained enough of the dirt factor to avoid turning retro. Grohl's vocals especially sounded more powerful than ever before, displaying a relaxed maturity that simply hadn't been present in any of his previous recordings. The climactic final verse particularly found Grohl's screamed melody imbued with a hitherto unheard depth.

"I think my voice sounds good on record," reluctantly admitted Grohl in *Kerrang!* when questioned about his initial insecurity about his vocal abilities. "It works in the studio. And I feel a lot more comfortable singing now, because I've had it blaring out at me from monitors for the last year. But no, I still hate it." [6]

As a part of their promotional tour for the single, Foo Fighters dropped into Radio 1 to record a special set of cover versions at the Maida Vale studios. One of the songs recorded was 'Drive Me Wild' a cover of a song by Vanity 6, but originally penned by Prince. Foo Fighters have over the years attempted on numerous occasions to cover Prince's 'Purple Rain', but have never managed to get past the first verse. Other songs recorded for the session were 'Baker Street' (without the famous sax intro), 'Friend Of A Friend' and 'Requiem'. While 'Baker Street' was originally by Gerry

Rafferty and 'Requiem' by Killing Joke, 'Friend Of A Friend' wasn't strictly speaking a cover version. It was, in fact, one of the songs by the aforementioned Late!, whose cassette album *Pocketwatch* had provided the impetus for Foo Fighters all those years ago.

The band had opted to do 'Friend Of A Friend' instead of covering 'Carry On My Wayward Son' by Kansas – but only because Grohl had forgotten the words! The versions were rarely as good as the originals, with Grohl occasionally slipping into cheesy cabaret delivery. On 'Requiem', one of the few chances the band had to let rip, they watered the song down. Grohl's vocals paled into insignificance next to the magnificent original version. Only 'Drive Me Wild' really worked because the band were able to infect it with enough of the Foo Fighters' sound so as to make it their own.

The second Foo Fighters album, *The Colour And The Shape* appeared early in May. Arguably, this represented the first album by the band rather than a solo Grohl project - even though the band had been present for the mix of *Foo Fighters* and Grohl had rather generously included his band mates in a share of royalties for a record they had never actually appeared on - taking Grohl's reputation for being generous to a new high.

However, the added input of the entire band turned out to be one of the album's failings. Quite simply, it lacked the focus of its predecessor. Where *Foo Fighters* had used the axis of simple, yet bold, grungy rock songs as its core, *The Colour And The Shape* was almost self-conscious in its desire to break out of the previous album's mould. Which meant embracing everyone from Metallica to The Velvet Underground, from Journey to The Dickies; and that was, in rock terms, some distance to travel.

Ironically, in attempting to traverse this distance, Foo Fighter's all too often resorted to formula in order to retain a Foo Fighters sound. The result was an album that wants to fly, but was all too often brought down to earth with an embarrassed, apologetic bump. *The Colour And The Shape* was polite where it needed to be belligerent, unassuming where it needed to shock. And when the band did go all out for that gut-wrenching rock attack, they seemingly cut the kill short with a friendly smile and a knowing wink. It was essentially the physical embodiment of Grohl's favourable public persona.

As such, the album encompassed the dilemmas that Grohl faced. In his need to be seen as the anti-star everyman, he had actually created a device that protected, and yet restricted, the band. His no-nonsense, all-smiling ordinariness had translated into the band's songs creating an album that almost, but not quite, stands out. The good guy you share a drink with after the game; the dependable mate who never lets you down – but also never sparks your life with unbridled excitement.

The Colour And The Shape is the anti-rock star rock album, borne out of the circus that Nirvana became. Like the geeky half-cousin that tries too hard, but not hard enough. The irony in all of this of course was that *The Colour And The Shape* wasn't a bad album. It just wasn't the album it should have been when you consider the combined forces at work. It lacked that free-falling edginess that had marked out producer Gil Norton's best work with The Pixies; it lacked the vulnerability that ran through the heart of Grohl's finest moments and it failed to ignite with the kind of loose limbed petulance that fans of Smear would have expected. If a group of master chefs were brought together and then told they could only make meatloaf, it would have tasted like *The Colour And The Shape;* tasty, but not the gourmet meal you might have expected.

Even more ironic was that fact that the production shone like a 1980s metal act; drums were crisp, tight and thunderous, guitars cleaned up of the excess, distant sounding distortion and instead glistening with bright melody. The vocals too were pushed to the fore with ADT (automatic double tracking) used liberally to beef up Grohl's voice. Like the band themselves, the songs weren't that excessive so as to benefit from such a cock-rock sound.

"There are so many amazing rock 'n' roll stereotypes that make for good bands and we're trying to squash everyone by making ourselves into the most boring fucking band in the world," said Grohl at the time. "A lot of rock bands aren't nice. I think this is probably the first time I've ever talked about another band in an unkind manner, but that band Sleeper... every time Louise (Wener) does an interview it's fucking front page. Is it just because she talks about fucking and drinking?

Well, it's always fun to watch other people try and pull off the rock attitude. We're probably the worst band in the world for those big quotes next to the picture. We're not going to say, 'I like fuckin' shaggin' in a fuckin' aeroplane. And after shaggin', fuckin', smokin' fuckin' grrrmmmphhh...' We're not a very rocking band in that sense. If we were drinking alcohol, that might be a different story... I don't think we're special, and it's been one of my goals to make people feel comfortable with us."

Had he ever considered taking on a rock persona? It might have given *The Colour And The Shape* a wilder outlook. "I'm too boring and unimaginative a person to think up an interesting fuckin' persona. I'd probably end up dressing like Bootsy Collins – 'I'm a rock star, look at my glasses!' I mean, God. When I was just seven I thought Kiss were cool."

In fact Grohl still thought Kiss were cool. The sing-and-chant-along choruses that Grohl specialised in came from the same lineage as Kiss' 'I Want to Rock 'n' Roll All Night'... only Foo Fighters didn't "party every day".

Interestingly *The Colour And The Shape* actually included two tracks from the original sessions with William Goldsmith's drumming still intact. Well, almost two tracks. He featured on the entire opener 'Doll', but was only present on the slow section of 'Up In Arms'. All other drum tracks came courtesy of Grohl.

'Doll' opened the album with a lilting country rocker that fell somewhere between The Lemonheads and Lynard Skynard in ballad mode. It also introduced the overriding theme of the album, dealing with loss. Specifically the loss of his long-term relationship with ex-wife Jennifer Youngblood, the loss of anonymity he had enjoyed before (with Nirvana everyone wanted the singer not the drummer, with Foo Fighters everyone wants the ex-drummer) and finally the loss of friendship (either through tragedy or negligence).

'Monkey Wrench' followed with its 1980s power punk heart beating to a defiant pose. "I'd rather leave than suffer this." Following on Grohl dealt with losing touch with old school friend Johnny Park. In the appropriately titled 'Hey, Johnny Park!' he asked the protagonist to get in touch. However the lyrics were underscored with a sense of bitterness. Musically 'Hey, Johnny Park!' sounded like Metallica covering Husker Du, with Grohl – presumably inadvertently – adopting an uncannily close imitation of Metallica's James Hetfield.

'My Poor Brain' is the first example of the infuriating nature of the album. Starting with a cacophony of frequency snatches and wireless sounds, it opened out into a glorious high-pitched melody over a simple strummed guitar motif, only to ergot into a clichéd neo-grunge chorus, complete with screeched vocals and guitars repeating a near-feedback refrain. Quite simply the track, which had originally been called 'Chicken Darby', lacked the courage to take either the verse or the chorus to their illogical extremes. Instead, Foo Fighters opted for the near-apologetic chorus angst to counter balance the verse's sweetness.

Lyrically, 'My Poor Brain' once again dealt with the breakdown of a close relationship. Although this time the mood was less about defiance than acceptance of an impossible situation. Of the album's rockers, 'Wind Up' was perhaps one of the most effective. Built around an ascending, circular riff, it found Smear's guitars flying off in blazing Fugazi-esque machine gun staccato. Simple, but effective.

However, 'Up In Arms' featured the same failings that coloured 'My Poor Brain', thanks to a Neil Young-style country intro that, far too predictably, opened up into power punk pastiche. Sadly, this time the song sounded far too much like Green Day. Only the song's theme of separation and reconciliation could be easily attributed to Grohl.

'Up In Arms' faded directly into the album's first true rock epic 'My Hero'. Again coloured a lighter shade of Metallica, the song thundered along to Grohl's powerhouse rolling drums and a searing guitar motif over which the vocal melody moved between a cynical sneer and open-mouthed awe.

The song also introduced the theme of loss of anonymity. Here he faced the hero worshipping aspect being a rock star from the fan's viewpoint. He subsequently used the soapbox to declare his hero to be ordinary.

Many critics mistakenly believed the song to be about Cobain. However it was in fact about the situations that Foo Fighters had increasingly found themselves in, and their oft stated desire to remain normal, 'nice' people. Among the inevitable aspects of the hero worship Grohl and his band were now witnessing was the hanger-on, the fan that thinks they're the band's best friend. "We come into town and there's people waiting outside every hotel," explained Mendel. "How do they know where we're staying? Don't know, but they're always there."

"And they always go straight for Pat," added Grohl. "What was that one girl's name? She offered Pat a psychic reading and he was like, 'Oh, thank you very much, but no...' And then she started showing up at every show. Like, 'Oh, I came to visit my mom - in Minneapolis. Next day, Indiana, she shows up outside the hotel. 'Dave! Dave!', she's going, 'Tell Pat I'm here! I'm waiting outside.' Then Chicago, then Denver... As far as you can go, and she's still there." [7]

Next track on *The Colour And The Shape* was the Beatles bar room sing-a-long 'See You'. One of the album's lighter moments, it is perhaps surprising that it also represents an album high point thanks to its sheer honesty. Neither a rocker, nor a grunge-by-numbers throwaway, this represented a moment of respite from the continuous onslaught of unsubtle dynamics. Furthermore it was one of the few tracks that had the courage of its convictions, never changing tack mid-way through to satisfy the rocker's needs.

'Enough Space' found Foo Fighters firing on all cylinders and delivering a hardcore-meets-metal workout. The song title referred to Grohl's boredom at always being asked about sci-fi. When he named his band and label he had never predicted quite how many people would assume him to be obsessed with outer space.

"Every time we got together to do an interview, or every time we read a feature on the band, it had more to do with UFOs and science fiction than the music," he says. "I'm a sci-fi buff; I'm a UFO buff. I named the band Foo Fighters. I named the record company Roswell Records because of the UFO crash in New Mexico. So, for good reason, people suppose I'm obsessed with outer space, which I'm just *not*. I love reading about it, I love science fiction movies, but I don't pray to the alien god in my fucking pyramid temple. It just doesn't happen. So I just thought, enough of this space shit." [8]

The situation wasn't helped by the fact that when he did offer up quotes about sci-fi, they tended to make more interesting reading than his continuous talk on only being one person in a whole band. "I used to want to see a UFO when I was a kid," he once told *Kerrang!* "I used to lie in the back garden at night and I wanted them to come and abduct me. 'Please, get me out of here!'

I had amazing UFO dreams. There was one dream where I was standing outside my house looking up at the sky and I suddenly realised that it wasn't the sky - it's this huge disc and the bottom of it is like a mirror. I can see the cars next to me in the bottom of this thing, forty feet above my head. It wasn't scary. I was just like, 'Take me! Take me!'

"UFOs are an escape. I sure fucking hope there's something else out there. There has to be. It's the romantic idea of staring up at the stars and knowing that someone's staring back at you." [9]

It was with the final four tracks that the album finally lived up to its promise. 'February Stars' - an aching slow jam that opened with a country lament, complete with honey dipped harmonies, before building towards an epic impassioned climax. 'Everlong' followed with one of Grohl's most touching and passionate songs to date, thanks to its undulating riffs and dejected melody. Again, the guitar hooklines sounded like 1980s out-takes, but this time around the combined force of the arrangements, Grohl's vocals, the drum track and the overall melody gelled into a solid whole. Suddenly the Foo Fighters sounded once again like they knew where they were heading, and made no apologies for the route they were taking. It was a cathartic moment amidst the album's over self-consciousness.

'Walking After You' again found the band wandering through Velvet Underground territory, specifically echoing 'Pale Blue Eyes', but this time taking things to a satisfying conclusion. Essentially a ballad for a spurned lover who refuses to let go, its acoustic guitar interplay brought out a new depth and sensitivity to Foo Fighters. Beautiful.

Concluding track 'New Way Home' offers a rare moment of insight into Grohl's personality with the line, 'I love this leash that holds me when I try to run'. Despite his life in music he has always clung to the concept of family. Each band he has been in is recalled with warmth. However, as soon as the cracks show, he feels insecure. This transposes itself in the Foo Fighters with his aforementioned admission that he loves the security of the tour bus and the sound of his friends making popcorn. Grohl likes things in their place, where he can find some security from the knowledge of their whereabouts.

A one-time promoter from Capitol (who preferred to remain anonymous), confirmed Grohl's need for security. "It's like he admires everyone else around him but doesn't admit his own central role," she said. "And if he does accept it he thinks he's turned into a rock star and lost it. So he keeps people close and surrounds himself with normality in a strange world."

Grohl's niceness means that people feel like they are cheating on him if they talk out of line. It is inadvertently an effective tool for controlling things. As a result, most third party interviews come with the request of anonymity.

Musically, 'New Way Home' was a stunning combination of searing guitars, pounding drums and growled vocals. Again the mood was epic; again the song was all about building towards the climax, but this time round it sounded like the band had achieved what they really wanted to do. It was the work of a unit breaking away from the sonic, if not the personal, leash.

Two other tracks were recorded during *The Colour And The Shape* sessions; the tender acoustic 'Dear Lover', and the feedback-drenched hardcore assault, "The Colour and the Shape', which although essentially the title track was left off at the last moment. 'Dear Lover' would turn up on the *Scream 2* soundtrack while 'The Colour and the Shape' had been the B-side of CD#1 of the 'Monkey Wrench' single.

The Colour And The Shape may not have been the masterpiece that the band had striven towards, but it bode well for the future. In those moments that it reached its potential, it sounded far and away superior to the band's contemporaries. "I don't want to yank my own crank, but this record is great!" declared Grohl at the time. Unfortunately, not all of the press agreed.

"Most of this second album follows a predictable US grunge rock formula. Grohl may be a superb hard-rock drummer, but his gruff, weather-beaten vocals leave the guitars with too much to do in terms of carrying any melody lines. The resulting racket lacks nothing in terms of spirit, but has simply been played too many times before," wrote the UK's *Daily Mail*, while *The Independent* went further by using the album to illustrate the creative lull being experienced by US rock bands at this time. "…this is pleasant enough grunge-pop, energetic and melodic in roughly equal parts," they wrote, "but there is a touch of desperation about the album, as if Dave Grohl and his cronies realise that there's not much mileage left in this kind of lumpen, overwrought American rock."

Select was even more scathing: "Sadly, *The Colour And The Shape* does Dave Grohl's reputation only sporadic favours. At its best, it shows him battling for singularity in a genre that's stuck in reputation and cliché. At its worst, it puts remarkably little distance between Foo Fighters and any run-of-the-mill band with tattoos, big shorts, bleached hair and a bug up their ass."

It wasn't all negative however. *The Sunday Times* declared that "Grohl has perfected the sound attempted on the first album, a winning combination of bouncy pop with chugging, shredding rock that keeps the tune to the fore even when the amps are turned up."

Kerrang! were so blown away by the album that they voted it their '#1 Album of the Year' in 1997 and one of their chosen '100 ALBUMS YOU MUST HEAR BEFORE YOU DIE' in a January, 1998 issue: "*The Colour And The Shape* sees Dave Grohl striding boldly away from his legacy and his band trampolining (sic) gleefully on all preconceptions. Truly Foo-king special..."

A few years later Grohl summed up the sessions for *The Colour And The Shape* as if it had in fact been pure torture. Largely because he refused to use the labour saving Pro-Tools software to tighten up the drum tracks. "*The Colour And The Shape*. That one. That was WORK. That was real fuckin' work.... that record was before ProTools really kicked in. It was done on straight tape, but Gil Norton was used to doing ProTools here and there and I objected to it with the drums. I thought, 'No, I don't want to do that. Let's just try and get good takes.' And in order to get a good take according to Gil, or a take that's good enough for Gil, like 'Monkey Wrench', I played that song, I don't even know how many times, for like eight-and-a-half hours. Over and over and over and over and over again. So that I would come into the studio to listen back and think, 'Dude, WHAT are you hearing? What is wrong with that? I honestly think I can't make it any better than that.'" [10]

On May 19, Foo Fighters set out on a tour of UK, US and Europe in support of *The Colour And The Shape*. The tour would find the band playing over one hundred gigs in almost as many cities, heavily featured in all of the European festival line-ups (usually supporting the Prodigy) and retaining the tag of the hardest working band in the world.

Foo Fighters were faced with a huge battle with this tour. *The Colour And The Shape* had arrived in a year when the full backlash against the post-grunge alt-rock scene in the US was in swing. Of the original Seattle bands, few had delivered the global success they were tipped to achieve. Furthermore the copyists had taken the original sound and turned it into an adult-friendly MTV rock banality. They were no better than Bon Jovi.

The reaction to this increasingly toothless sound came in the shape of so-called electronica. In 1997, Prodigy had delivered *The Fat of the Land*, the greatest hard dance album of all-time, which had gone to #1 in twenty-three countries around the world. In the US, the electronica invasion was in full swing, while in the UK the media's obsessions had become split between electronica and alt-prog rockers Radiohead. More poignantly in regard to Grohl's self-recording ethos, the Prodigy's mastermind Liam Howlett had recorded much of that global smash album from his own home studio. Suddenly, *Foo Fighters* seemed limp by comparison.

Foo Fighters simply didn't fit anymore. They certainly weren't a poor imitation of grunge, like Bush for instance, and they had no intention of recreating old Nirvana tracks, like just about every other alt-rock band. They were still an MTV-friendly proposition, but many felt that somehow their days were surely numbered.

Ironically, it was the electronica invasion that allowed the band to move beyond the alt-rock circuit. Thanks to many dates with the Prodigy, Foo Fighters were able to access a brand new audience, while the Prodigy - who were at this time plying their trademarked electronic punk sound - were able to access a rock crowd through the Foos.

The 1997 world tour kicked off in the UK at Cambridge's Corn Exchange on May 19. In the days that followed Foo Fighters took in Wolverhampton Civic Hall, Nottingham Rock City, Leeds Town and Country, Glasgow Barrowlands, Manchester Apollo and the Guildhall in Southampton, ending the UK leg with two dates at London's Astoria.

In their review of the first night at The Astoria, *The Times* declared the Foos to be "a thrilling dose of assault-rock 'n' roll at its finest", while arguing that Grohl appeared to have developed a "commanding stage presence." It was certainly true that he had moved on from the endless hair flailing and goofing around that marked out the earlier shows. His interaction with the audience became more effective and his movements less frenetic. On stage it was becoming more and more the Grohl show. Not even Pat Smear could match his growing aura.

Midway through the UK leg of the tour, *The Colour And The Shape* was released in the US. The following week, the second single from the album, 'Everlong' was released, featuring B-sides that were recorded live at the BBC for an April 1997 session and on May 25 at Manchester's Apollo, again for a BBC Radio 1 broadcast. Released as another two CD set, Part 1 featured 'Drive Me Wild' from the BBC *Evening Session* and 'See You' from Manchester. While Part 2 found 'Requiem' being lifted from the session and 'I'll Stick Around' being taken from the live show.

The band opened the US leg of the tour on June 7, following a one-day stop off in Paris to play at L'Arapaho. The first date of the US tour was at Randalls Island in New York to play the second Tibetan Freedom Festival. The tour would take in dates in Mansfield, Irvine and New York before landing in Washington on July 9, at the 9:30 Club for a homecoming show that brought all of his family and old friends out to see the Foo Fighters show.

Hyperactive as ever, Grohl darted from person to person, smiling and generally acting the congenial host. Constantly by his side was his mother, who has remained supportive throughout the years, turning up to numerous Foo shows - just as she had with his previous bands. Grohl was centre stage and loving it.

"I always shoot myself in the foot when I play in Washington," explained Grohl at the gig. "Because I call everyone I know and tell them to come down and hang out, and I'm so excited to see everybody, but then of course there's not time to spend with everyone, and by the time I go on I think, 'My God, my whole soccer team from when I was in fifth grade is here and I haven't had a chance to talk to them.' But that's the way it goes and I hope people understand." [11]

It was clear by this stage that Grohl had metamorphosed into an enigmatic band leader ("I don't like to say that," he argues. "Foo Fighters wasn't *my* band. It was my demo tape, and that became the band") and a skilled interviewer. His handling of the press would find him disarming awkward questions with a smile, followed by a polite refusal to answer any questions he didn't like. These usually revolved around the inevitable questions about Kurt Cobain and Nirvana.

Two things were immediately apparent. When Grohl wanted to talk about something, he was a funny and enthusiastic interviewee. Bring up any subject that he didn't want to discuss and he'd stop talking altogether. Surprisingly he never came over as moody, or belligerent, just a professional man who had drawn a line through the past and was living very much for the present.

On July 26, the Foos' touring machine flew to Yamanashi, Japan for the Fuji Rock Festival. A hugely popular gig with bands, due not only to the fantastic crowds but also the breathtaking festival site at the foot of Mount Fuji, the show was the epitome of organisation. People were bussed into the location, their tickets checked with utmost efficiency and speed, while the stage management itself ran like clockwork, each change-over handled with speed and the absolute minimum of fuss.

Furthermore the security was second to none. There was no blagging your way past Japanese guards who stood by the backstage entrance. Without the correct pass you could have been the lead singer in the headlining band and you still wouldn't have got past. Backstage itself was strictly limited to band and crew only – this being one festival that didn't turn into an industry schmooze from beginning to end.

Foo Fighters were booked to play alongside Prodigy, Rage Against The Machine, Beck, The Red Hot Chili Peppers and Green Day among others. However, this year's Mount Fuji Festival was to prove to be a particularly memorable one.

Grohl recalls why: "Oh my God... It was us and the Chili

Peppers, Beck, Green Day, Prodigy... a ton of really great bands and on the first day a fucking typhoon hit. The show went on and I'm on the stage, the rain's coming in sideways so hard I can't open my eyes. I'm standing in a puddle, holding an electric guitar, with about 60 million watts of power running through everything, thinking for sure I was about to die. They had to cancel the second day because the stage was sinking into the ground. I totally fucking loved it. It was insane." [12]

On August 28, following festival dates around Europe (including Chelmsford and Leeds) the band arrived in Seattle to play the Bumbershoot Festival. Given the fact that the gig was in the home town of Sub Pop and the grunge phenomenon, a place which both Grohl and Mendel had called home for a number of years, inevitably the show was the subject of huge speculation as to who might guest with the Foos. Eddie Vedder was a favourite.

The band's set brought together the best moments from the first two albums with highlights coming in the shape of a resounding version of 'Alone + Easy Target' and stunning takes on 'February Stars' and 'Everlong'. For the encore they were joined by Krist Novoselic to play versions of Prince's 'Purple Rain' and Led Zeppelin's 'Communication Breakdown'. The crowd were at first stunned and then responded with an almost deafening roar.

A few days later on September 4, Foo Fighters were booked to play the MTV Video Awards being held at Radio City Music Hall. The band was to play a three song set including 'Monkey Wrench', 'My Hero' and 'Everlong'. Two songs in, Pat Smear threw his guitar to the ground and walked off stage. He had quit the band, literally there and then in front of the MTV cameras, only to return with his replacement in tow, one Franz Stahl! "That last song was my last with the band," he announced to the crowd. "I'd like to introduce Franz Stahl who will be taking over. Rock on guys. FOO FIGHTERS!" Possibly one of the greatest band splits of all-time?!

Stahl had quit his band Wool to join Foo Fighters. "Ultimately it's great to be back again with Dave, being friends in a musical sense," explained Stahl after the show. "I think my brightest moments playing music were with Dave. I saw when Taylor joined Foo Fighters, there was a spark, an infusion of energy that reminded me of a time Dave came over to the basement to audition for Scream."

Grohl's reunion with his long time friend became somewhat overshadowed by the speculation that surrounded Smear's departure. According to the rumours, it was due to a power struggle between Grohl and Smear. Other observers suggested that Grohl's relationship with Louise Post of Veruca Salt had caused the friction. Grohl steadfastly dismissed the rumours as a "bunch of internet crap".

"The rumours had been going round for a really long time." he continued. "Pat decided he wanted to leave a while ago, but he agreed to finish out some of the touring. So we did the American tour and the European tour. Pat's going on. He's doing his own thing. It's cool."

Talking about the departures of both Smear and Goldsmith, Grohl argued that the main reason behind the changes were due to the constant touring. Grohl may have been a hyperactive guy with a love of constant touring, but the rest of the band on the other hand needed to take a break occasionally.

"Pat had never really toured other than with Nirvana – he'd never been in a band for more than a year so his career in Foo Fighters was as long as he'd ever experienced. When Pat left it was understood that we were gonna continue. When all bands start they always make a pact that if one person quits they're gonna break up, but it never really works out that way, particularly when things are going so well." [13]

Among the rumours that surrounded Smear's very public resignation was the suggestion that he was totally against the Foo Fighters' next move, playing as support to the Rolling Stones. It was an act that was totally against Smear's punk principles. Only a few years earlier, Grohl had derided U2's Bono for suggesting that

Nirvana support them. Now he was happy to play opener for the world's biggest rock dinosaurs. Had Grohl lost his principles in pursuit of success on the long rock 'n' roll ladder?

However, rock historians will tell you that the Rolling Stones were originally one of the music world's most incendiary and visceral bands; others might argue that the tag of rock dinosaur was a churlish criticism of a legendary band whose main crime was to stay together and get older.

Clearly Grohl had very different principles with Foo Fighters than he had had with Nirvana. However, these principles were not tempered by egotism or the need for stardom. He simply wanted to get his music heard by as many different people as possible. Watching the band side stage at both their Chelmsford and Leeds V97 Festival dates, I was struck by how relatively small the band actually were at this stage.

On both occasions they played the mid-afternoon slot drawing crowds of around a thousand. This was in stark contrast to the Prodigy who attracted an unprecedented crowd, rammed together as far as you could see – it was obvious that Foo Fighters had some way to go before they could compete on this level. It was important for them to escape the baggage of grunge once and for all. If the bright and overblown production on *The Colour And The Shape* had failed to do this, then it was down to the Foo's vibrant live experience. Playing with the Rolling Stones would bring them to another new audience. Why not?

If opening for The Stones had come as a shock to fans of the band, then two events that drew the year to a close would have people baffled. One involved hip hop impresario Puff Daddy, the other involved bottle blond drummer Roger Taylor from pomp rock deities Queen. The Puff Daddy (aka Sean Coombes) situation came about when the hip hop producer asked the Foo Fighters' frontman to work with him on a rock version of his theme to the movie *It's All About The Benjamins*. In the end Grohl played drums, bass and guitar on two versions of the track.

A month after the release of the title track as a single, Foo

Fighters were joined on stage by Queen's Roger Taylor to play a version of 'Sheer Heart Attack'. Thus closing the year in the same way it had begun, with Grohl playing on stage with his heroes.

So, from Bowie to Queen in twelve uneasy months. 1997 would be remembered as a year when Foo Fighters lost members but gained swathes of new fans, in spite of the prevailing anti–grunge climate. It also became clear throughout this campaign that as long as Grohl wanted the band to continue, it would do so. True, the year would also be remembered for a disappointing second album. However it wasn't all bad. *The Colour And The Shape* had remained in the US *Billboard* Top 100 all year and would feature in those listings for the twelve months to come. A few remaining hardened critics might not yet be convinced, but an increasingly adoring public at large were showing ever more obvious signs of being totally converted.

6

THERE IS NOTHING LEFT TO LOSE

ANOTHER DRUMMER JOKE
Why are drummers always the first to arrive anywhere?
Because they keep speeding up.

"It sucked!" exclaimed new Foos guitarist Franz Stahl when questioned about that first gig at New York's Radio City Hall for the MTV Music Awards. "When you're nervous and sweaty, it's kind of hard to play, and I was so nervous I think I managed to make everyone else nervous."

Franz had known for quite sometime that he would be stepping into the breach to take over from Pat Smear. The call had come earlier in the summer of 1997, but he went on tour to Japan instead. On his return, he was hurriedly rushed into rehearsal rooms where, after only one hour he had mastered one song, 'Everlong'. Then, after another six days of hectic rehearsals, he was thrown into the gig arena, with an hour's worth of songs under his belt.

"I'm still not at the point where my hand can play without thinking," said Stahl shortly after his debut. "It's still kind of awkward, but I have a grace period. I can fuck up for a while because I'm the new guy."[1]

When Stahl became a Foo Fighter, he was following in the footsteps of one of punk rock's legends. However, he joined a band that was racked with disquiet. The public face of the band had been one of an easy-going gang, who all got along like the best of buddies, who enjoyed nothing more than swapping their tour bus for a sweaty van, just to get that closeness of a gang. But it wasn't true.

The departure of Goldsmith had made this abundantly clear. Not so much through his absence, but via his replacement. When Taylor Hawkins, joined he gelled immediately with Grohl. So much so that people started joking that they had been separated at birth.

The two drummers shared the same passion for music, the same hyperactive sense of humour and above all the same level of energy for pursuing the dream of being in a band and making music. The drum duo quickly started to act like a unit that was almost separate from the others. It wasn't a conscious thing, just something to do with chemistry.

"Taylor and I are best, best friends in the world," Grohl would later admit. "He is like my brother. He is my best friend I ever had in life. He's the greatest guy in the world. As friends we communicate by not even having to speak at times. Other times I reveal to him more than anyone. We're really close, so when it comes to doing drums... He's a phenomenal drummer, just amazing. So, when I write songs, I can hear sort of what's going on in my head as far as the rhythm or the accents or drumming in general. I don't want to impose on him. I don't want to go, 'This is exactly how it should go.' You just try to relay the accents. 'Feel that right there? Look at how I'm strumming the guitar. It's a kick drum that should be right there 'cause I want to catch that thing.' I'll say things like that." [2]

Mendel, the philosophical one, was able to assimilate the new band dynamics into his worldview. Smear on the other hand didn't have the same nature. And, as it turned out, his departure hadn't been as amicable as that *MTV* speech had suggested. Indeed, his input in the Foos recording was even called into question.

Grohl later said, "We were between a rock and a hard place then. We were under his thumb. There are some songs he didn't even play on that record. (*The Colour And The Shape*)" [3]

So when Franz rejoined his old friend, it wasn't a case of rekindling the Scream flame. That belonged very much in the past. It was more a case of fitting in and finding a way to work with an altogether new beast.

"At this point, I have a good idea of what my role is, but I haven't fully melded into being a member of the band yet," said Stahl. "But I can't wait to start recording and writing songs, leaving my mark on tape and playing my own parts. It's been a while since I've really been working with people. In Wool, we would all bring things to the table and hash them out, and I think it's going to be like that in this situation. And I think there could be even more all-around input. But, in truth, I'm not thinking about that much either right now. I'm really just trying to mesh in as a member, not create any waves, and learn the music." [4]

It was to prove to be a hard task. Stahl would find a strong link with Mendel and, when they were on the road there was always his brother Pete to hang out with, who was a part of the Foo Fighters' crew at this stage.

Grohl's admiration for Stahl had not diminished in the years since Scream. He still regarded Stahl as one of the guitarists he admired most. "When we started this band, had Franz and Pete not been in Wool, Franz would have been the guitar player (for Foos). When Wool broke up, I knew someday I'd be playing with him again… I've spent more time with him than with any other guitar player in my life. He taught me so much about playing, and on top of that he's a great songwriter and an amazing vocalist. "It might sound mean, but this version of the band is absolutely the best. I'm really looking forward to hitting the road with these guys." [5]

Foo Fighters started 1998 in much the same way as they had left 1997; on the road. Grohl's excitement at his latest version of the band translated into increasingly fired up shows, with Stahl's guitar work proving a tighter, and at times more aggressive foil for Grohl's melodies. It was clear that the four piece were enjoying playing together.

What was also apparent was how the loss of Smear had forced Grohl to become more dynamic onstage. In many ways, Smear had been a crutch for Grohl to hide his insecurities behind. In his mind the renowned guitarist was the focal point of the band. It was a situation that suited him. He still suffered from stage fright and harboured huge doubts as to whether he could cut it as a frontman. With Smear firmly planted in his mind as the Foo Fighter everyone was looking at, he could overcome his nerves and doubts by subconsciously living in Smear's shadow.

With Smear's departure, however, the role of focal point lay squarely on Grohl's shoulders for the first time since the band's inception. Or indeed, the first time since he started playing in bands. "When he split, I did feel extra responsibility, but it was strange because he was the focal point, yet he never did interviews. When he first left and you listened to the band, I don't think you could really tell that he wasn't there. Now you can tell he's gone though, because in the last eight months we've become the best band we've ever been – live *and* in the studio. I think that Franz's guitar playing is so much more contained and precise and powerful. When Pat left, I expected people to be holding up 'Where's Pat?' signs; I expected there to be some sort of backlash, or a lot of people that were upset about him leaving, but not once have I seen anyone say, 'We miss Pat'. That sounds awful, but it's true. Actually, after he left, the band started getting more popular, so I don't know what that has to do with! It seemed like he split right at the wrong time, 'cos everything started going so well for us. But he still gets to sit at home and he gets the cheques, so he's psyched." [6]

Grohl's reticence to step into the limelight not only stemmed from his own insecurities, but also his punk ideologies. He was still fiercely anti-star. In fact, despite living amid the hell of Hollywood celebrity (and reportedly dating Winona Ryder at this time) he had never embraced the celebrity ethos.

As a result he worked overtime at pushing this image that his band were just ordinary people. This translated into rarely having to deal with the problems of being pestered by the tabloids or stalked by the public. In fact, he was able to live a relatively normal life – if spending ninety per cent of your time on a tour bus can be considered normal!

"I don't get accosted by people, I don't have a stalker and I don't have a hard time in public," he says. "I think one of the reasons I don't is (a) we're not that popular a band, (b) I was the drummer of Nirvana with long hair – no one knew what I looked like, even when I was in that band nobody recognised me and lastly (c) most people see me as an anti–celebrity, just a normal guy. Wow, that guy won the lottery, how come he gets to be on fucking *Saturday Night Live*, how come he gets to be on *MTV*. He doesn't look any different to anyone else. So whenever people accost me on the street it's 'Hey Dave, how are ya? What's up Grohl? How's it going?' It's never bodyguards and security."

The motivation behind his anti-celebrity stance was, he admitted, due to those punk roots. Although, as has already been noted, the everyman image also acted as an effective defence mechanism against the more negative and invasive elements of the media.

"I hate to go back to the punk rock all the time but when I was twelve, thirteen-years-old in the Washington DC hardcore scene, there wasn't any such thing as a rock star," he continued. "The people in the bands were the people who were selling you the T-shirts after the show. The people in the bands were the ones driving the vans or hanging out with you or sleeping on your floor. Your favourite bands, the singer's taking a shower in your house because they couldn't afford a motel. That idea still sticks with me. That's the way I've always seen the whole thing. There shouldn't really be any difference. And I still hate to see fucking egotistical rock stars who consider themselves better than anybody else just because they play an instrument. It's ridiculous. Even horrible bands. It blows me away that anyone would consider themselves any better than anyone else because of something that they do. To consider yourself badass for being a fucking drummer..." he trails off in disbelief at the whole idea.

Despite his claims to be just an ordinary Joe, Grohl did receive more than his fair share of attention from fans. He may suggest that this was typified by people saying, "Hi Dave", but the reality was a little more akin to pop star worship at times.

Many of the band's shows or TV appearances became hunting grounds for the more obsessive fans who would scream his name at the tops of their voices, pleading with him to acknowledge them. It was a situation that he clearly found uncomfortable.

"I still never expect it; it just happens. You have to figure, well, these people probably really like your music, so it's pretty flattering. But it gets a little weird. You hear one of them go, 'Oh my God! I can't believe I touched him!' and it's like 'Oh please! Would you just relax? Give me a break! Would you like to come and watch me take a shit?'"

Another interesting aspect to his anti-star position was the fact that he felt little affinity with his contemporaries who were being hailed as stars. For him 'stars' at this time (1998) had little to do with music, but image and PR. He did however have some respect for the old-school rock stars. "I've always thought of the rock star term as fucking derogatory man, it's gross. When I think of rock stars of yesteryear, they sort of seem like superhero cartoon characters. When I think about rock stars today, I think they're arseholes! When someone is termed 'one of the last true rock stars', to me it seems like they're saying they're one of the last true arseholes', you know? In order to be a good rock star today you have to be arrogant, very career-driven and everywhere all the time – in all the right places and dealing with all the right people.

It used to be that rock stars had something to do with music; they were people that were exceptional and really excelled in whatever they were doing. Whether it was John Bonham, Jimmy Page, Ozzy Osbourne or Tony Iommi or whoever – they were doing something that was new and meaningful and wonderful and different. Today it just seems like this person got lucky 'cos they had a hit single and their face is on the cover of every magazine, and that gives them licence to fucking mouth off, which grosses me out. It should be secondary – it doesn't have anything to do with the music anymore, it has to do with the image. That's what I think is wrong." [7]

On January 21 the anti-star Foo Fighters arrived in Tokyo, Japan to play two dates at Blitz. The opening night, the first of the Pacific Rim stage of the tour, went without a hitch. However, the following night Grohl became violently ill nine songs into a nineteen-song set and was forced to leave the stage. He never made it back again.

Missing a gig through illness was almost unheard of for Grohl. In the years since he first started playing in bands he had never missed or abandoned a gig for anything. In fact, had he been a blue-collar worker, he would have been the one clocking in the hours and popping cold remedies rather than take a day off work. To say his approach to being in a band was almost the epitome of the protestant work ethic wasn't an understatement. Witness the fact that he has always found it almost impossible to take a holiday. Sure he's hyperactive, but he's also the one who takes care of things, the provider. And if he gets ill, everything around him suffers.

In support of the winter 1998 tour, Foo Fighters had released their third single from *The Colour And The Shape*. 'My Hero' was perhaps an obvious choice of single thanks to its radio friendly hooklines. The CD release in the UK proved to be the beginning of the band's use of new technology as CD extras. The single included a cross platform enhanced CD portion, which featured the full-length 'Everlong' video, thirty seconds of the 'Monkey Wrench' video, and screenshots from a Brixton Academy show in November 1997. It was one of the first enhanced singles (the very first having come from south London dance-rock crossover act Transcendental Love Machine a year earlier).

Other tracks included on the single were 'Dear Lover' from the album sessions and 'Baker Street', the Gerry Rafferty song recorded by the band for their 1997 Radio 1 session. 'Baker Street' would later appear on the EMI artist's compilation *Come Again*.

Following their Japanese dates the band flew to Australia for shows in Brisbane, Sydney, Melbourne, Hobart, Adelaide and Perth before playing two dates in Auckland and Wellington, New Zealand. The band then travelled to New York for a one-off date at the Roseland Ballroom and an appearance on *The Howard Stern Show.*

During their rare few days off in March, they opted to go into the studio! Their first session was to record a new version of 'Walking After You' at Ocean Way Recording in Hollywood. This was followed by a session at Sound City Studios, Van Nuys, California, to record the new song 'A320'.

The reasons for the new version of 'Walking After You' was that it had been licensed for use in the *X-Files* movie. Grohl had wanted to provide the track with more emotion, having been unhappy with the original vocal track. However, he also had high hopes that this love song about his separation from Jennifer Youngblood would be the catalyst for, and soundtrack to, Mulder and Scully finally getting together!

"Having watched the show so much for so many years, you fall in love with the characters," he says. "And I guess you sorta expect them to fall in love with each other. 'Walking After You' is basically an intimate sort of love song where you're so dependent on someone else that you know, if they walk out on you, then... then you're walking after them. Because you need them. So I guess my dream was to give this to the *X-Files* and have them use it in a scene where Mulder and Scully finally get together (laughs). The love scene! It would be amazing to see that happen with a song that meant a lot to me playing in the background. That would be pretty beautiful." [8]

'Walking After You' would be released as a limited edition single in May 1998. The flipside featured Ween playing their song 'Beacon Light'. 'A320' on the other hand would eventually turn up on the soundtrack to the movie *Godzilla*.

"It *(Godzilla)* was fuckin' lame," laughed Grohl. "So we sat through the whole movie wondering where the hell they were going to put our song. It wasn't even in the movie! (Soundtracks are) more to promote the movie and act as a recovery fund if the movie does really poor." [9]

'A320' was produced by Jerry Harrison of Talking Heads fame.

It was a mid-tempo track that boasted gorgeous, Bowie-esque outro featuring Petra Hayden on violin, Benmont Tench on organ and Harrison on piano. It also offered an early glimpse at the more introspective nature of the tracks they would go on to record for the next Foos album, *There Is Nothing Left To Lose*.

'Walking After You' was issued on Atlantic Records as they owned the rights to the *X-Files* soundtrack. However there were other label changes going on in the background at this time. Grohl had severed ties between Roswell and Capitol, taking Foo Fighters with him. He was now looking for a new deal for his imprint. The generally accepted reason was that Grohl had included in his deal a "key man" clause that stated should company president Gary Gersh ever leave, then he could too. So when Gersh left in 1998, Grohl remained true to his word, and upped sticks.

As this was unfolding, however, Foo Fighters continued on their exhaustive world tour including the summer's many festival dates, which included a gig with Ozzy Osbourne at the legendary Ozzfest on June 20.

"I didn't realise what the gig was going to be at first," laughs Grohl at the memory. "I was just asked, 'Do you want to play with Ozzy?' and I was like 'Fuck yeah!' So I thought we would be supporting. Then I found out we were in the line-up for Ozzfest! The biggest fucking heavy metal festival! So I thought, 'fuck it, let's do it.'"

Although the audience were pretty hostile towards Foo Fighters, Ozzy himself treated them well. This hadn't been the case when the band had supported the Rolling Stones however. This date – which had after all caused so much friction - turned out to be a nightmare. The Stones attitude to their support act only underlined Grohl's dislike of the rock star mentality.

"They didn't give us a guest list, they reserved a hundred tickets that we could buy for $64 a piece," he exclaimed. "So if I wanted my sister or my girlfriend to come, I had to buy a fucking ticket. And they didn't give us a dressing room in the venue; we had to sit in the trailer out in the parking lot. That was fucked up, that was bullshit." [10]

Foo Fighters were a little less demanding however. In an industry famed for its excessive rider requirements, the Foos were unusually restrained. "We're not really too big on deli meats," said Grohl. "We like Kinder eggs - we end up just making the toys and throwing away the chocolate. Cigarettes are probably the weirdest things I insist on. I have friends who work at clubs, and they keep the riders that bands send and tack them on the fuckin' wall so I see the most ridiculous riders - fifteen boxes of Kleenex, a box of rubbers, some clean white socks, some underwear... buy your own fucking socks, man!" [11]

To play a heavy metal festival like Ozzfest wasn't such an unusual concept for Grohl. In the days pre-punk, he was a huge heavy metal fan and still harboured a love of many of those bands. His passion for the music stretched as far as speed metal, thrash, death metal and so on.

Not that this love of metal had effected his own stage persona. True, he was given to striking James Hetfield poses in moments of on stage self-depreciating humour, but the old punks still inspired his actions. For example, at the Midtown Music Festival in Atlanta, Georgia, on May 2, he stopped the band mid-song to make sure an apparently injured fan was all right. And when a girl mosher had her shirt torn off, he gave her the shirt off his own back!

In June, Foo Fighters joined the Edgefest Tour of Canada. The country had long held a strong fan base for the Foos, with *Foo Fighters* shifting in excess of 200,000 units, which represented double platinum sales. *The Colour And The Shape* was on the way to similar sales.

On the opening night in Montreal, Grohl took two $100 notes from his pocket before the band played 'Big Me' (which he described as "a stupid love song") and waved them in the air. He then asked for a girl and a guy to get on stage to see if they would kiss for the entire song. When they succeeded he gave them one hundred dollars each and then screamed "get the fuck off my stage!" repeatedly. Self-effacing humour or not, Grohl was turning into something of a showman.

Following the Edgefest tour, the band returned to the UK for what were to be their last gigs of the year. The first, a secret gig at London's Subterranea as a warm up for their performance at Reading Festival the following night. By playing a Reading Festival warm up at the Subterranea, the Foos were following in something of a tradition. Over the years bands that have used the small west London venue for secret pre-Reading gigs have included Red Hot Chili Peppers and Jane's Addiction.

The venue would also have been of interest to Grohl because in its previous incarnation as Acklam Hall, it was something of a punk and post-punk hangout; playing host to many of the bands Grohl had been into since discovering punk.

With the completion of the Subterranea and Reading Festival shows, the tour for *The Colour And The Shape* was finally over. The band returned to the US with thoughts already turning to recording the third album. However, Grohl had other things on his mind. First of all, he had agreed to produce Capitol Records artists Verbana. Secondly, he was growing tired of Hollywood and wanted to get out.

Verbana consisted of Anne Marie Griffin on guitar, bass and vocals, Les Nuby on drums, and Scott Bondy on guitar and vocals. Grohl had become a huge fan of theirs when they had supported Foo Fighters during their 1997 tour of the US: "...a return to good rock music... they have a great spirit and energy along with really catchy tunes. It's like a nasty, sexy Rolling Stones meets Debbie Does Dallas tuned down to a C."

Grohl produced the band's *Into The Pink* album, which echoed Nirvana's *Bleach* as much as it conjured up memories of early punk bands – with loads of pop melody thrown in for good measure. Sadly, the album was a huge disappointment, never fully moving beyond the monotony of a recording that was so one-level as to be virtually flat-lining.

Life in Los Angeles had become increasingly difficult for Grohl to come to terms with. The city was built around the concept of the velvet rope, which went against everything he held true. He hated the plasticity and many of the city's most celebrated characters left him completely cold and alienated.

As a result, numerous dilemmas which he had suppressed over the years came to the surface. Issues like his inability to face problems head on; his tendency towards an emotional distance; of course the psychological fall out from his break-up with his ex-wife Jennifer; and the ever-present post-traumatic shock which followed Cobain's death. He still thought about the Nirvana singer everyday, but more to the point, was continually forced to think and talk about it by journalists who would find ever more slippery ways of getting him to open up on the subject.

It was a period in which Grohl started asking a number of questions of himself. Inevitably perhaps, given the city he was living in, he sought answers through counselling. "I've gone to a few different therapists," he explained. "I'd go to one and they'd tell me one thing and I'd go to another and come out of it and my friend whose idea it was to go would say 'what did your therapist say?' And I'd say 'my therapist said this,' and this person would say, 'oh, you've got the wrong therapist. Go and see another one.' And they'd say an entirely different thing. I've never been a fan of therapy, although I can understand how it can be helpful but I had bad experiences with it because I just felt like I was being judged more than anything. I felt like I was in a confessional and that to me didn't seem very healthy."

Grohl subsequently returned to his hometown of Virginia "just 'cause of family. My mom and dad live around here and all my friends from high school." Grohl bought a house in Alexandria, Virginia and set about building a basement studio. To help in the process, he enlisted the services of long-time friend Adam Kasper.

"Well he's from Seattle and he had worked on some Nirvana

stuff. He worked on some mixes for *In Utero* and recorded us a couple times." [12] So Kasper moved to Grohl's house and got down to the hard work of creating the studio. It was completed by November 1998 when the band decamped to Virginia to start work on demo-ing new material.

Studio 606, as it was christened, is accessed via steep steps. On the descent the steps pass a Mardi Gras skeleton, complete with tux. The studio's name is announced by a sign that hangs on the door at the bottom of the stairs. Open it and you discover a room full of equipment stored under a low ceiling. Amplifiers, drums, mics are stacked everywhere. At the far end of this room is another door which opens into the mixing area. This room features walls that are plastered with evidence of Grohl's life in music. Gold and platinum discs for *Nevermind* and *Unplugged* sit next to awards for 500,000 sales of *Foo Fighters*. An advert for a New York Coliseum show with Nirvana, The Breeders and Half Japanese sits next to a photo of that venue displaying a 'SOLD OUT' notice. There is also an original show advert for Little Richard and Guitar Slim. Grohl's favoured chair is a luxurious loveseat. It is here that he sits while overdubbing guitar parts. Behind it, on the wall, sits his aforementioned framed Dischord royalty cheque.

Building the studio was important for Grohl, not only to demo the Foos, but also so he could continue recording his own material. In the years since that debut album, he had tried to find time to put down occasional ideas, many of which were unsuitable for either the band or even commercial release.

"I'm always recording some stuff. I even record speed metal songs or country ballads, just something to do if you've got an hour to spare, you know. Listen to it, laugh about it and erase it. It's great to see that you can do a complete speed metal song – writing, composing and recording it – in just one hour. I've got heaps of tapes at home that are just dealing with the question of how far you can push the rip-off of a Led Zeppelin riff! Nobody will ever hear that stuff, I'm just doing it for my own amusement!" [13]

As the band settled into the demo process in the newly finished

Grohl and his band–mates grew increasingly uncomfortable
with the media circus that revolved around Nirvana.

With Queen's Brian May at the 16th Annual Rock 'n' Roll
Hall of Fame concert, New York, 2001.

Grohl with an Australian fan, 2002.

The things you have to do to sell records nowadays –
Grohl takes the punk ethic a little too far...

Foos at the 49th Annual Grammys, failing to scoop the
'Best Dressed Rock Group' Award.

Chatting with the two most important women in his life,
mom Virginia and wife Jordyn, 2002.

Grohl's relationship with Taylor, both professionally and as a friend,
is famously close, despite the latter supposedly having the hardest
drummer's job in the world of rock.

Grohl playing the Devil in Tenacious D's film, *The Pick Of Destiny*, 2006.

The Tonight Show with Jay Leno, September 2006.

Dave and Jordyn attending the Clive Davis Pre-Grammy Awards party,
Los Angeles, 2008.

The Foo Fighters at Wembley Stadium, London.

Studio 606, problems started to emerge. They just weren't happy with the way things were sounding; the four band members simply weren't gelling musically.

Following a Christmas break, the band had reconvened at the studio to work on more new material. Progress was slow. The combination of the awkward band chemistry and the new studio's teething problems hampered the sessions.

Throughout 1999, Foo Fighters failed to come up with that next album. There were demos, but nothing that they could say they were particularly happy with. The only song that they were looking forward to recording was 'Aurora', one of the subsequent album's standout moments.

In early July 1999, the underlying friction in the band came to a head when Franz Stahl left. Stahl himself hadn't been comfortable with the new stuff. He was pushing in a harder direction, while the others were exploring less confrontational terrain.

"We were just going in two different directions musically, and the three of us had made a connection that we had never done before," says Grohl, who admits to shedding a few tears at his friend's departure. "It sucked. I love Franz, and I miss him. But the three of us were moving at pace and doing something we've never done. Nate and I were making this connection where he was complementing everything that I came up with. Taylor was so ready to go that he was playing like a madman. Our enthusiasm was really huge, and it seemed like most of the creative energy was coming from right here." [14]

"Franz leaving the band was a really traumatic experience for me. I cried after it happened," added Mendel. "But we all went through it together, and I feel like it made us closer. Right before we went in to record, we had this traumatic bonding experience that gave us cohesion. It sounds dorky, but there was a lot of hugging going on before we made this record." [15]

With the band now down to a three piece, they returned to Studio 606 for a period of intense creativity. The trio quickly locked into a unified idea of what the new album was going to be like. "Going in (finally to the studio) to make this album was the easiest yet," confirmed Grohl. "Taylor and Nate and I feel like we are the original line-up. We don't feel like this calico fucking paste -up of a band - Nate and I definitely have an unspoken musical relationship that is unlike anything I've ever experienced before. Taylor is not only my best friend in the world but the best drummer in the world and three of us realise that if anything happened to that, it would definitely be over."

Together the trio worked, rested and played day and night to get the songs right. The sessions were relaxed, but emotionally intense. Grohl, it was rumoured, was really cracking the whip.

"...cracking the whip only in that I think it is really important that each person have as much passion as the next," he argued. "Fortunately we do. The best (musicians) in the world struggle and it's frustrating, and that frustration becomes some weird energy or motivation that winds up making its way into the music. I think that is important. I think it's important to struggle to make an album. If it's too easy it just sounds too easy, ya know? The thing about recording is you're totally naked and under the microscope and then you have to challenge yourself. I think it's the most fun in the world. It's great - albums are like little journal entries or diaries. Once that song is on tape it will never, ever go away. It's forever and I think that's pretty fuckin' cool. But also as far as perfection goes, perfection is a subtlety. Perfection is not like, 'I want everything to be spot-on that click track. I want everything to be perfectly in time.' Perfection is something where you just feel it, it could be sloppy as hell... but it sounds fuckin' perfect to me. Also, I think everyone sort of cracks their own whip on themselves, saying, 'I'm not good enough.' I mean I have seen our bass player Nate throw his bass in the trashcan before." [16]

These rumours that Grohl was exercising his renowned dictatorial streak were completely unfounded as he actually felt complete respect and trust in his band mates. That feeling was mutual so the trio were able to bounce ideas off each other freely without ego ever getting in the way of the process. What transpired was arguably the Foo Fighters' first album as a true democracy. No power struggles, no musical differences, just locked-in creativity pushing towards a singular goal. Remarkably, Foo Fighters were still without a record deal.

In the month that followed the album's completion, Foo Fighters underwent a task that they had never had to face before; they auditioned for a new guitarist. After days of jamming with hopefuls they eventually settled on the relative unknown Chris Shifflett.

On September 3, the band played the first of three secret shows which they set up to ease Shifflett in. The first show took place at Troubador in LA, where they played under what was to turn out to be the suitably fitting pseudonym, Stacked Actors. The second secret gig was on September 15 at The Horseshoe Tavern in Toronto, followed two nights later with their final secret set at the Bowery Ballroom in New York. This latter was a showcase for industry and competition winners only. The band had used the lure of the tapes for their new album to open negotiations with interested record companies. Eventually, after a brief courting period with a few majors, Grohl opted for RCA. This gig was a celebration for the new label.

"It was interesting to see how much more fucked-up the business has gotten since 1991," Grohl said. "Now, the first thing you have to ask is: 'When is everyone getting fired? Has Seagram bought you yet?' That's the biggest difference, that and now everyone wears fucking Prada." [17]

So happy were RCA to have signed Foo Fighters that their A&R man, Bruce Flohr, could be seen down the front, moshing with the kids and singing along to the songs. "Bruce, you're scaring me," chuckled a bemused Grohl from the stage. "Can I tell you how psyched the whole company is about this band? It's almost too much for words," enthused Flohr at the time.

The RCA deal, like the previous contract with Capitol was with Roswell Records, allowing Grohl total control over Foo Fighters records. Not that he was unrealistic about how far he could go.

He knew that if they wanted to put out some of the heavier material that the band had worked on as a single, "… we'd have to fight like hell, but legally we could do it. But at the same time I look up to a lot of those people… I don't disrespect the people that work at RCA because they know what they're doing; they're there for a reason, just as I do what I do for a reason. It's a mutual relationship. There are times when it's tough and there are times when it's great. And we feel really lucky that they don't mind that we make albums in the basement, ya know? Not many people are fortunate enough to do that." [18]

A few weeks after that secret industry gig, the band flew to Australia to play a tour in support of the first new single, 'Learn to Fly' which was released there on October 18. The single was issued in the UK a week later.

Although Grohl had since declared his dislike for the song, 'Learn to Fly' has become classed as one of the Foo Fighters' true classics, thanks largely to its addictive hookline. The UK release of the single was again a double pack with The Obsessed's 'Iron and Stone' and Pink Floyd's 'Have A Cigar' on Part 1, and 'Make A Bet' (a *The Colour And The Shape* out-take) and 'Have A Cigar' on Part 2. 'Have A Cigar' featured Hawkins on vocals and lead guitar by Hawkins, Mendel and Adam Kasper.

The video for the single marked the beginning of Grohl's association with the semi-spoof band Tenacious D, featuring top Hollywood actor Jack Black, who Grohl would go on to produce an album for. "I was in Los Angeles a few years back and a friend of mine who worked at that club The Viper Room called me and was said, 'Man, you gotta get down here on Sunday night. This band's playing and you gotta see them.' So I kinda blew them off the first weekend. Second weekend I couldn't make it. Then I finally got down there expecting it to be just a band. There weren't that many people there, maybe about twenty five or thirty people. And Jack and Kyle (Gass) got up on stage just with acoustic guitars. I was doubled up laughing, I felt like I was on acid. It was the funniest thing I ever saw. I swear to God." [19]

On November 2, Foo Fighters' third album *There Is Nothing Left To Lose* was finally issued. It included a tattoo and an enhanced portion. The cover had a picture of the back of Grohl's head, where the nape of his neck now boasted a 'FF' tattoo.

There Is Nothing Left To Lose proved to be the best Foo Fighters album yet. Neither restricted by the insecurities of *Foo Fighters*, nor flawed by the inadequacies and power struggles of *The Colour And The Shape*, this album was the sound of the band working towards a common goal. To rediscover the American rock legacy and transform it through the energy of post-hardcore power pop.

Hence, through the album's eleven tracks the band embraced artists like Lynard Skynard, Joe Walsh-era Eagles, Peter Frampton, Kiss and even Foreigner and Journey, among many others, and reworked them with the tuneful force of a latterday Bob Mould. Gone were the Metallica poses and the 1980s rock sheen that had marked out the previous album. In its place were a series of wistful, contemplative epics. Indeed the out-and-out rockers were as few and far between as the predictable grunge-isms.

"To be in a band means to go through different phases, each album reflects another phase," explained Grohl. "You know I've always admired Bowie. He is a chameleon who refocuses with every album, he's always and forever changing his style and that's really fascinating!"[20]

There Is Nothing Left To Lose opened with the misleading thunder of 'Stacked Actors' with its belting distorted bass, rippling guitars and powerhouse vocals. It proved to be the only moment on the album that in any way hinted at the band's history. What followed was a far more tuneful and mellow affair than on previous outings. However that opening number did turn heads, not only with its brilliant melody, but also with the lyrics which some speculated were about his soured relationship with both Hollywood and, perhaps, Courtney Love (Grohl did not confirm this).

"I think the most important thing about writing songs is to refuse the specifics because that takes away the opportunity for some listener to relate to the song," he says in defence of the lyrics. "'Stacked Actors' – I wrote that song about everything that is fake and everything that is plastic and glamorous and unreal. So if that pertains to anyone that comes to mind, then there you go. And I'm sure a lot of people can relate to it and forward that message on to a number of disgusting celebrities. But specifics are fucking boring, y'know. Whatever, it'll be the subject of speculation forever. But I knew when I was writing it that, oh God, this'll become one of those songs that I'll have to explain at length every time."

The track that followed, 'Breakout', was a power pop stomper with a sensitive touch. Its phased bass line intro, picked guitars and feedback refrains introduced some of Grohl's most sublime melodies yet. 'Learn To Fly' was a moment of stunning beauty captured in just less than four minutes thanks to its understated guitar and bass interplay and joyous, almost spiritual chorus.

'Gimme Stitches' was a sly and raunchy look back to the glam stomp of T-Rex and the Stones, but without the former's lip gloss action and the latter's arrogance. It came in like a dirty 'Gimme Shelter' and went out like 'Let It Bleed' stripped bare of its glimmering paintwork. The chorus proved to be another case of Grohl snatching the most addictive hookline from the burning embers of power chord rock. A classic Grohl hookline in fact.

'Generator' was the least effective track of the set, thanks to its kitsch voice box refrain that echoed Peter Frampton's 'Show Me The Way'. What followed however was the track that Grohl is on record as thinking of as "the greatest song ever written!" That song was 'Aurora', the only song that had survived those earliest sessions. With its luscious chord changes and aching melody it proved to be a high point on what was an album with few lows. "'Aurora' was never (initially) going to be on *There's Nothing Left To Lose*, and yet it ended up getting on and it's my favourite on the album," admitted Grohl later.

'Live-In Skin' followed with its seductive rolling bass and liquid melody, while 'Next Year' offered his take on The Eagles with jangling guitars and camp fire harmonies that are one step away from being a trucking soundtrack.

'Headwire' was somewhat surreally reminiscent of The Police thanks to its shimmering guitar motifs, while 'Ain't It The Life' luxuriated in slide guitar–drenched, trad-country rock. The mellow mood was smashed with 'MIA', the band's final slab of visceral, guitar drenched rock. If slightly reminiscent of Foreigner, it still managed to capture that Foo Fighters essence

There Is Nothing Left To Lose was an important album for Foo Fighters because it taught them how powerful music could be without resorting to dynamics, histrionics or grunge. The power for this mellow, contemplative set came from the sheer level of emotion and the arrangements the band used to convey these feelings.

Part of the reason for the albums relaxed atmosphere was simply due to the way it was recorded. The laid-back environment of Alexandria and the lack of pressure from the record company created a notably more relaxed recording schedule.

"We had demo-ed maybe twelve or thirteen songs and then threw them away. Went 'No!'" explained Grohl. "We took it easy on that album. It was spring time and we would wake up, have breakfast, go out and shoot hoops for a couple of hours, come inside, listen to what we had done the night before, maybe put down a guitar track, and go have a BBQ. It was really, really mellow and it was great. One of the things about the album that I love so much is it sounds very mellow.

(It) was kind of a response to all the music that you were hearing on the radio. You were hearing albums that were so incredibly produced, people just taking advantage of ProTools. Auto-tune on the vocals, drumming that was obviously looped, and shit like that. It's cheating basically... I mean I know that there are bands that we have toured with like that. I watched the singer struggle to stay in tune every night. Then their new album comes out and it's fuckin' like Pavarotti. That's not him, that's Bill Gates... Well, kind of." [21]

If one thing stood out on the album it was the mark that

Hawkins had placed with his own drumming style. His rhythmic approach was far more subtle than Grohl's, while he was able to move from brutally pounding to gently stroking with the ease of a well-oiled machine. It was a factor that gave *There Is Nothing Left To Lose* a whole new dimension compared to the band's previous albums.

"William was a bit too influenced by my own style and Taylor was influenced by a lot of other drummers," explained Grohl. "Taylor is pretty much an individualist," said Mendel, "which is fine by me. That the songs work out and sound good, you've got to have a certain style, sure, but Taylor has a very individual touch and he's really doing his own thing but always keeps it within the frame of the song. It's hard to explain, his style is a bit rougher, edgier."

"He's got a different drive," concluded Grohl. "He's faster, the guy's hyperactive and an unbelievably powerful drummer who's favouring a rather complicated style. He's stressing different parts of the songs that William did, but he's always within the context of the song, you know." [22]

The press response to *There Is Nothing Left To Lose* was mixed, with many finding the mellow Foos hard to take. However, there were plenty that were ready to heap huge amounts of praise on the band.

"If not quite as bold as its title implies, *There Is Nothing Left To Lose* nonetheless marks a departure, with greater emphasis on melody and actual singing," wrote *Rolling Stone*'s Greg Kot, "(where once he was) blessed with a vocal range that consisted of two tones - conversational and catastrophic."

In the UK, *Kerrang!* Initially complained that "compared to *The Colour And The Shape*, this is a very one-dimensional album," before going on to lavish the album with belated praise! "Grohl has seemingly discovered where his biggest strength lies - tugging at heart-strings rather than slashing at powerchords - and has decided to focus on that instead of trying to do everything all at once. Relaxed, tuneful and mature, what *There Is Nothing Left To Lose* lacks in variety and aggression, it makes up for in big-hearted tenderness. Foo Fighters have hit the mark once again."

There were plenty of fans who agreed with such plaudits. Two months later, *There Is Nothing Left To Lose* would be certified platinum.

The album's release heralded the start of a two-year tour that would take Foo Fighters all over the world a number of times. In the few short months that followed the secret industry gig at New York's Bowery Ballroom, they would play no less than thirty-nine shows.

On November 6, the band broke up their tour with an appearance on *Saturday Night Live*, for which they played 'Learn To Fly' and 'Stacked Actors'. During the performance Grohl wore a shirt that had been bought for him that day by REM's Michael Stipe!

"I've never worn something like this before," he told *NME*'s Victoria Segal before the show. "I called a friend of mine today on her cellphone and said 'what are you doing?' and she said 'shopping with Michael Stipe!' As a joke I said 'tell him to pick me out a shirt to wear for *Saturday Night Live*.' And he did. It actually fits – he did a really good job. I don't know if I'm gonna wear it, but it's pretty comfortable."

A few days later the band would extend their previous Queen connections at London's Brixton Academy. Roger Taylor and Brian May joined the band onstage for a rendition of the Queen song 'Now I'm Here' (one of Hawkins' favourite bands ever).

On December 9, the band played one of their most unusual sets yet at Seattle's Key Arena. Mendel had been taken ill and was forced to pull out of the gig. The band played as a trio with Shifflett on bass duties for openers 'Monkey Wrench' and 'Everlong'. Then Justin Medal-Johnson from Beck's band took over bass for 'Learn To Fly'. Back as a trio again, Grohl, Hawkins and Shifflett played 'Ain't It The Life' and 'Breakout' before being joined onstage by one Krist Novoselic who played bass on 'Big Me', a cover of Foghat's 'I Just Want To Make Love To You' and finally 'I'll Stick Around'.

Two subsequent gigs in San Francisco and Phoenix were cancelled due to Mendel's illness, although they managed to play one date in between at Anaheim Pond in California. The show marked a brief reunion with Pat Smear who guested on 'Stacked Actors'.

The millennium closed with Grohl on an all-time high musically. The latest Foos album had remained in charts all over the world and was continually gaining him a new audience. Its on-going organic critical and commercial momentum would see it eventually gaining recognition at the Grammy Awards in 2001, when *There Is Nothing Left To Lose* was given the coveted award for 'Rock Album Of The Year'.

And yet, despite this revered critical acclaim adding to the band's exponentially expanding commercial success, Grohl was already talking about his retirement from Foo Fighters. "I don't see myself doing this past one more record," he said late in 1999. "Playing in a rock band is so fleeting and I've been so fortunate with the past ten years of my life. I feel fortunate every day that I get to do this, but there's a whole lot more to life than rock music, that's for sure."

Yet once again, just when events seemed to be turning to the Foo Fighters' favour, behind the scenes there were more dramatic twists about to unfold. In the two years that would pass before the band's fourth album, Foo Fighters would have to face yet another abandoned album session, Grohl's rumoured departure to join Queens of the Stone Age and finally, Taylor Hawkin's much-publicised collapse.

7

DONE, I'M DONE AND THEN
I'M ON TO THE NEXT ONE

ANOTHER DRUMMER JOKE...
What do you call a drummer who overcomes the premature demise
of a world-famous band, launches his own band in the role of
singer, songwriter and label owner, shares out the royalties to his
band even though they didn't play on the debut album, produces
a well received solo movie soundtrack, watches as his band almost
implodes, scraps two albums in their early stages (one after it has
been completed), guests on a world tour with a friend's band,
instigates a heavy metal fantasy project, provides drums for one of
his favourite bands as a teenager and then gets the satisfaction
of watching his own band come back from the brink and deliver
an album that would finally put them into the big league of
stadium-filling acts?

Hyperactive.

As the new millennium dawned, Foo Fighters found themselves
facing a barrage of criticism. Not for their music, but for
their decision to organise and play a benefit gig at The Palace
in Los Angeles for Alive And Well, an "alternative AIDS
information group".

The sold-out show that was organised by Mendel featured
a speech by Alive And Well founder Christine Maggiore, whose
theories about the virus have been somewhat controversial. It was
her belief that AIDS may be caused by HIV-related medication,
anal sex, stress and drug use. Fans of the band were also given free
copies of Maggiore's self-published book, *What If Everything You
Thought You Knew About AIDS Was Wrong?*

Mendel's support for Maggiore's group came after he had read her book and become completely swayed by the arguments. However, there were many opponents of her opinions and this show led to several intensely negative appraisals of both Alive And Well and the Foo Fighters support.

Mendel was suitably moved to write a letter on the Mojo-Wire website in defence of the band's actions, in which he explained why he believed the theories of Maggiore (as against much of the established theories about HIV) and why they had played the benefit. Essentially, the band's support of Maggiore came from their humanitarian stance, something that had been borne out by the amount of benefit gigs they had played over the years.

Amid the Alive And Well controversy, Foo Fighters launched their Big Day out tour of Australia with the release of 'Stacked Actors' as an Australia-only single. The single included 'Floaty' and 'Ain't It The Life' from the sessions in Holland in November 1999. Other tracks played at this acoustic performance were 'Breakout', 'Next Year', 'My Hero', 'Everlong', 'Learn To Fly' and a cover of Elton John's 'Tiny Dancer'. The latter found Grohl talking to the audience about how the movie *Almost Famous* had introduced him to the song. He also talked about his aim to do a performance piece for the song. He then encouraged the audience to count him in and sing along with the chorus before shouting over the audience applause, "Hey this is my show!" The Australian tour came to an end on February 6. This was followed by a brief break in which Grohl laid down a number of heavy metal tracks at his Studio 606.

Following the cancellation of three dates in Brazil under mysterious circumstances, the band would embark on a brief European tour. On Feb 26, however, coinciding with the Brazilian cancellations the band were invited to play on *The Dave Letterman Show* – the host's first following heart surgery. Letterman requested 'Everlong', introducing the Foos as "my favourite band playing my favourite song".

The rest of 2000 found the band locked into a relentless touring schedule, punctuated by (band and solo) demo-ing. The tour would include the usual barrage of festival dates, an arena tour in support of the Red Hot Chili Peppers (when they would play in -store and radio acoustic sessions in the afternoons before the gig) and endless club and concert hall dates all over the world. The tour was gruelling to say the least.

"Sometimes when you're on the road for a long time, it feels like it doesn't really matter about going home any more," Grohl unusually complained mid-way through the Chili Peppers tour. "It's kinda sad. That's when depression creeps in…. At this point in time when we go to McDonalds, I don't need to look at the pictures that go with the number for the Value Meals. I just know what they are. A number 9 is a fish fillet, a number 2 is a double cheeseburger, a number 1 is a Big Mac. Don't you think that's scary?" [1]

The shows themselves weren't the boring part however. Grohl admitted that the lead up to each gig was a stressful time, while the after-show was totally boring. The gig however was where he and the band could let off steam and give it their best shot… and put up with occasional hecklers!

"The last time we played 'February Stars'," laughed Shifflet, "it was hard for Dave to get his ego big enough to go out and play a beautiful, pretty song like that, but he did it. Afterwards, there was this total silence, until some guy shouted, 'BORING!'" "I'm never playing that song ever again," concluded Grohl.

At another gig, one dissenter decided to throw things at Grohl throughout the show. Eventually, Grohl got him onstage and in front of the entire audience made him sit there as he counted out the guy's entrance money and gave it back to him.

It wasn't all work however. On his days off, Grohl checked out gigs by local bands and even listened to the occasional demo. One he received came with a photo of a lank-haired guy with a bloodied nose. It was his first introduction to Andrew WK, whom he subsequently invited to play with Foo Fighters and helped to get a recording contract.

"Andrew WK is a true American hero," says Grohl. "He's our saviour from the Midwest. It's hard to explain Andrew – only because you've never really seen anything like it before. You know, all I got was the demo and the promo shot which was Andrew with the worst bloody nose you've ever seen in your life and, in some bizarre way, it was the sexiest photo I've ever seen of a man in my life. My girlfriend immediately had the biggest crush on him. So it was a love-hate relationship with Andrew.

We had him do a few shows with us and it's just Andrew with a CD player and a microphone jumping around like a teenager in his bedroom singing along to Sweet songs. There's no gloom and doom – it's all about partying until you puke." (2)

During this period, Grohl also launched his latest band, the fantasy heavy metal band Probot, which had come about as a direct reaction to the laid-back sounds of *There Is Nothing Left To Lose*. Or more to the point, the MOR balladry of 'Learn To Fly' that he had grown utterly sick of. The only cure for this sickness was a good dose of loud noise.

"I just felt like, goddamn it, I gotta get back in the studio just to prove to myself that I can do something else other than AM-radio, alternative McDonald's pop. So, I started writing these things. I didn't know what I was doing, they didn't sound like Foo Fighters songs to me."

With seven tracks recorded with the help of Adam Kasper, Grohl already knew that he would be the wrong person to sing the songs. He needed a genuine metal singer, or it would all end up sounding too melodic.

"You know, it's really strange but in the studio we can come up with something that's really dark and hard, like a Voivoid tune and I'll still end up writing a pretty melody. I suppose it's just me, I can't help it. It's what I do," he laughed.

The solution to the Probot problem came to him after he was invited to sing 'Goodbye Lament' on Black Sabbath guitarist Tommy Iommi's solo album. Seeing the veteran guitarist enlisting the support of twelve different singers, Grohl decided to use a similar angle for the Probot project. Only his twist on the theme was that he would only use underground heavy metal singers from bands between the years 1984 and 1990.

"I went about trying to choose my favourite vocalists who happened to be from that genre at that time, I love people like King Diamond and Snake from Voivoids."

The proposed album's twelve tracks would go on to feature among others, Soulfly's Max Cavalera, Slayer's Tom Araya, Cathedral's Lee Dorrian, Mike Dean from Corrosion of Conformity, King Diamond, Celtic Frost's Thomas Gabriel Warrior and Motörhead's legendary Lemmy – warts and all.

"Lemmy. What more is there to say? He is God," genuflected Grohl to *Kerrang! Online*. "He is the reason. He is the last man standing, and no one even comes close. That guy is a true rock 'n' roller. Everyone else is just trying. I can't even begin to explain how fucking life-altering a day in the studio with Lemmy really is. He walks in, kicks the shit out of a song, and then he's gone... like the goddamned Lone Ranger. He is the coolest person I've ever recorded with in my entire life."

The Lemmy collaboration, 'Shake Your Blood', would be recorded early in 2001. "He said he always hated it when people called (Motörhead) a heavy metal band because he felt they were a rock band. He loves Little Richard. We talked about Little Richard a bunch. After meeting him, I don't think I've ever met a rock 'n' roller in my life. He's just so fucking great, man... just the total lack of pretension. Absolute genuine rock 'n' roll. It was like my make-a-wish foundation with Lemmy.

He comes in wearing this Civil War coat with long tails, the tightest black jeans possible, and these white boots. He's just like, 'Hey man, let's have a drink.' We sat down. I had a couple Jack and Cokes with him, before lunchtime. He's like, 'Here's the lyrics.' He had three different versions and having Lemmy singing this stuff in my ear was just so great. He went into the studio and went through the vocals like *that*." [3]

Despite rumours that the album would be released through either Roadrunner or Grohl's own Roswell Records (through RCA), Probot initially remained in the can with no concrete plans for its issue. Early in 2003 however, underground metal imprint Southern Lord Records announced that they had signed Probot with a release schedule and super-cool underground marketing campaign. "There's a certain kind of person that will like the Probot record and there aren't that many of those people.... I mean, it's not meant to, like, make money," Grohl said of the album. More later.

During 2000, Foo Fighters would issue three more singles from *There Is Nothing Left To Lose*, although they were already growing tired of the album's mellow atmosphere and longed to release some heavier material. In March they issued 'Generator'. The limited edition single was coupled with 'Ain't It The Life' and 'Floaty' from the 2 Meter Sessions, and 'Breakout' recorded live by the BBC at Glasgow's Barrowlands in 1999.

The next single was 'Breakout' which appeared as a two CD set on September 11. Part 1 was backed with studio out-take 'Iron & Stone' and a live version of 'Learn To Fly' recorded in Australia. Part 2 featured 'Monkey Wrench' and 'Stacked Actors' from the same Australian gig.

The final single of the year came in December with 'Next Year', another two CD set. Part 1 was backed with two more tracks, 'Big Me' and 'Next Year'. Part 2 on the other hand came with 'Baker Street' (again) and an enhanced portion containing the video for the 'Next Year'.

On January 3, 2001, Foo Fighters continued their gradual rise to critical approval by receiving no less than three Grammy nominations. *There Is Nothing Left To Lose* was shortlisted for 'Best Rock Album', while the brilliant 'Learn To Fly' was nominated for 'Best Short Form Music Video', and for 'Best Rock Performance by A Duo or Group With Vocal'. And this despite the fact that Grohl was sick of the song! A month later at the actual award ceremony, the first two nominations succeeded in bagging the Foos a brace of Grammys.

The 'Learn To Fly' video was indeed deserving of the award and is typical of the hilarious videos the band often shoot – yet somehow Grohl does this in a way that never dilutes the seriousness of his band or makes them look like a novelty act (Madness had perfected this approach back in the early 1980s). The video for 'Learn To Fly' was shot in the cabin of an aeroplane, featuring the band in a number of cameo roles with Tenacious D planting drugs in the in-flight coffee percolator. Grohl played a flight captain, a very camp attendant, a large blonde woman, a pig-tailed girl, an FBI officer and himself.

The twist in the video is that the crew and passengers all get stoned from drinking the coffee – except the rock band who turned down caffeine in favour of alcohol. As a consequence the band is forced to find the plane's manual, take up the controls and "learn to fly back home"!

These weren't the only awards to go the Foo Fighters' way in the early part of 2001. On February 20, Grohl cemented his multi-instrumental reputation by winning the 'Gibson Guitar Award' for Best Rock Guitarist, then a few months later in May, 'Learn To Fly' was again honoured, this time at the BMI Awards. The release had been confirmed as the single most-played song on US college radio.

With Foo Fighters scheduled to take a break in the early part of the summer, Grohl predictably took it upon himself to work on other material. Among these would be recording drum tracks for the forthcoming album by Queens of the Stone Age.

Born from the ashes of legendary thrash metal outfit Kyuss, the Queens of the Stone Age duo of Josh Homme and Nick Oliveri took the dark metal pulse of their former life and incorporated contorted soul flavours and psychedelic twists to create a unique take on the rock genre.

Their self-titled 1998 debut album ploughed a territory that was instantly recognisable as belonging to Kyuss. However, it was with their second collection, *Rated R* that the Californian duo truly staked their claim on a new territory in the rock 'n' roll landscape. *Rated R* was an amorphous (con)fusion of *Psychedelic Shack*-era Temptations, Hawkwind's heavier moments, Husker Du's melodies and Metallica's power. An album without compromises, it lit up an otherwise dull rock arena upon its release.

To support the album, the band toured the world, including a support slot on the US leg of the Foo Fighters' 2000 tour. The Foos and QOTSA instantly struck up a mutual appreciation society and when they came to record their third album, *Song For The Deaf,* they approached Grohl to guest.

The mutual admiration between Josh Homme/Nick Oliveri and Grohl stretched back much further than just the Foos or QOTSA. Grohl has admitted that he was a huge fan of Kyuss, playing that band's album *Blues For The Red Sun* at least three times a day when it came out. Kyuss on the other hand paid tribute to Nirvana on 'Day One,' a secret track on *And The Circus Leaves Town,* the band's final album released in 1995.

"I've known those guys for a long time," said Grohl. "I was a huge fan of the first Queens album and jokingly, when asked what was my greatest disappointment of 2001, I said that I hadn't been asked to play on their record. So they were nice enough to ask when it came time to make another record. One thing we have in common is a love of early Black Flag. In one of the songs that we recorded – I think it's called 'Song For The Deaf' – there's a nod to an early Black Flag record: the drum riff is me paying tribute to Bill Stevenson." [4]

"I don't think he realised how much we liked his band," added Homme of his band's feelings towards Grohl. "It was one of those things where he would come out to our shows, it was cool, we kind of like mutually respected him and liked each other's bands. He was one of the early supporters, it was cool to play with him."

In the end, Grohl played on all but one of the album's tracks. It was, he says, the best record he had ever been involved with. "Josh (Homme, Queens' guitarist) should talk about this because I don't want him and Nick (Oliveri, Queens' bassist) to tag-team my ass," he laughed. "But I'll just say that it's my favourite album that I've ever played drums on. When I jammed with Nick and Josh, it almost sounded like I was back in 1992 playing on a Kyuss record. It was fucking amazing. They let me go off on this album like never before. It rocks ten times harder than anything they've ever done." [5]

Suitably inspired by the Queens sessions, Grohl immediately went into the studio to mix the fantasy metal band project Probot. What was interesting about both Probot and Queens of the Stone Age was that, despite his own success, Grohl had never lost that fan attitude. In some ways this harked back to his inferiority complex, that he would in some way be surprised that artists he liked, respected him enough to ask him to play drums for them. Grohl seemed almost blind to the idea that these people were his contemporaries and that the respect went both ways.

Respect however was something he was rapidly losing for the Foo Fighters situation. Not only had the touring gone on too long, but also he was growing ever more tired of playing the old songs. Even the thought of recording the next album was starting to feel like a contractual obligation, rather than something he longed to do.

In August however, the band were dealt an almost catastrophic blow. Taylor Hawkins collapsed and was hospitalised only two dates into their UK and Ireland tour. The initial reason was "exhaustion", however this turned out to be a euphemism for what appeared to be a drugs overdose. Bad memories came flooding back to Grohl.

Foo Fighters were forced to cancel gigs at London's Kentish Town Forum on August 27, Edinburgh Corn Exchange on August 30, and in September 1, Slane Castle in Dublin. As it turned out Hawkins' drug abuse wasn't anything to do with the chemicals usually associated with the rock 'n' roll life. Malicious rumours had it that he'd taken large amounts of cocaine, endured a heart attack and was rushed to intensive care. It was, apparently touch and go whether or not he would make it through. All nonsense of course. The actual problem was far more innocent.

When confronted with this (unfounded) rumour by journalist Ian Winwood – who wished to clear up all the gossip - Hawkins reactions were a mixture of humour and contempt.

"No, that's not true." Hawkins exclaimed. "It wasn't cocaine, but it was drugs. I don't want to say what kind." Hawkins also confirmed that the collapse wasn't due to heroin before admitting, "I was addicted to painkillers. That was my addiction."

"What kind of painkillers?"

"Just fucking painkillers, okay? It doesn't matter what they were; all that matters is that I had a problem with them. It was a situation that had gotten out of control for me. That's all. And last summer I took too many of them and I went into a coma for two days. It was very serious. I've been into rehab and I've cleaned up. It's all in the past. It's over now and I've come through what happened. End of story.

But, believe me, I'm not proud of what happened. I don't want to celebrate it and I don't want to dwell on it. I'm happy to clear up what happened but that's it. It ends there. I can see why you're asking me about it, because if the roles were reversed I'd ask you about it. It's something that people want to know about, and in other situations I'd want to know about it too. People love this kind of story. But it's such a cliché. Member of a rock band - the drummer of a rock band, no less - takes too many drugs, becomes ill, has to go into rehab. If you spell it out like that, it's just so embarrassing. It's so obvious."

The refreshingly honest Hawkins was out of action for a number of weeks, forcing the band to take an unscheduled sabbatical. Their only task during this period was the re-recording of 'Make A Bet', an out-take from the sessions for *The Colour And The Shape*. The new version was called 'Win Or Lose', and it was given to the soundtrack for the movie *Out Cold*. Grohl would also take the opportunity to lay down twenty drum tracks for the Tenacious D album. It took him one and a half days! He would also play a demon in their 'Tribute' video in April of the following year.

In December, a fully fit Hawkins returned to the fold for a series of demo sessions at Grohl's Studio 606. The intention was to lay down the last of the tracks for the next album, before decamping to a larger studio to record them properly. The final task of the year came with the release of 'The One' on the soundtrack for the movie *Orange County*. The track was issued as a single in Australia.

2001 had been a year of extremes for Grohl. On the one hand his Probot and Queens of the Stone Age work had given him a huge boost. On the other, Hawkins' collapse and the boredom of touring had seen him testing that famed emotional distance.

"What happened (in 2001) didn't really have anything to do with the band. We just wanted things to happen naturally and not force it. For a band that's been so glamour and drama free, for something like that to happen was something of a shock. We're pretty boring people. We don't lead the rock 'n' roll life style that people imagine every band must have."

In March 2002, the band went into Conway Studios in Los Angeles to start recording their fourth album which had already been demo-ed at Grohl's place. They had also worked a lot at Hawkins' own home studio in Topanga Canyon, LA.

"The whole idea of building a home studio is just to be in complete control of everything," Grohl explained. "I will never work another way again. There's just no way. There's no clock on the wall, it's your fucking house, which also means that you decide who's allowed to come by the studio and who's not. Our routine up here (Hawkins' studio) has been ridiculous. We come out here at ten o'clock in the morning and swim for two hours. Then we play for two hours, then we have a BBQ for two hours, then we jump in the pool again." [6]

Among the numerous working titles for the album were *Attica*, *Tom Petty*, *Knucklehead*, *Spooky Tune*, *Full Mount*, *Lonely Is You*, and *Tears For Beers*. The songs were a definite reaction to *There Is*

Nothing Left To Lose, having turned out far heavier than the predecessor's acoustic-driven mellow numbers which were "written lying on the bed in front of the television with an acoustic guitar.

All of those songs on the last album were written on acoustic guitars, even 'Breakout' and 'Stacked Actors'. A lot of this stuff that we've been writing now has been written with everything on *11*! We have guitar leads on our songs now!" Grohl laughed. "And that's Shifflett, not me! We have this new fast song that we decided to give to Shifflett for a lead break. We were recording live in the room down there, and I can't really hear Shifflett's amp. When I went back and listened, he was shredding this fucking 'Yngwie' lead! I was like, 'Oh my God! Who *are* you? I didn't know you could do that!" [7]

Such was the positivity that surrounded the demos that Grohl said he could see the album hitting the stores later in the year. "Now we've done the demo-ing, I really don't think it's going to take long. The eighteen or nineteen songs we have are so close to being finished. Hopefully (we'll) have it finished by the beginning of November."

It wasn't to be that easy though. When the band listened to the unmixed album they hated it. It was, they thought, just Foo Fighters by numbers, with no development or contrast. They immediately binned the album. It has since come to be known as the *Million Dollar Demo.*

"When we were making the first version of the record, it felt like we were making an album for the sake of making another album, not necessarily making another record because we were dying to do it," he later explained. "It was a little too forced because the motivation was unclear, it wasn't as pure as having these songs we couldn't wait to get out – it was a little blurry, a little more scattered than that. If we had felt trapped in that position for our second or third album we might not be around to make the fourth record.

It was the absolute correct thing to [bin it]. It just didn't have that attitude and energy the band thrive on – it had songs that sounded like singles and that's not necessarily what keeps a band alive forever.

We realised we wanted to be in this band for a long time to come and two years ago we didn't necessarily feel that way, it seemed it would be okay if we just stopped. And after Taylor went down in London we realised we didn't want it to end ever. Yeah, because you get to the point where you realise rock music isn't the most important thing in the world. To me at least. Playing the game, doing interviews and such is just playing the game. And making music is bigger than that but even bigger and more important than that is health and happiness and family, the bigger picture. (Laughs) We're getting old."

With so much dissatisfaction in the Foo's camp, Grohl decided he needed to do something that would help him clear his head. Then the opportunity came for him to tour with Queens of the Stone Age. He agreed to do it.

"It was the best thing I could have done. Back home, there was tension between Taylor and I, between Nate and I. This gave us all a rest. Our album had turned into a responsibility, an obligation. You could hear in the music that we didn't feel lucky to be in the band," stated Dave. Getting behind the drums again was an obvious escape. "That's where I feel most comfortable. I love singing and playing the guitar – but playing the drums, I never have to think or concentrate on what I'm doing. All the pressures were taken away.

I'd recorded 'Songs For The Deaf' last summer and I was helping them to find another drummer. I thought I'd found one for them but I just had to play one show. I had to prove to myself that I could do it after eight years, that I hadn't lost that part of myself. We played in Los Angeles and it was amazing. The connection that Josh (Homme) and Nick (Oliveri) and I have is really incredible. We don't have to speak, we look in each other's eyes and we know what happens."

Grohl initially only agreed to play a one-off gig at LA's Troubadour Club. It was the first time that he had played drums on stage for eight years. "That show was so important to me because it was the first time I'd played drums in a band since Nirvana. Because of the way that band ended, anything to do with Nirvana has now become somehow legendary… But everything becomes spoken in these hushed tones. Like Kurt. Kurt's become a legend, but he was just a man… because I was the drummer in Nirvana people seem to consider me a legendary drummer. Let me tell you, I am not a great drummer, not by a long way.

And so the gig with Queens was the most pressure I've felt in a long time. It was like I was playing in a great rock band with the weight of having been the drummer in another great band weighing on my shoulders.

You know, the reason I didn't just join another band after Nirvana ended was because of the feeling I had playing in Queens of the Stone Age, which was just the greatest feeling. And that's the feeling I needed. All of that bullshit that has to do with the urban myth of Nirvana – the band that imploded, the band that broke down, the band that ended in tragedy and despair. After going through all that chaos and misery and pain as it happened, having to go into a miserable situation again would have been a bad idea." [8]

Queens of the Stone Age played dates on that year's Coechella Festival in the US before decamping to Europe. The solidarity between Grohl and the guys from QOTSA was obvious.

"We're like, 'You can have as many bands as you want. I have three bands, why shouldn't you?'" explained Oliveri. "If he's into it, which he is, I hope he stays. He's one of my favourite drummers of all time. He's got a signature beat, and I don't know many drummers that have that, you know, the 'Teen Spirit' beat. That's Dave Grohl's beat as far as I'm concerned. I've never heard that beat before. I've heard it after he did it, but I never heard it before he did it. So I'd say it's his. It's amazing, dude. He's from one of my favourite bands of all time and I'm fucking counting my blessings. I haven't taken my bass home to practice in years, but I've been taking my bass home – trying to stay strong with my fucking chops and shit." [9]

With Foo Fighters' fourth album languishing in the trash and Grohl out on a tour of the US, Japan and the UK with Queens of the Stone Age, the future of Grohl's band seemed to be in genuine doubt. *NME* actually ran a news story headlined, 'Are the Foos about to split?' One thing was for certain – Grohl was having a great time rediscovering the joy of playing drums live. However he was also using the gigs to run away from the tension between the members of Foo Fighters and muse on whether or not they had the will to continue. With QOTSA, he didn't have to think about writing songs, signing cheques or doing interviews. All he was there to do was play drums.

"He's a great songwriter," argued Oliveri. "He's a great singer and a guitar player, but he's a better drummer as far as I'm concerned. I tell him that to his face, so it's not anything I'm just talking shit about. He's one of the best rock drummers. He should be behind the kit. He should be hitting the skins. He's a madman." [10]

"I was worried – for about a week," confirmed Hawkins at the start of Grohl's tenure with QOTSA, "and I think Dave's made that new Queens album a hundred times better than it would have been."

At the time, Grohl was having such a good time with Queens of the Stone Age that he was close to joining full-time. In his role as a drummer he was able to enjoy playing for the sake of the music, and being as good as he could be. There were no pressures of entertaining the crowd, none of the stress of being a reluctant frontman.

"Behind a drum kit is where he fuckin' should be," Josh Homme said at the time, emphasising the points already made by Oliveri. "Dave's an amazing player; he played his fuckin' ass off. I think that he is a drummer first, and people have sort of forgotten that."

On the subject of Grohl becoming a full time Queen, Homme and Oliveri confirmed that it wasn't a part of their game plan, let alone his. "You know there is so much finality, people are saying that we are Yoko-ing Foo Fighters," argued Homme. "It's so much more casual than that. You can be in this band and do that band as well. It doesn't have the finality of the Bible."

"We have set up Queens where there are a bunch of different members, one in and out," added Oliveri. "Dave isn't going to stay forever, but there is an open door for him to come and jam with us, because he is one of our favourite drummers. He's an honorary member." "He has the badge and the patch and the sweatshirt," concluded Homme.

"It was a split hair decision," suggested Grohl. "I'm not so career -minded that I have a plan… I mean, if Linkin Park called me up and asked me to record with them I'd probably say 'no'. But while we were recording with Foo Fighters and we were getting stuck trying to deliver this thing to a schedule, I just said, 'Fuck it, I'm going to go off and play with Queens of the Stone Age for a while and see how I feel when I get back.' The thing is that I don't have to do this career thing. I'm free to do what I want to do.

I think everyone was uncertain whether I would come back. I know that I was," admitted Grohl. "And I was having a blast every night playing drums with those guys. But at the end of the day I had to come back because much as I loved Queens, they're not family. These guys are family. This is where my heart has always been. I know I'm a better drummer than anything. And it's twelve other people [crew], not just the guys onstage." [11]

The Queens of the Stone Age tour suitably rejuvenated Grohl so between legs of the tour he went back into Studio 606 to record another album. They subsequently wrote and recorded fourteen tracks in a matter of days. "That's how you should make a record. I listen to it now and I think it's the best record we've ever made, the first one that reminds me of the band," exclaimed Grohl. Only one track survived the original album session, 'Tired of You', which featured Queen guitarist Brian May.

Still the rumours persisted that the band were on the verge of splitting. "I had no idea anyone was concerned," claims Grohl. "Hearing the rumours about the demise of the band, we had no idea people were paying attention. We come home from being on the road and we feel like we just disappear. Unless we're on tour in front of people it just doesn't seem like it matters. But it was pretty funny. In some areas of the world it got blown up into a virtual scandal and it just wasn't."

On July 11, Foo Fighters embarked on a three-date stay in Dublin, Ireland before heading off to the T In The Park Festival in Scotland. They returned to the US for three weeks, during which time they filmed the video for 'All My Life', the first single from the forthcoming fourth album. Grohl was the director, as he had been for 'Monkey Wrench'.

Following the video shoot the band returned once more to Europe where they played one night in Cologne, Germany, before going to the UK for the album photo shoot, rehearsals and then an appearance at Reading Festival on August 24. The following night they played Leeds Festival, with a gig at London's Astoria taking place the night after.

On August 27 they played at the *Kerrang!* Awards where they were honoured with the prestigious 'Hall of Fame Award'. They subsequently played a low-key show at London's ULU.

September saw the band embarking on a six-week promo tour of UK, France, Germany, Japan and Australia. During which a limited edition single of only 2,500 copies was released on Sessions Records. The single featured 'All My Life' and a version of The Ramones' 'Danny Says' with Shifflet on vocals.

The full release of 'All My Life' came a month later. A fast-paced rocker with Grohl's breathy, tense vocals leading into a glorious anthemic chorus – all thundering drums, slashing guitars and rolling bass – it proved to be one of the band's finest tracks so far. If Foo Fighters really had been on the verge of calling it a day, then this single suggested otherwise.

Yet another double pack single, Part 1 of 'All My Life' featured a version of Psychedelic Furs' second single 'Sister Europe', 'Win or Lose' (the remake of 'Make Bet') and the director's cut of the video for 'All My Life'. Part 2 was backed with The Ramones cover 'Danny Says' and 'The One', the movie soundtrack for *Orange County*.

On October 22, Foo Fighters' fourth album *One By One* finally hit the stores, a mere twelve months later than originally anticipated. The wait had been worth it. The album went to the #1 spot in the UK on first week of release. Ironically the much anticipated and highly controversial compilation of his previous band Nirvana only reached #3 – *One By One*'s sales figures of 91,500 beat Nirvana's first week total by 7000. *Nirvana* would topple *One By One* from the top a week later.

Grohl himself was barely able to contain his excitement at the way the album turned out. After the lows of having to scrap the original effort, this new version was beyond even his lofty expectations.

"Well, I love the record… I listen to the sound and it reminds me of the four of us playing together. It's very simple. We didn't stray too far away from the true sound of the band so to me it's the best one yet. The songs are more advanced and interesting. It's lyrically more mature than anything we've ever done. It's just nice. It feels like we're growing into ourselves."[12]

As with *There Is Nothing Left To Lose*, the opening track was somewhat misleading. 'All My Life' chugged in like Survivor's 'Eye Of The Tiger' before turning into one of the band's fiercest onslaughts. Hawkins ricocheting rim shots and machine gun staccato rolls created a new sense of urgency for the band.

"That song suits us and the album well," explained Grohl. "Sometimes it's angry and dark in a romantic, but not necessarily depressing, way. It's important that the band do something different every time. One of the reasons why we threw away a lot of the songs from the first sessions was because they sounded too much like singles that we would write: big chorus, fast tempo, sweet melody over hard guitars. It didn't challenge the band or the listener. The idea is to try and stretch your days, your life and try to make everything last as long as possible." [13]

If 'All My Life' was misleading, then what followed was clearly put there to send the listener in completely the wrong direction. 'Low' represented the band's heaviest and hardest record to date. A slab of angry pulsing hardcore with guitars, bass and drums careering like a runaway eighteen-wheeler, burning rubber across scorched earth, with bitter sweet melodies teasing like a sneering, contorted nursery rhyme. It was even better than the opening track.

And then just as the energy seemed to be getting cranked up even higher, 'Have It All' came in with a dislocated, springy guitar melody that sounded like UK punk outfit Wire covering 'My Sherona', before walking dangerously close to middle of the road territory with super smooth chorus harmonies, only to be rescued with a blinding display of drum and guitar interplay bringing the song to a close.

"I thought 'Have It All' was going to be the most screaming, fucking rock song we've ever done," laughed Grohl. "And then I came up with that beautiful melody like fucked-up Beach Boys or something. That's always what happens. And maybe that's what our band sounds like. Those two ingredients complement each other well. Maybe that's what we do the best. I can't write something that sounds like White Zombie, or Slayer, or Motörhead. I just can't do it."[14]

'Times Like These' followed with Grohl singing "I'm a one way motorway" over a backing that verged on latter-day Manic Street Preachers delivering an AOR take on Guns N' Roses' 'Sweet Child of Mine'. Surprisingly, however, the track worked, with Grohl's impassioned vocals pushing the band into gloriously emotional waters. A song about positivity, about finding the light in a dark place, it could have been the soundtrack to the previous year.

Of the next track, 'Disenchanted Lullaby', Grohl suggested that unpredictability was the key to the album, thanks to the way the song's smooth windswept verse melody erupted into a chest -beating chorus. "It's always nice to have a little jab at the end of a chorus. That's the melancholy, the bittersweet. This album is less predictable than anything we've ever done," he said. [15]

If people were looking for any signs of Grohl's time with Queens of the Stone Age having a long-term influence on him, it came with 'Disenchanted Lullaby'. On 'Tired Of You' the track that followed however, the band sounded like tight-rope walkers traversing the thin line between love lost and found. They were deep in Neil Young territory, delivering a hopelessly melancholic love song. It was the only track to have survived the original sessions.

"What we do is not conducive to a grounded, stable life. You're cursed by this love of what you do," explained Grohl of the nature of the lyrics. "We're just wanderers, which would make anyone write songs about wanting to be in love forever. It's just the nature of what we do – but shit, it makes for good songs." [16]

'Halo' featured Hawkins' drum again thundering from wall to wall, underlining the song's epic grandeur with hyperactive energy. Indeed, this album amply displayed just how great a drummer Hawkins really was. He had clearly enjoyed the process. "You pray you're gonna make it/And then when you're done you keep fucking up," sang Grohl in what could have been a typically self-depreciating comment on his life in music. Never able to sit still, always moving from album to scrapped album to finished album, project to project, leaving in his wake a trail of solid and at times stunning work. But none of it living up to his own expectations. Witness the number of times Grohl had scrapped Foo Fighters albums for not achieving the levels he required. Each one a "fuck up" in Grohl's perfectionist mind.

'Lonely As You' was the sound of the Beach Boys playing with, well Queens of the Stone Age, all sweetness and psychedelia with a haunting underbelly of utter darkness. 'Overdrive' followed with what was the most formulaic song on the album thanks to its hum -a-long guitar hooks, head-bobbing pop melody and stadium-sized chorus hook.

'Burn Away' was a mid-tempo classic rock stomper featuring bottom heavy guitars winding around Grohl's melody, while closing track 'Come Back' found the band at their most expansive, pushing the boundaries of the Foo formula to their very extreme and fusing them with Lynard Skynard (again). The chorus cry of 'I will come back' also found Grohl re-deploying his James Hetfield growl.

Perhaps not their best album, *One By One* did however contain some of the band's best songs. It also showed the Foos gaining a new maturity which hovered between the downside of simple acceptance of their own limitations, and on the positive, the ambition to take their sound far beyond the Nirvana straight jacket; their historical references owing far more to US rock than UK punk. Indeed, of all of the Foos' records, this one had the least to do with Grohl's previous band.

The media were impressed. "Grohl's task, which he has taken on with grace and persistence, is to make rock that sets its own stakes high and doesn't get stuck looking back," wrote *Rolling Stone*'s Jon Pareles. "Whatever their genesis, the songs are stronger and broader than autobiography... It's rock that draws power from its determination to struggle onward."

This single-minded determination lay at the heart of the making of the album. That the initial album was dropped, that he even went on tour with the Queens, had as much to do with his need to let everyone know that he could do these things, as any desire to rejuvenate his love of music.

"One of the things I love about being in Foo Fighters is we really call all the shots," he says. "We take advice from people when we want to know how to go about touring but at the end of the day we have this veto power that a lot of other bands don't and I think that's what kept the band alive as long as it has and will keep us for years to come in the future hopefully. So long as you do it on your own terms and your pace you can make it last a lifetime. And as long as you're doing it for the right reasons."

The release of *One By One* was marked by an in-store gig at Virgin Megastore in Hollywood. During the mixing of the album and through all of the Queens time, Grohl had lived in Los Angeles again. However this time round he had come to terms with the nature of the city.

"There are things about Los Angeles that I like now," he admits. "I've just discovered neighbourhoods whereas before it was this swingin' singles fuckin' tequila party every night. And my sister lives here now so I have family here. Just mellowing myself, it seems Los Angeles has mellowed as well. I don't really go out any more – every once in a while I'll come down to a bar down the street and hang out with a bunch of friends, but when Queens of the Stone Age aren't in town there really aren't many people to hang out with. Nobody fun... or that much fun."

In the months that followed, Grohl and the Foo Fighters would find themselves once again traversing the globe, this time in support of *One By One*. February 23, 2003, would see them once again winning critical recognition at The Grammys, scooping the 'Best Hard Rock Song' gong for 'All My Life'.

In March, Grohl would embark on another guest appearance. This time it was with his teenage heroes Killing Joke, whom he had met in New Zealand. The resulting album *The Death and Resurrection Show* proved to be Killing Joke's finest since their debut self-titled collection. Grohl's drums added a power that many felt had been missing on the band's latter 1980s recordings.

"He's such a powerful drummer," says Killing Joke guitarist Geordie. "He really added a lot of energy to the songs. It was good for me to have that kind of power 'cos it meant my guitars could get even more fired up, y'know what I mean? It's a fucking huge album, and Dave's a big part of that."

"The drums in Killing Joke are always Killing Joke drums," singer Jaz Coleman explained to *Metal Hammer*. "They're always played a certain way... big tom-tom patterns." Despite Killing Joke embarking on a world tour, there were no plans for Grohl to join them.

Besides, Dave Grohl's crammed diary was already filled with Foo Fighters dates on a tour that would find the band finally headlining their own stadium and festival dates. They had come a long way since that low turn out at V97! Most notable perhaps was a forthcoming truly barn-storming set at V2003, when anyone present would struggle to disagree that the Foos stole the show from under the noses of other huge bands such as Coldplay and the Red Hot Chili Peppers. It had been a long and at times treacherous path to mainstream, stadium-filling acclaim, but Foo Fighters had finally made it.

Ever the modest type, Grohl admits to being surprised by their success. "We've been perfectly happy in our own little corner of the world. I'm surprised at the response we're getting in England especially. I just never imagined it getting to that point. Having it happen later rather than sooner is surprising to me. The fact we're doing this arena tour that's sold out is a surprise, because I've always felt that this band would remain in its own comfortable corner forever. The ambition is more inward than that. The aspiration is just more about making records and performing. Be it to 700 people or 70,000 people."

As the Foo Fighters' stadium and festival tour wound round the globe, they released two more singles from *One By One*. On January 6, 2003, 'Times Like These' was issued. As was customary for Foo Fighters singles, it came as a double pack. Part 1 included unreleased track 'Life Of Illusion' and a live rendition of B-52s 'Planet Claire' – with Fred Schneider paying back Grohl's respectful and accurate imitation on 'Watter-Fred', by providing vocals. Part 2 included another unreleased track 'Normal', along with a live version of 'Learn To Fly'. Both CDs included enhanced parts.

The summer 2003 tour was supported by the release of 'Low'. This time Part 1 included a live version of 'Enough Space' and the video for 'Low'. Part 2 included live song 'Never Talking To You Again'. There was also a DVD release of the single taking full advantage of a controversial, MTV-banned video.

This notorious promo featured Grohl and Tenacious D's Jack Black as two rednecks on a drinking session in a motel. Events gradually degenerate until the duo end up dressed in women's clothes. Like a low budget fusion of the 'Squeal piggy squeal' scene in *Deliverance* and the motel scenes in *Reservoir Dogs,* the video was both funny and sad at the same time. The guilty looks on the men's faces the next day was the perfect side-splitting climax.

According to Grohl, his new fiancée - MTV producer Jordyn Blum - thought the movie was very funny. She even helped pick out his clothes for the cross-dressing part. Whatever the truth, the sleazy goings-on in the promo didn't put her off him and on August 2, 2003, they were marred at Grohl's house in Woodland Hills, near Los Angeles. The ceremony was typical of Grohl. The guests were his friends and family. The band was present, as were crew and Krist Novoselic. However, the only person who could be remotely described as a celebrity was basketball player Codi Bryant. This was one wedding that wasn't destined for the pages of *Hello.*

"My biggest hero is Neil Young. He's living the life I hope I can have one day," explained Grohl to *USA Today*. "He's living on a beautiful farm with his beautiful children and his beautiful wife. He plays concerts now and then. He still makes records. His love of music hasn't diminished. And he's remained a real person."

8

LOOKING FOR RELIEF IN
YOUR MISERABLE LIFE?

ANOTHER DRUMMER JOKE... THE LAST LAUGH
What do you call someone who hangs around with musicians?
A drummer.

"When I was 16 I wasn't the singer of the Foo Fighters or the drummer of Nirvana. I was a fan of heavy music. I still am!"

There comes a time in every successful artist's story when they feel compelled to explore fresh avenues. Not necessarily for artistic reasons, rather more the need to recapture the essence of why they started playing music in the first place.

So people turn to their record collections and scrap books in a vanity-drenched attempt at cavorting once more with the wide-eyed arrogance of youth. It's like a first draft of the mid-life crisis script, the demo for the hell that may follow in a few years. The curse of the thirty-something grappling with the reality of responsibility and the sound of their carefree youthful selves sprinting into the distance. It's the rabbit-in-the-headlights shock of a new generation taking over your terrain, your spaces, but with completely different frames of reference. It's the sheer white panic of becoming redundant.

Rock 'n' roll is the worst for this. Despite the fact that the genre is itself an old beast lumbering towards a pensionable age, it keeps its youthful veneer through constant reinvention. And yet its entire make-up is, in youth culture terms, ancient.

Artists deal with these eternal youth obsessions through numerous forms of idiocy. Whether this be via trendy threads and over-worked hairstyles, or through attempts at embracing new sounds from the street, the result is all too often like the effect of the tail wagging the dog. Leaders becoming followers and therefore lose the essence of what made them so good in the first place.

And then there are those who invite the young pretenders into the palace to admire the crown. The artists who get the freshest faces on the block into the studio to collaborate or contribute to tracks, just to provide the desperate air of the zeitgeist in partial effect. Events such as these, of course, become the mainstay of the information hungry music press, desperate to get in on the latest album sessions. However, the reality of the finished product rarely lives up to the fantasy. What makes the new breed so good rarely transposes to the vision of the old guard. It's all a question of ego.

Such achingly familiar attempts at supping from the fountain of youth more often than not relate to older post-midlife crisis rock stars. The group we're interested in is the one young enough to remember why they became musicians in the first place. The kids who dropped out and rebelled against an imaginary mainstream in order to embrace the falsified outsider-ness of rock 'n' roll.

We're interested in the self-elected outlaws of the community whose romanticised existence was intended to shake the very foundations of society until they woke up one day and realised that their band, their music, their rebellion had become their day job. So they attempt to grasp at the last remaining vestiges of youth they possess and embrace that which they loved when they were starting out.

More often than not, this wave of nostalgia, tainted with a faint whiff of fear, manifests itself in an album of cover versions of songs from their youth. All too often these are dreadful affairs with barely a hint of face-saving integrity about them. In some cases, however, this re-visiting of the artist's teen self involves inviting older heroes to record with them (thus asserting their own youth while underlining the respect that originals have for their music). Occasionally musicians form supergroups with those people they respect.

Dave Grohl is no exception to the shock of time elapsed. By 2000, he had grown tired of the increasingly mainstream route the Foo Fighters were taking. He still believed in the band and its music, but he had grown to feel that they had become more like the Eagles than the bands he loved to listen to. Inevitably, the man who had once exclaimed that "those early Trouble records fucking changed my life", now started to question the direction he was taking with his music.

"The early Voivod records and Corrosion of Conformity's *Animosity*, and the D.R.I. seven-inch that I bought from the singer out of his van in 1983 — that's the kind of stuff that laid the foundation of the music that I make today… (*There's Nothing Left to Lose*) … was a pretty mellow record for us. It was about exploring low-level dynamics and melody, and simple arrangements and acoustic guitars — it was more about those things than about hitting the Turbo Rat and turning it up to ten. So we went out and played a lot of those songs live, and they were pretty mellow. I would find myself listening to Sepultura's *Chaos A.D.* before going onstage, and then singing a song like 'Learn to Fly'. Which I thought was kind of funny — like, what am I doing with my life, man?" [7]

That the Foo Fighters had come from punk, hardcore and underground metal wasn't hard to see for anyone — including the man behind the band. So in the days off from touring 1999's *There's Nothing Left to Lose*, he invited Foos producer Adam Kasper to his home studio to record some tracks that were as far from mellow Foos as you could imagine.

"I'm like, man, I've gotta fucking record some riffs. I've gotta get in there and do something heavy. As much as I love this acoustic guitar shit, I've just gotta feel it in my bones again." [3]

So Grohl and Kasper just kicked back, relaxed and tried to recapture the carefree riffing of their previous selves.

"I would sit on the couch, drinking beers and watching TV with the fucking Explorer and a little Peavey practice amp next to me, just playing around. If I came up with something that sparked my interest, I'd say to Adam, 'Come on, let's go downstairs!' I'd sit down at the drums and go through a quick arrangement off the top of my head. I didn't adhere to any sort of conventional song structure. I just thought, *Well, maybe that's a verse; maybe that's a chorus. I don't care, let's just record it!* And then I'd get out of there and put some bass on it, put some guitar stuff on it. Forty-five minutes later, you've got a track. I didn't really take it that seriously. So then I'd go back upstairs, grab a couple more beers, come up with another riff, go downstairs and do it again. Within three days, I had seven songs that were basically just riff instrumentals, with no suggestion of melody or vocals or anything." [7]

Thus was the aforementioned Probot finally realised. Sonically it was like Neil Young's musicians that Grohl has so openly admired, making the leap from the laidback melancholia of *Harvest* to the somnambulist rock of *Zuma* and then on to the angry feedback assault of *Rust Never Sleeps* in a matter of two years rather than decades. Neither *There's Nothing Left To Lose* nor the less acoustic, but equally mainstream album, *One by One* (that arrived during the four year process of recording *Probot*), could have prepared the listener for its sheer visceral, snot-nosed adolescent attack.

In February 2004, the world finally got to hear the results of Grohl's heavy-metal project, Probot — the name of an obscure character in *Star Wars Episode V — The Empire Strikes Back*. "I had no idea [about that]," Grohl said at the time, "I was in Las Vegas and I was walking through one of these memorabilia stores that has signed movie posters and knick-knacks and collectible crap. I walked past this one display that had a lot of antique toys in it, and there was an original toy from *The Empire Strikes Back* ... it was a gun turret and Probot. I lost my mind! I had no idea that it was anything at all. I never knew what it was. I thought I made up the word. And the only reason why I'm calling the record that is because when I recorded the first seven songs I wrote the word 'Probot' on the spine of the reel in my basement so that it wouldn't get lost among all my other Foo Fighter tapes." [1]

Albeit accidentally named after a piece of film memorabilia, *Probot* was the perfect monicker for Grohl's long talked about nostalgia project. Not so exciting, however, was the choice of musical genre that he was intending to rediscover. Rather than go to the punk and hardcore tracks of his early teens, he searched back to the heavy metal soundtrack of his post-punk wake up call. The records that many punks denied ever liking.

"I discovered all of these bands through the punk rock scene, so in 1982, when I started listening to hardcore, anything that was fast and loud, screaming-out-of-control rebellious, I would listen to – whether it was MDC or Flipper or Bad Brains – and then that gave way to Venom and Slayer and getting really into Motörhead." [2]

The man whose near-hyperactive manner leads him to tap out drum patterns on his legs when he's being questioned, found a natural affinity for all that is dark and hard in metal. He even admits to having been mildly attracted to the satanic aspects of the music genre!

"Did I sacrifice virgins at an altar and drink the blood of a lamb? Well, no, I didn't. But I thought it was kinda cool that someone did. And a lot of those bands shared the political ideals that punk rock bands did – Sepultura, Corrosion Of Conformity, D.R.I. were socially or politically motivated, somewhat. And then [there were] bands like Venom that just wanted to get wasted!"

So often the butt of jokes in the music community, heavy metal shares with Goth an assumed affinity with 'outsiderness'. It embraces the oppositional stance that most rebels against the perceived mainstream. So metal fans worldwide have often garnered negative attention from a media who increase sales through the invention of moral panics. The oppositional position that metal takes is often geographically and socially defined. As a result, U.S. metallers like Slayer will take a stance against right-wing Christian beliefs and attack mainstream morality as a way of attacking the heart of the American dream. In 1996, the parents of Elyse Marie Pahler took satanic death metal band Slayer to court in the US after their fifteen year old daughter was murdered in what was alleged to be a satanic ritual imitating the band's lyrics. The case was dismissed by a Californian judge in 2001.

Italy has a strong Satanist scene in music, fuelled by such outsiders' feelings towards the Catholic church. Even Norway – famously liberal and easy-going – was shocked by the murder and violence surrounding the country's Black Metal scene and bands such as Mayhem, as well as the various arson attacks on churches. Ozzy Osbourne's 'Suicide Solution' is a more obvious mainstream example – but suffice to say, metal has long been used as a folk devil for society's moral panics.

Okay, so it could be argued that the above instances of extreme behaviour are out of the ordinary. It could also be argued that some of these bands played death-metal, a particular strain of the genre that took the fantasy aspects of the sound out of comic books and turned them into reality. The fact is that by the time Grohl launched his *Probot* project, the metal genre had become best known for either its extreme stupidity, or its tendency, in the shape of the more mainstream acts, towards big hair and bad videos. So why would Grohl chose to deliver a metal opus now? Was it a case of potential career suicide?

Grohl maintains he never lost his love of metal. True, as a youngster he agreed with a friend that they would never listen to that kind of music again after they'd first heard punk. But when he found his friend playing an old metal album a few months later, he realised that such a narrowly dogmatic approach to music was a bad thing. He dug out the old albums and embraced his love for metal once more. He even used it as a badge to underline his punk credentials.

"In suburban Virginia where I grew up, I was one of only two punk kids at the high school. I used to do the morning announcements right after first period, and you could start with a little music, so I would slip in a little Metallica at fuckin' eight o'clock in the morning. I think people thought it was kinda cute." [6]

Years later and Grohl was still trying to be the cute kid slipping some Metallica in between news bulletins. But this time Metallica was *Probot,* and the news bulletins were Foo Fighters records.

"To this day, I'm almost 35 years old, and I still feel like I'm seventeen" he told *Guitar World* in 2003. "My world really hasn't changed so much. I mean, I might walk down the street and meet people all day long that recognise me, but man, I still deliver bagels to my mom in the morning, and I still do beer bongs at night. And the passion for music hasn't changed, either. It still really burns inside of me, and I think the same thing goes for all of the people on the album. It's just a love of music that drives you, you know? It's like an addiction, and it's the greatest high in the world."

The actual *Probot* project was very much Grohl writing as a way of showing respect to the hardcore and metal of his youth. He played all of the music with the exception of a few guest over-dubs and approached a wish list of singers to be involved. Those included on the finished album were Cronos (Venom), Lemmy (Motörhead), Max Cavalera (Sepultura/Soulfly), Tom G Warrior (Celtic Frost/The Apollyon Sun), Mike Dean (Corrosion of Conformity), Kurt Brecht (D.R.I.J), Snake (Voivod), Wino (Saint Vitus/The Obsessed/The Hidden Hand), Lee Dorrian (Napalm Death/Cathedral), Eric Wagner (Trouble) and King Diamond (Mercyful Fate). An extra hidden track included a vocal performance from comedian and friend Jack Black.

The only singers from Grohl's wish list not to appear on the album were Tom Araya of Slayer and Phil Anselmo from Pantera, and latterly of Down and Superjoint Ritual.

"Everyone of these people who I asked," he explained, "has a lot to do, and some of them live on the other side of this planet. I sent packages with tapes and hoped that that addressee would like them. That's why it took three years from the first take until the last take. I also sent a tape to Tom Araya, but it didn't work in the end. It wasn't easy to fill his place. It had to be someone who fits into the family. It took a while, but then I thought of Kurt Brecht from D.R.I., Corrosion Of Conformity and the Cro-Mags – these were the three best bands from the punk or hardcore side, that in reality were making metal." [7]

This last statement from Grohl gets to the heart of the problem that runs throughout *Probot* as a long-term proposition. Grohl's approach to genre is extremely liquid. As a musician he sees the natural links between all types of metal, hardcore, punk and so on.

However these musical forms are all too often followed vehemently by musical obsessives who will separate out genres into small sub-genres, which are defined by something as arbitrary as guitar sound or drum patterns. Each genre subsequently develops its own life beyond the musical form and subsequently perceived subcultures and scenes develop.

Grohl's approach is, however, far more pragmatic in that it allows for the fact that no one remains within one strain of a genre. Furthermore, no single form of music is separated from another, genre isn't as simple as the racking of styles in a record store. It's also true to say that no subculture exists in a vacuum untouched and uninvolved with mainstream culture. Music culture cannot ever be seen as being homologous, and Grohl understands this. Which is why he can make the switch from extreme to mellow and back to extreme, noise so swiftly. It's all a part of the same thing to him. It all comes from those bands he grew up with.

There was another contradictory aspect to *Probot* in that it presented a challenge to the perceived ideas of rock music history. The music press likes to present a notion of genres having a defined moment of birth and death. Subsequently they obsess with finding the first recorded music of a new genre and then declare its death with the onset of new sound, or a fresh style. Grunge and metal are good examples of this.

Grunge was clearly defined by the media as having emerged at a particular moment in time, in a clearly isolated geographical place and somehow separated from anything but the coolest antecedents. It was the sound of Generation X living out slacker realities through a soundtrack that drew on hardcore punk, the Stooges, MC5, glam era Bowie and at a push, the bluesier elements of Led Zeppelin. Furthermore the arrival of grunge was mediated as being the final death knell of Eighties heavy metal. As *Independent* journalist Ben Thompson suggested in 2004, this meeting of the zeitgeist and the newly redundant was most clearly represented when Nirvana and Guns N' Roses almost got into a fight at the 1992 MTV awards.

Thompson quite correctly argued however, "There was much

more at stake than just the usual clash of rock-star egos. The confrontation between old-school, macho Goliath and new-school, dress-wearing David seemed to mark a historic shift in rock's balance of power." [4]

For Grohl now to be seen to embrace that which his band had come to overthrow, seemed to many to be somewhat hypocritical. But this accusation would ignore the fact that Nirvana (like many of the grunge élite) had always admitted to liking a far more diverse selection of musicians than the media would allow into the very narrow definition of grunge. Not only did these catholic tastes extend to aspects of hardcore and metal, but even to the opposite extremes of disco! Indeed Cobain's journals clearly depict his pen drawn image of Parisian disco musician Cerrone 'saving the world!'

Marc Cerrone explains the effect this had on him personally, "When I first saw this I felt like... wow! I remember that in the period that Kurt was big I was frustrated. Everyone thought disco was has-been music. So when this guy's diaries are published, I discover that back at the time when I was thought of a has-been, this guy, who everyone loved, was doing cartoons of me. I was like... wow!"

This wide open view to the machinations of genre and understanding of histories are what also marks Grohl's own musical position out. He realises that genres aren't born separated from history, he also understands that music doesn't die, rather it occasionally fades away. This is how he can so easily make generic shifts. However, the point he does make, and one that reveals much about the true motivation behind *Probot*, is one of authenticity. A concept that he brings down to the simple duality of a good/bad taste culture.

"To me, there was good metal and there was bad metal. Good metal was Voivod and Motörhead and Trouble and Merciful Fate and Sepultura. And then there were a few bands whose time was up, and none of them had anything to do with that scene at all. When it comes to good metal and bad metal, it's pretty obvious which bands were ready to trade their guitars in for shovels." [11]

This need for authenticity extends deep into the make up of the *Probot* concept. It was his reaction against the mundanity of radio friendly rock, a position that in itself would have abhorred the younger Grohl. Indeed the Foo Fighters' stadium sized tours and mainstream hits would have represented the epitome of what he would maybe have been against.

So authenticity lies at the very heart of the album, from its choice of singers to its marketing through independent metal label Southern Lord. It was every inch the embracing of 'real' musical values over the fake values of the industry. He even declares that he didn't care if it made money or not, that money wasn't a concern to him. Neither was it a concern for his favourite musicians from his youth.

This position was most clearly revealed to *Guitar World* when pushed about the ironic images of metal in popular couture at the time.

"Well, see, that's something that we've been very sensitive to throughout the whole project. Rock music has become kind of in vogue, and rock cliché has become kind of in vogue and the irony of rock has become kind of chic, you know? You start seeing supermodels in Motörhead t-shirts, or pop stars wearing fucking MC5 shirts. But to me, rock 'n' roll has never been a fashion thing, and metal has never been ironic.

But with this *Probot* record, all of these people are still making music for all the right reasons, and that's really important to me. Before Nirvana became popular, I was happy because I loved doing it. If that meant going without food for two or three days, or playing in front of seven people a night, it didn't matter to me, man. I was just going for it because I loved it. And then after Nirvana became popular, it was the same thing. It still is." [5]

The sense of family, or community is the most important aspect to *Probot*. In this project Grohl gets to reclaim his place in the underground while also realigning himself to the ideologies of his past life. It's an act that reaffirms his position as a free thinking individual who, despite being signed to a major label and playing in a huge rock band, still thinks like someone on the fringes looking in.

With no single stylistic focal point and numerous vocalists on board, the *Probot* project sounded disjointed at best, and at worst a fantasy folly of someone successful enough to make music without any need for financial reward. Much as he might romanticise about his days being a penniless musician with Scream traveling around Europe in the back of a van for the love of music, it was only with the success of his later bands that he was able to indulge in this fantasy. In fact it's a fantasy that clings to his role as a fan – a position that has been a feature of his entire career. "The list of vocalists just read like a dream come true, it was my fucking record collection." Indeed, Grohl has confessed to having listened to Voivod's 1988 album *Dimension Hatross* every day for a year, and that it was his dream to go to a C.O.C. or Voivod gig, end up playing drums for them there and then. "I had this fantasy that I would go to their show, something would happen to their drummer, and they'd call into the mike: 'Is there anyone out there who knows our songs?' And I would step up and just fucking shred through a whole set."[9]

Perhaps the truest test of the authenticity, or honesty of *Probot* lay not in Grohl's ambitions but in the reactions of those who actually got involved. In many ways the album was as much a way of paying respect to them, as it was a dream work-out for him.

The production of the album would provide few clues as to the reaction of the guest vocalists beyond the fact they'd agreed to do it. Much of the album was recorded via parts being Fed Ex'd all over the world and with Grohl rarely meeting his idols during this process. Very little critical hype built up around the album. The project was limited to rumour and idle talk. Of all of the guests involved, only two made it into the studio to work directly with Grohl: Motörhead's Lemmy and Wino (real name Scott Weinrich) from the Obsessed.

"The Obsessed were local D.C. area heroes," explained Grohl with an obvious fan's admiration. "They were not unlike Motörhead in that they were a band that both the punks and the metalheads liked. You would see the Obsessed on a bill with 45 Grave or Void or local hardcore bands, you know? And everybody had a lot of respect for them, because they were heavy as fuck, man. Wino wound up being in St. Vitus and Spirit Caravan, and the guy is a fucking legend. I mean, he's unbelievably talented, and his conviction and integrity are still rooted in the local scene and in the underground, which is an aesthetic that I wanted to adhere to with this album. I really wanted to make sure that everything still had that spirit and that vibe.

"I went into the studio with Wino. And there's nothing cooler than seeing one of your heroes stand in front of a mic with his hands on his belt buckle, singing a song like that. It was unreal!" [7]

Wino himself was equally excited by the *Probot* proposal. Not simply because it was being put together by his old friend, but also due to the line-up of legends on the album.

"I was pretty honoured that he asked me, but surprised at the same time," explained the man who is famed for his tattoos and wild stare. "I was proud to be included in his list of inspirational people. I thought the Nirvana stuff was great," he said " I thought moving to the Foo Fighters was very logical and I was very happy to see him have the success that he has."

Talking to *Kerrang!*, Voivod frontman Snake (real name Denis Belanger), was similarly non-committal about the Foos, preferring instead to focus on Grohl's personality and love for the music being represented by *Probot*. "I think Dave is really good because he made it big and successful," Snake noted. "But he has so much respect for the bands that were there. He's a wonderful guy, always has a smile on his face." [9]

If the inclusion of Wino in the line-up drew a direct line to Grohl's teenage years, then the addition of Lee Dorrian (Napalm Death/Cathedral) was his link to the true international underground community of the Eighties hardcore/metal scene. Grohl had first met Lee when Scream played at a gig in Birmingham being promoted by the then-Napalm Death man. As was normal at gigs like these throughout Europe, the band stayed with the promoter – in this case, Lee's minimally furnished flat.

"Oh god," Lee recalls, "Dave stayed at my flat when there was no furniture, no carpet, all the windows were broken and we just slept on the floor. I remember Dave from then, he was a cool guy."[9]

Lee lost touch with Dave as the two of them went on to enjoy differing levels of success with their own bands. A few years later, however, when Dave was playing with Queens of the Stone Age, Grohl sent a message back to Lee via Greg Stahl.

"Greg and I were out in London on one of our wrecking spree weeks and the Foo Fighters were playing with Queens Of The Stone Age. Greg went backstage to say hello and when he came stumbling back to meet me in the pub later he said that Dave wanted me to be on his record. I thought that was just Greg being drunk, but then I got an email. Fucking hell, it was true. Then I heard the music Dave sent me and it was a double 'Wow,' because it was proper doom. It wasn't just some guy making up a track, it was proper ... fucking ... doom. For someone like Dave to ask me to be on his record and then to come up with music like that, I was overwhelmed a little bit," he admits. [9]

If any of the guests on the *Probot* album had any misgivings about the project then they left it to one man to express them. Nordic legend Cronos admitted to being at least a little unsure of the proposal to work with a musician better known these days for his 'soft rock' anthems.

"At the beginning, Dave sent me an email, in which the first hundred lines he was talking about how much he loves Venom and how often he's seen us play live. A real fan letter! Back then he was only playing with the idea of recording a metal album with all his metal heroes and Venom having a part in it. He wrote that he'd have to get something off his chest. I answered instantly 'Of course, man. Send this shit over! Let's fucking do it!' It was very, very strange. I didn't know what to expect at all. Would this shit be hard or not? Until now I've only done the hard sound – and that won't ever change! But when I got Dave's package and heard the tape ... Fucking hell, this was heavy shit!

This guy has metal balls! I mean, I don't know what it's like to do commercial pop music, but he seems to miss something. That has to be frustrating, if you want to scream, but you have to sing. That's why the *Probot* record is so fucking heavy as fuck!" [10]

But it was the involvement of Lemmy that quickly took on legendary proportions with Grohl describing being in the same studio as the man "like meeting the fifth Beatle".

Grohl continued: "I met Lemmy once, years ago, but I was walking out of a strip club and he was at the video poker machine. I said, 'Hey, man, I've got a lot of respect for you' and then I ran away before he could say anything. For 'Shake Your Blood' he came into the studio and drank a half a [small bottle] of Jack Daniel's before he even got in front of a microphone. He sang it twice, and it was genius. He nailed the bass in two takes. When we were done he said, 'Who wants to go look at some tits?'" [1]

The eleven track, self-titled *Probot* album was released on February 10, 2004. A two-track seven inch single containing the cuts 'Centuries Of Sin' (featuring Cronos of Venom) and 'Emerald Lies' (featuring Wino), limited to the satanistic joke of 6,666 copies, preceded the album release. As did a video to accompany the Lemmy track 'Shake Your Blood' — a song that was criticised as being a dead ringer for Motörhead's 'Ace of Spades' ("I wanna be the drummer in Motörhead for one day, you know? So I wrote a track that's a simple rock song - straight to the point, no filler or fluff, just something that sounds like Lemmy should be singing on it." said Grohl at the time).

In many ways, the video could be the one aspect of the entire *Probot* package that smells of ironic pastiche. In an attempt to capture the frequent sexism of the metal scene, the band (Grohl on drums, ever the fanboy in a Motörhead t-shirt, Lemmy on bass and turtle neck growling vocals, Wino on guitar) perform the song amid seventy scantily clad, tattooed women all recruited through the Suicide Girls website. With the girls performing various forms of S&M on each other and generally "making out" the scene was one of pure adolescent fantasy — and ironically the very thing that the other guys in Nirvana found uncomfortable about the metal genre.

Grohl made no apologies for it though. He was, after all, living out a lifelong dream of drumming with Lemmy. Talking to *Guitar World* he exclaimed, "Dude, I could've wrapped my car around a tree on the way home, and I would have been *totally* cool with it!" [2]

Despite any obvious cynical observations, however, *Probot* was largely a success with metal heads appreciating it for what it was. The album was perhaps understandably less well received by fans of the Foo Fighters who had grown used to a far more sanitised, anodyne form of rock. Following TV appearances on MTV and Fuse TV, Grohl returned to the Foos camp newly invigorated, and the experience of laying down some hard and heavy tracks suggested a change in direction for the day job.

"I believe *Probot* is good for Dave, to break out of the rock star-routine. Because he simply is a rock star," suggested Lee Dorrien. And its certainly true that the pressures of being a recognizable star had had a profound effect on Grohl, the man who preferred to step out of the spotlight and hang out in normalsville with his mates.

"I don't wanna be like (a rock star)" he has said, "even when I was young, I wanted to be a rocker, but not a rock star. I could've never been a part of U2 or The Police. What I make ... there is just no option to become famous. There's people that want exactly that, who behave like stars. I have never dealt with that. I mean if you listened to *Bleach* would you have thought that Nirvana were gonna be huge? I didn't. I didn't know anyone who knew it. In our wet dreams we thought of 700 people in a full club." [7]

So with the Foo Fighters about to enter the recording arena once again, Grohl was displaying the dichotomy of his position for all to see. At heart he's the fanboy, still in awe of those artists whom he worshipped as a teen ("If you would have told me that I could take a photo of Cronos and me when I was sixteen, I would've shit my pants"). He's still the underground troubadour with a desire to make honest, no bullshit music. But to many his band epitomises mainstream MTV rock. It was a thought that had even crossed Grohl's mind in the two years leading up to the release of *Probot*.

Back in 2002, as the band headlined the main stage at the Carling

Weekend Reading and Leeds Festivals, Grohl was struck by the dilemma posed by 55,000 people singing his band's songs back to him. Exciting as it felt at the time, later in the day he started to consider the other side of the coin. "We had reached this peak and suddenly we were enormous. We were playing arenas in the UK, we were headlining Reading. We went to Australia and we headlined the Big Day Out festival over there. We had this huge, big, long set list of songs that everyone knew. We had this massive production that we dragged around the world. We had moments in the show where people would sing along. And it was great – of course it was – but do you know what? I never imagined it reaching [such a] point. Not for a second. And when it happened it got me thinking... about what it meant for us. We'd reached a level and it meant something. It was just a question of what? Did it mean it was time for us to take one of those four year breaks? Or did it mean it was time for us to try something different?" When asked if that included splitting up he confided, "Well, yeah, that was one of the things I wondered about. I did think about going out at the top."[12]

The only way for Foo Fighters to move forward would be to take the lessons learned with *Probot*, the boredom endured through the nightly performances of 'Learn To Fly' and the experience of feeling like his band risked turning into the Eagles, and turn them on their head.

If the Foo Fighters creative position appeared to be slightly schizophrenic at this point, then what followed would not only exaggerate the suggestion, but also confound all but the most adoring fan.

9

ALWAYS WAS THE LUCKY ONE

ANOTHER DRUMMER JOKE
Why do drummers have kids?
They're not too good at the rhythm method.

May 2005, Radio One Big Weekend, Herrington Park, Sunderland, United Kingdom.

It's mid–May, a month that promises the first hints of blue skies and summer warmth. Here in Sunderland however, the Gods of the weather are waging a war on Radio 1's mini festival. In the space of a few hours, the North East of England is whipped by gale force winds, burned by sharp spells of sunshine, blistered by pelting hail stones and half–drowned in rivers of mud. It's like Woodstock, Glastonbury and a mud wrestling championship on a small scale. All that's missing is a bloody great tsunami to wash Herrington Park out to the North Sea.

In his band's bus, Grohl sits ashen faced. He is suffering from severe laryngitis and his doctor has ordered him to refrain from talking for at least a week. Already he's been forced to cancel a secret warm–up date and an MTV shoot for the Foo Fighters. His only thought is to keep quiet to allow his voice enough of a return for him to play in Sunderland's newly acquired swamp. Not even the sight of self-styled Foo Fighters uber-fan, Radio One's eternal student Jo Wiley, can tempt him away from his vow of silence.

With lank hair falling across his unshaven face and hoody sleeves pulled over his hands, he huddles into his chair. Only able to manage a shrug and a faint smile in acknowledgement of visitors as he tucks into his warming medicated drink.

A few hours later, he announces to a baying crowd that the

doctor's had warned him not to sing tonight, but all he wanted to do was play some loud rock 'n' roll to the people of Sunderland. And that's exactly what he does. For the next thirty minutes, the Foo Fighters are the single most electrifying band on the planet. They steamroll through a greatest hits package that reminds the crowd of what a potent force they are live. When they introduce 'Best of You, you can be forgiven for forgetting that only a year earlier this band had seemed on the brink of collapse. It's the first time the forthcoming new single has been played live to a UK crowd and already it sounds like classic Foo Fighters. Suddenly the Foo's future looks bright.

But to understand the place where they are with 'Best of You', it's necessary to look back again. Back to the days when Grohl was missing in action on his numerous guest sessions, and more importantly, back to *Probot* – the sound of the man letting off steam and getting back to some kind of nostalgic reality.

The four year period between initial recording and final release of *Probot* represented a shaky time for the Foo Fighters. The band's leader Dave Grohl was increasingly smitten with the idea of drumming again and found himself being willingly spirited away to supply drums for a series of bands. Furthermore his love for Queens of the Stone Age was starting to out shine his feelings for the day job. Perhaps unsurprisingly the album recorded in the middle of this malaise, *One by One,* proved to be such a hit and miss affair, with the band later universally claiming it to be a turkey.

Far from being inspired by Grohl's metal musings, it was an album which showed the growing schizophrenia in the band's make up. On the one hand, they were a rock band who had the desire to play hard and loud. On the other, there was this whole west coast MOR rock balladeering side to them, which they also clearly loved. Grohl may have admitted to feeling like the band had turned into the Eagles on *There is Nothing Left to Lose* but at least this stage of the band's career had an honest and clearly definable direction. *One by One* was nearing Foo Fighters pastiche in that it tried to cover both aspects of their sound, but ultimately took neither to its concluding extreme.

"It was a traumatic period," Hawkins explained to *Blender.* "We were just happy we got it done." Grohl however was less charitable towards the album. In the same interview he argued, "Half of it is chud. There was a lot of filler. I didn't realise it when we were recording, or when we were mixing, but I realised it when we started playing shows, and half that album was completely deleted from the set list. That's just a tell tale sign."

Much is made of Grohl's extra curricular activities at this time but it is important to note that the rest of the band also explored their own projects. Many band members also returned to a pre-Foo Fighters type of music – the need to get back to the roots of why they joined bands in the first place being as real for Mendel in particular as it was for Grohl.

As the longest surviving member of the Foo Fighters, it is perhaps Mendel's relationship with Grohl that best illustrates the inter-band chemistry. Hawkins and Grohl, meanwhile, suggest themselves that their friendship is more like that of siblings.

Grohl: "I'm like the uptight guy, and you're like the 'No way, it's cool!' guy."

Hawkins: "[Bad Religion's] Brian Baker thinks it's homoerotic. He thinks we're lovers."

Grohl: "We're kind of like brothers." [1]

Schifflet all too often appears to be distant from Grohl's leadership, although he has admitted that he was a little unsure of what Grohl thought of his guitar parts on *One by One*, as the band leader wasn't actually present for much of the album's recording – preferring instead to tour with Queens of the Stone Age.

However, Mendel is the member of the band who appears to feel most comfortable challenging Grohl. This is perhaps due to the pair's friendship stretching back to their Washington hardcore days, or simply due to Mendel's longevity in the Foos (he was after all one of the first people Grohl called to play in a band in order to tour his self-played debut album).

This closeness has resulted in an occasionally tempestuous relationship between singer and bassist with the situation boiling over when the band came together to rehearse for their stint at Coachella. The question was a simple one – how committed was Grohl to the Foo Fighters? The answer wasn't so simple however.

Talking to *Kerrang!* Grohl explained, "There was a moment when I thought, 'Well, that was fun and we've had a good run at the thing.' I've always thought that bands shouldn't last forever, there's always an expiration date. So, yeah, for a minute I thought we should call it quits and end it on a high note. But, there's a lot more to being in a band than just being in a band. It's such a big part of your life and at that time the band was our life and it had been my life for eight or nine years. I know it's a clichéd analogy, but it's like a marriage, an unspoken foundation, and it's something you know you rely on. Even if you're not there doing it every day, just knowing it's there in the back of your mind sort of props you up and keeps you going.

"When I was out with Queens of the Stone Age, I felt like I was losing some of that and it didn't feel right; I didn't feel solid or balanced," Grohl continued. "To me the band is more than just making records. The studio represents what I love about the band because we can hide away and shut ourselves off from the outside world. Even if we don't go out on tour for a year and we don't see each other every day, I really feel like some of my closest friends are the guys in the band. I don't go looking for new friends or new family because I have them here." (15)

Of the family that Grohl had been vacationing from, the first to explore his own side project was Nate Mendel whose band The Fire Theft featured former members of his old group Sunny Day Real Estate. Mendel was joined by singer, guitarist Jeremy Enigk and drummer William Goldsmith. The latter, of course, had also endured a brief and ultimately disastrous time in the Foo Fighters, however the friendship between Mendel and Goldsmith had overcome any initial problems that followed his departure from Grohl's band.

The Fire Theft released their eponymous debut album in September 2003. The *Hands on You* EP followed it in January 2004. Stylistically the band drew obvious comparisons with Sunny Day Real Estate, or more pertinently their Mendel-less third album *The*

Rising Tide. Although obviously still owing a huge debt to the original Emo sound of DC hardcore act Rites of Spring, The Fire Theft introduced a greater sense of melody and dynamic.

A tour to promote the album followed its release but the band have sadly remained dormant since. There have been rumours of a second album, but the originally muted February 2008 release date failed to materialise.

During this period, Chris Shiflett went back to his punk roots with the band Jackson. Initially featuring Shiflett, his brother Scott on bass and drummer Pete Parada, they played their first date in April 2003 at the King Kong Club in Los Angeles before releasing a self-titled EP. Soon after, Parada left to concentrate on his other band Saves the Day and was replaced by Cary LaScala. Also joining the band around this time was Doug Sangalang who suggested the name change to Jackson United after the original moniker had proved too difficult to copyright – not least because a band of that name based in Paris had already released a brace of singles on a UK major. As legend has it, the United part of the name was proposed in celebration of Shiflett's love of football ... or soccer as he might have called it.

In late 2004, the band released their debut eclectic punk album *Western Ballads*. Ironically, despite Schiflett's brother having left before its release (his role was taken by Omen Starr), the album actually featured only the original line-up.

In more recent times, the band has again consisted of only the Schiflett brothers, as LaScala and Starr moved to pastures new when the Foo Fighters were reactivated in 2005. Drumming duties have since then fallen to Taylor Hawkins and Dave Grohl although it is not clear whether either has contributed to the band's as yet unreleased second album *Harmony and Dissidence* (originally pencilled in for a January 2008 street date), although the band do promise a huge array of star guests.

Perhaps unsurprisingly, given his much publicised problem with prescription Vicodin, (the powerful painkiller that has publicly affected the lives of Matthew Perry from *Friends* and Jack Osbourne among many others) Taylor Hawkins was the slowest to get out of the traps in the solo project race.

"I did have a hard time with that shit," explained Hawkins in 2005. "I've been to the doctors over the last few years, once recently with lower back pain because of all the mountain biking and drumming I'm doing and not sitting properly. They're just so eager to give out these really strong painkillers, and it's overkill, man, because it's just legal heroin. It has become such a party drug in a way. They should clamp down on it and they should ask questions." [12]

Coming back from the harrowing experience provided Hawkins with a fresh outlook on his music career and, taking a leaf from Grohl's book, he increasingly guested for other bands (including on US prog rock band Coheed and Cambria's Nick Raskulinecz produced album *Good Apollo, I'm Burning Star IV Volume Two: No World for Tomorrow* in 2007). His first non-Foos outing came in 2003 when he got together with bassist Chris Chaney (from the final incarnation of Jane's Addiction) and guitarist Gannin Arnold. Together the trio started demoing tracks in a home studio owned by friend Drew Hester. Rumours abounded that the band, known as Taylor Hawkins and the Coattail Riders were like 'Rush meets the Bee Gees'.

"I think it [was] Oscar Wilde who said, 'Why go on vacation when working's so much more fun?' I'm no good when I have nothing to do. I really wanted to make a record and have a project outside of the Foo Fighters, because we do take breaks. So I had to kind of create another little environment for myself to keep busy and excited," he said.

An album was recorded in 2004, but it didn't see the light of day until March 2006. Its twelve tracks (including hidden track 'Perfect Day') were clearly influenced by Hawkins' childhood heroes. "I hear a lot of stuff [in my work], I hear The Police, I hear early prog-rock stuff from the Seventies, I hear Queen and Devo – everything I grew up listening to is on there. I don't think I'm John Lennon, but I like writing songs and making music, I really do."

The end result owed much to Hawkins' love of Eighties music with the tracks shifting between lightweight Jane's Addiction, west coast rock, later Genesis, Queen and even country and western in an often unfocused mélange. Hawkins' vocals proved to be less impressive than his drumming thanks to his throaty monotone delivery; however, some of the album's more experimental instrumental passages do shine through an otherwise lacklustre set.

With the Foo Fighters now locked into their own outside adventures, it seemed as if the band would never come back from the fracturing effects of the disappointing *One by One*. But Grohl had other ideas. He had to bring the family back together and his way was via a creative hub, a studio complex the band could call home.

It was an important decision. Up until now all of their biggest disappointments had come through recording in ill-suited studios. Only Grohl's basement set-up in Virginia had proven particularly fruitful in latter years, but for the band it was always Dave's place. They needed a group focus and in September 2003 they took over an 8,000 square foot industrial complex in the leafy San Fernando Valley suburbs of Reseda and Northridge, California. An area otherwise known as the porn capital of the USA where any number of the area's warehouses will at any one time be hosting low-budget skin flicks. Even in their move into band real estate, the Foo Fighters managed to pull off rock 'n' roll with effortless ease!

"Before it was built," guitarist Chris Shiflett explained to *Clash* magazine, "Dave was saying, 'Yeah, we can store the gear there, we can rehearse there, make the albums there, we can do press there, photo shoots ... blah blah blah' and it's really actually turned into that. It is the all-purpose Foo Fighter hub."

Studio 606 is exactly that – over £350,000 worth of space, temperature controlled at a constant 72 degrees, where the band can quite literally work, rest and play. Only ten minutes drive away from Grohl's Encino home, hidden behind a Jehovah's Witness Kingdom Hall and opposite a tyre shop, the studio's eight-foot gate opens to reveal a highly secured building. In one entrance lies a huge warehouse where the band's touring equipment is stored. Another leads you into a voluminous room where the band can rehearse.

The recreation room/kitchen houses toys, guitars, lava lamps and a huge leather sofa festooned with cushions with covers made by Grohl's mum from his old tour T-shirts including Slayer, Sonic Youth and Genesis.

"I got that (early Eighties Genesis t-shirt) when I was thirteen. I worked that concert. Actually, what I was really doing was spending the whole day looking for pot" Grohl chuckles. [9]

In the office area, table tennis and an Addams family pinball machine shares space with Apple Macs while out front, there's a basketball court. In the corridors the band's trophies are in clear view. Silver, gold and platinum discs for albums representing an estimated value of thirty million sales, stretching as far back as Nirvana's *Nevermind* and including some bands Grohl has guested for – one for Queens Of The Stone Age's *Songs for the Deaf*, another for Jack Black's Tenacious D project. Then there are the Foo Fighters' discs, loads of them from all over the globe, a reminder of just how universally successful the band are.

But it's not only Grohl related success signifiers that adorn the nerve centre's walls. In some areas framed photos and posters of favorite artists take pride of place. Most notable perhaps are the Nirvana photos which sit happily alongside the usual canonic list of rockers like The Who and an abundance of images of Led Zeppelin.

Zeppelin's influence on Studio 606 even leaves its imprint in the design of the facility itself. It's modeled on the Polar Studios, the Abba-owned luxurious wood-panelled rock 'n' roll playhouse facilities in Stockholm where Zeppelin recorded their swansong *In Through The Out Door* in the winter of 1978.

Grohl's taste for metal is also everywhere to be seen. A poster for the Mötley Crüe reunion tour gazes down upon the overflowing ashtray festooned mixing desk, just above a toy version of Mötley Crüe's drumkit in pride of place.

In 1999, veteran Detroit rocker Iggy Pop told me he'd bought a house out in Miami in order to be able to "piss on a piece of my own land". In Studio 606 Grohl and Co. had a property that they could piss on for the next twenty years and still not cover its surface. As rock 'n' roll statements go, Studio 606 is near unbeatable.

The first album to come out of this bricks and mortar symbol of band solidarity was in many ways their most ambitious to date. *In Your Honor* attacked the musical schizophrenia of the rocker who likes a ballad, the balladeer who likes to rock by splitting the two Foo Fighters character traits right down the middle. A two-disc set, it featured one rock album and one acoustic. And it was an arrangement that allowed the band to exploit their oppositional tendencies to the fullest – in total separation.

"That was pretty conscious and we knew we could do it, 'cos we were making the double record, so both acoustic and rock dynamics had to be extreme. We wanted them separate so we went as far as we could in each direction. After we'd recorded the acoustic record, we realised it had kept getting bigger and bigger, so we had to push the rock stuff even more to keep that distance between the two of 'em. We even went back into the studio with the rock record to make the rock stuff more rock!" [6]

Despite retaining a radio friendliness throughout, the album was the sound of the band exploring these extremes. Sure they might be able to take things further out as individuals (although the solo efforts suggest not) but collectively the Foos never wander too far from the easy-to-listen-to mainstream. Not unlike Nirvana in fact, a band whose obsession with the classic pop tones of the Beach Boys was as important as their love of punk rock.

"I don't know if it's because I'm getting older, or if I'm just becoming a fucking snob, but I'm so disappointed with what people are being fed musically these days," Dave explained of his inspiration for the new album. "It's junk food, it's so bad. And bands that people rely on are starting to fail. I wish every band could do what we're allowed to do, because we're allowed to simply be ourselves."[9]

Drawn from a possible forty recorded songs, the end result was the band sounding harder *and* softer than ever before. But never do the two extremes meet. A Foo Fighters concept album if you will, albeit one that investigated the band's creative psyche. Inevitably critics immediately drew comparisons to Guns N' Roses' indulgent *Use Your Illusion* twin discs as well as other double set concept pieces. The double, or triple, album is all too often seen as proof of an artist's self-important indulgence.

"It's inevitable that, in every band's career, they get the itch to do the pretentious, *White Album* freak-out. But it was time to flex a little bit. Besides, you know how bands say they're making a double album, but just release one and then another six months later ... Well, we just saved you eighteen fucking dollars!" [1]

Of course such generalisations about multi-disc releases ignores the fact that bands come up with certain gems that may not fit into the confines of a single album. In fact, the single disc can be so creatively restrictive as to be more conceptual than the double, or triple, set. *In Your Honor* however, was more like two separate albums, each tightly defined, with no room for flab or filler. Less the sound of a band not knowing when to stop than the sound of Grohl and friends furiously working in a focused way for the joy of the actual process.

As a statement of intent, the album's opening title track couldn't have been more perfect. A full throttle droned guitar assault that explodes one minute forty seconds in, when a drum finally piles on some militaristic rolls. It's only in the final third of the track that guitars start to riff towards the crescendo. With no clear chorus or identifiably typical Foos structure, 'In Your Honor' screams at you to listen and, above all, feel. It's a song of celebration, defiance and anger, and it offers the first real sign that Grohl's extra-curricular activities (which by this stage had grown to include stints with Garbage and Nine Inch Nails) had had a huge impact on his approach to capturing power with the song structure.

If previous Foo Fighters releases had been restricted by a self-imposed style hierarchy, then this song found Grohl defying even his own best judgement of what a Foos song should be. As such, it is perhaps the band's bravest statement. Grohl, who always had a self-conscious concept of what a Foo Fighters tune should sound like defended the song by suggesting that at the end of the day it was still the same four people playing "so it just is a Foo Fighters song, whether it sounds like Carcass or fucking Ry Cooder."

Talking specifically about 'In Your Honor' to *Kerrang!* Grohl argued, "It's really fucking cool to have just three minutes of noise and then rolling drums for a minute and a half and then into full-on thrash! It's fucking awesome. I remember when we were rehearsing it, our guitar tech came in and said, 'What the fuck is that?' I said 'That's the song we're opening the show with for the next two years and he said, 'Wow, after 'All My Life' I didn't know how you guys were going to open a show ever again!'" [15]

With the track that followed, 'No Way Back', the band were in more familiar territory, despite Grohl's trademark melodic vocal delivery (from a whisper to a growl, but always with a tune) and typically addictive chorus – the song maintained an unusual aggression.

If the album's aim was to toy with people's perceptions of what the Foo Fighters were, then 'Best of You' directly challenged the concept of their typical single. The first single on the album, released a month after that infamous Sunderland show in June 2005, employed the quiet/loud tricks of old but with added twists. Screamed vocals start with an impassioned cry and build from there, while the band builds through a series of textured riffs gradually reaching a thundering climax. 'Monkey Wrench' this was not.

Interestingly the song was also his most overtly party political track ever – a celebration of the sense of camaraderie he encountered while on the campaign trail for Democratic Presidential Candidate John Kerry. Grohl was moved to take action following the Bush campaign's use of Foo Fighters' 'Times Like These'. The thought that Bush might get into office again was intolerable to Grohl, but the suggestion that Grohl's own composition might have inadvertently helped incensed him.

"I've never been an outwardly political person. I've always voted, I've always been active in my community. But I've never had it make its way into the music. But I was in John Kerry's motorcade, and we went from town to town through middle America. I would play acoustic shows at these rallies, and nobody knew who I was. What inspired me most wasn't necessarily political. It was the strength of community and human will. Seeing so many people come out because they either desperately needed to be rescued or they genuinely wanted change. It really hit me. I'd never been so deeply involved in something so important. It was unbelievably inspirational."

When Bush did succeed, Grohl was clear in his opinions, saying he was "Fucking pissed, really fucking upset. My immediate reaction was, 'Fuck it all, let's riot! Fuck you world! I fucking hate everyone that didn't vote for Kerry!' But that's ridiculous. You have to do something to make things better. As John Kerry said when he conceded defeat, 'Just keep fighting the good fight.'" (14)

From here the loud album in the double set continues down an increasingly familiar path. 'DOA' is another 'knobs turned up to eleven' rock out with a sing-along chorus about death. 'Hell' finds the band riffing through harmonics before being driven by frenetic drums and winding melody. 'The Last Song' employs the Foos trick of the band holding back on a monotone riff before finding a rushing release through a driving drum break tightly wound in the coils of melodic guitar riffs. Lyrically the chorus found Cobain reference watchers rushing to make the over obvious accusation – that Grohl was publicly declaring the end of his link to the Nirvana legacy. It was suggested that this was the moment when Grohl decided to stand-alone from his past.

It was a ludicrous suggestion that ignored the fact that the Foo Fighters had by now out lasted and *out-sold* his previous band. Also Grohl was at pains to point out that he was Nirvana's sixth drummer and only in the band for a short time. To him, Nirvana were as much history as Freak Baby, Mission Impossible or Dain Bramage.

The links to Nirvana's legacy were perhaps made all the more exaggerated by the final release of the long disputed box set of Nirvana rarities, *With the Lights Out,* six months earlier. Compiling the set was an act of closure for both Grohl and Novoselic, but it reignited Nirvana in the hearts of the fans.

Elsewhere on *In Your Honor*'s heavy disc, the band retained their resolution to rock harder than before. Only on the strummed intro to 'The Deepest Blues Are Back' do they hit a mellow note, but this is soon crushed with the screamed build into the chorus. Other tracks like 'Free Me' and 'The Sign' are full on riffing hardcore metal juggernauts while 'End Over End' and 'Resolve' sit in familiar Foos territory – albeit in a heavier form than fans were used to.

If the loud album had contained few real surprises beyond the fact that it featured no acoustic ballads, then the quiet, contemplative disc two was a revelation. And one that the critics immediately picked up on. Far from simply being the Foo Fighters unplugged with songs played on acoustic instruments, the songs here were constructed with the necessary mellowness as a central theme. Whether achieving this end involved the use of strings, mellotron, piano or percussion was neither here nor there – it was a case of using the right sounds for the right effect.

Inspired by Tom Petty's solo work on *She's The One,* the acoustic album came from Grohl's desire to write a movie soundtrack. "After we finished touring for the last record I thought, Okay, I'm in my mid-to-late thirties now. Do I really want to run around festival stages screaming my head off every night? I don't know, maybe it's time to start playing some [mellower] music. So I thought that, rather than just jump back into the album cycle, I'd see if I could find a movie that needs a score. One of my favorite albums of all time is Ry Cooder's *Paris, Texas.* I love that album – I've listened to it for years and years. So I envisioned finding a project that I could turn into my own version of *Paris, Texas.* After about a month of writing I thought, wait a second, this could be a killer Foo Fighters record. I'd hate to have pulled a solo album out of my ass in the middle of the best time of our lives as a band, so instead it became a Foo Fighters project." [3]

Given the space to breath, the band's approach to the acoustic album found them embracing space, timbre and texture to a far greater degree than ever before. Opener 'Still' featured echoing ambient swathes and picking guitar with a lyric that captured Grohl following an unusually clear narrative.

"'Still' is probably the first song I ever wrote that comes close to any sort of storytelling," he said. "It's about my being a kid, going to the lake by my house on a Saturday morning and seeing all these ambulances and fire trucks because someone decided to kill himself by sitting on the train tracks. When you're a child, you're so naive, you have no idea what's really going on, and you start to explore and find yourself playing with pieces of the .... it's a pretty gory story, actually, but it happened." [3]

Elsewhere 'Another Round' featured Zeppelin's John Paul Jones playing mellotron over a guitar riff and harmonica solo that was distinctly Neil Young in flavour, as was 'Over and Out' which featured a six-year-old guitar part and an occasional Young-esque vibrato in Grohl's voice. 'What If I Do?' had all of the trademarks of a classic Foo Fighters ballad; contemplative verse sung over picked guitars and uplifting sing-along chorus, while 'Miracle' recalled late Eighties grunge precursors The Smithereens, albeit an acoustic version (and with a beautiful, melancholic violin refrain) in the same way that 'On the Mend' recalled Grohl's own 'Touch' soundtrack and Nirvana's quieter pop moments as on 'Polly'.

Final track 'Razor' presented Josh Homme's picked minor chords and Grohl's sombre vocals celebrating the beauty of the razorblade. Orginally debuted acoustically at the January 2005 Tsunami Benefit at the Wiltern in LA (Grohl introduced the track by saying he'd just written it that morning), 'Razor' is a breathtakingly beautiful song which was perhaps the only moment that the project truly recalled Ry Cooder's *Paris, Texas* opus.

Standout moments of the album come courtesy of the surprise elements. First of all 'Virginia Moon' jumps out due to the fact it's a bossa nova, and through the inclusion of guest vocalist Norah Jones.

"When I mentioned her name, everybody was like, 'Really?' I think the only person who wholeheartedly approved was our guitar tech, who's had a borderline stalking crush on her for years!" Grohl said at the time.

"But she came in, did her thing, and it fit perfectly," Hawkins added. "We didn't use it [just] because it's her. I mean, if you listen to it, it works."

The band had in fact demoed the song some years back but

decided it was wrong for them at that time. Here it was back again and sounding decidedly coffee bar.

"It's just my lame attempt at recreating 'The Girl From Ipanema'" he told *Guitar World Acoustic.* "We'd actually tried to turn that into a rock song back when we were making 'There Is Nothing Left To Lose', and it just sounded completely ludicrous. There was no way it would work."

Perhaps the obvious other standout is the reworking of his *Late!* song 'Friend of a Friend', a track originally written about his new band Nirvana in the first few weeks of living with Cobain. Inevitably the inclusion of what was the first song Grohl had written on acoustic guitar brought even more questions about his previous band. Not least because it included the word 'nevermind' in the lyric, despite the fact that it predated the album considerably.

"I was nervous about putting it on the record. Pretty much any song I write people are usually willing to pick it apart for specific references, obvious references. Whether it's Courtney or Kurt or Nirvana or whatever. And it's not that simple. There are a lot of other people in my life that I love and hate. It's not just the two.

Of any song that I've ever written, 'Friend Of A Friend' is most blatantly about my time in Nirvana," he concedes. "I wrote the song about Krist [Novoselic] and Kurt and me. I don't even think I ever played it for them. It was just one of those things." Talking about the extreme loneliness of time that inspired the song he added, "God it was quiet, I had nothing better to do than think with a guitar in my lap. And it was a dark, rainy winter. The sun would come up at 8.30 in the morning, and go down at two in the afternoon, and those were the hours I slept. I didn't see daylight for months. It was fucking depressing."[14]

The final standout moment came with the Hawkin's sung 'Cold Day In The Sun' which is Eagles–lite, a pure slice of west coast rock fluff. To some critics, it was perhaps one of the worst songs the Foo Fighters had ever recorded.

In Your Honor was met with huge acclaim from fans and critics alike with discussions raging about the stronger acoustic aspect to the double set. In many ways the album represents the first time that the band had achieved exactly what they'd set out to do.

The main criticism was that the acoustic set becomes too anodyne after a while, its sweetness outshining the darker shadows and ultimately creating a slight blandness. The very thing that Grohl set out to do was to separate the heavy and the soft in order to reveal more in the music. Ironically in the end he arguably masked the styles through too much sameness. Listening to the album through the iPod in shuffle mode, brings out more power and texture than does the official schizophrenic approach.

However, of all of the Foo Fighters' albums, it's the acoustic set in which Grohl claimed to have the most pride at this time. Rather than a sideline, he considered it to be a huge achievement that heralded a fresh approach and proved the band could have longevity long after their stadium anthems might have lost their appeal.

"Have you any idea how proud I am of this album?" Grohl asked at the time, "and the thing I'm most proud of is the fact that it opens doors for us musically. When I listen to some bands who have been around for ten or fifteen years like, God bless 'em, the Ramones or Green Day or AC/DC, those bands have made a career out of making music that wrestles with one dynamic. And they're known as being the kind of bands that can do that one thing. But fuck that, I don't want to be that band. I want to be a band who *can* do fucking anything. Because we can do fucking anything." [7]

In the short term, however, the band had to get on the road to promote the album. They all relished the straightforward rock gigs, however, the muted acoustic shows found Hawkins perhaps a little less excited, fearing, "People would throw piss at us."

Happy or not, the acoustic live show would mark the next phase of the Foo Fighters' growth.

10

WHAT IF I SAY I'M NOT LIKE THE OTHERS?

ANOTHER DRUMMER JOKE - THE LAST LAUGH
What's the first thing a drummer says when he moves to LA?
"Would you like fries with that, sir?"

It is said that you haven't made it in rock until you've been the subject of a death rumour. The history of music is littered with them. From Paul McCartney to Michael Jackson and taking in Bruce Springsteen, and Paul Weller among many others, the rumours have been a continual feature on the landscape of pop mythology.

In May 2006, Grohl himself became the subject of one such rumour mill. Slightly bemused by the story, he explained, "I got a phone message from a friend saying 'Er, I guess… Jordyn… this is maybe… for you. I'm so sorry to hear what happened.' I heard this message and went 'What the fuck?' They were leaving a message on my cell phone saying 'I'm sorry Dave died.'

That was weird, but I guess I've finally graduated to that status of being an internet rumour. It weirded me out a bit, but it's stupid. I'm like a cockroach, don't worry, I'll be around for a long time."

Strangely Grohl was the subject of a second death rumour in February 2007 when his band's Wikipedia entry was amended to include the date of his passing.

However, Grohl was most certainly alive and well and in the year that followed *In Your Honor*, the Foo Fighters pursued an equally schizophrenic path. Their famed live show embarked on the customary world tour, with arenas getting larger and larger. Notable among these dates was the June show at London's Hyde Park. "When they asked us to play Hyde Park I was, like, 'Wait!

Isn't that place huge?'" he said at the time. "But I thought, 'Well, if we get 30,000 people, it'll still be the biggest show we've ever played.'" As it turned out, 85,000 watched the band run through a storming set that included 'Breakout', 'All My Life', 'Monkey Wrench', 'Best Of You' and 'Learn To Fly'. Motörhead's Lemmy joined the band for a run-through of *Probot*'s 'Shake Your Blood' and Queen's Roger Taylor joined them for a storming 'Tie Your Mother Down'. If any doubts remained that the Foo Fighters had become the live band everyone loved to see, then this was the decider.

Given their status as the world's favorite rock band then, it was somewhat ironic that they chose to present their first live album, not as a representation of the adrenalised rock Foos, but the mellow acoustic version. In November 2006, Grohl's band released *Skin and Bones*, an album recorded live in Hollywood during the summer when the band were on a short acoustic tour in support of Bob Dylan – the man once charged with selling out his folk roots when he went electric.

There were inevitable comparisons with *MTV Unplugged*. Indeed, the performance drew an almost accidental line direct to an era when MTV *Unplugged* represented unmissable and eminently watchable TV. In an era where bands are encouraged to offer acoustic versions of songs for cell phone adverts and live DVDs are as obligatory as the quirky cover version, it's hard to imagine the cultural worth of MTV's show. However, it was valued as a performance where the artists could stand or fall on talent alone and no amount of orchestration could hide the egg on the artist's ego when things didn't work out.

Of course, one of the classic *Unplugged* shows was by Nirvana, the live CD of the show largely considered to be essential listening. If Grohl was tired of the comparisons with his old band then he seemed to sleep walk into this one.

Sadly, for many observers, the Foo Fighters acoustic outing had the opposite effect to the Nirvana one. Where the latter's acoustic performance revealed an almost painful frailty between moments of near-transcendental beauty and hitherto hidden depths, *Skin and Bones* revealed a band with limitations. Many of their songs appear inch deep, surface glossed for the adult ear. Normally powerful hooks are reduced to slow riffing while Grohl's voice feels one-dimensional throughout, his husky charm lost to the faux chocolate box arrangements.

"It seems like I've joined a new band because it's very different to anything we've ever done." Grohl said on the eve of the acoustic tour. "Plus we have an extended band, including a keyboard player, a violinist, and Pat Smear playing guitar. It's like our own little mini orchestra. The few times that I've played acoustic by myself it's been really moving and we're trying to capture those moments throughout the set."

If the album had been intended to be a powerfully moving statement, then it failed. Not only that but it denied the band's fans what they really wanted, the full throttle live experience. Admittedly a download only version of the Hyde Park show was made available a couple of weeks later, but this hardly compensated for the disappointment.

Skin and Bones was accompanied by the release of a double DVD that featured both the Hollywood and the Hyde Park shows. Not as good as their patchy 2003 live DVD *Everywhere But Home* (which included the highlight of the band's old style acoustic performances as extras), the *Skin and Bones* set revealed the extent to which the band's intimacy seemed to have been lost.

In many ways the performance was testament to the inherent problems on the preceding double album. In its attempts to remove the two sides from the coin, the band lost a necessary edge. It became obvious that the band now had to find a way of bringing the two extremes back together in a happy marriage.

The apparent sleepiness inherent in *Skin and Bones* may have also had a lot to do with the mellowing effects of fatherhood. On April 15, 2006, Dave and Jordyn Grohl had a daughter, named Violet after Dave's grandmother. "Her name is Violet Maye Grohl," he beamed a few weeks later. "She was six pounds, fifteen ounces, she's got blue eyes, dark hair and she's fucking cute. She's six weeks old and she's already smiling and laughing.

"I spend hours upon hours just talking to her," he continues. "It's kind of embarrassing, I think she's gonna look like her mother and act like me, which is fucking trouble! I've wanted a child for a long time. I can change a diaper in fucking five seconds, but the first couple I was fumbling and got shit all over myself!" [4]

Despite the huge Hyde Park show, it was perhaps the band's Live Earth performance that really cemented the Foos as a genuine generation-leaping mainstream phenomenon. To see Grohl sprinting around the stage, engaging the audience, delivering his addictive songs, it only took him twenty minutes to become the household name he always threatened to be. Basically he stole the show.

"Well, I mean, when you only have twenty minutes, it's easy to run it into the red the whole time," he later told *Clash* magazine. "I think that the Live Earth show was special in that everyone was there for the right reasons and the songs made sense in the context of the evening; 'Best Of You', 'Times Like These' and 'My Hero' – I think all of those people were singing those songs with me for the same reasons. It was just that time of the night where everything needed to come together and fortunately we were there to witness it happening. But it was fun man, that was a fun gig. I was a little nervous, going on after the Pussycat Dolls and before Madonna. I missed a lot of the show - I only saw a few of the bands - but you walk out from that curtain and you see Wembley Stadium with all of those people and it's like jumping into a cold lake, like 'Holy fuckin' shit this is HUGE!' Not to mention two billion people watching it on television! So you walk the lip of the stage and you take a look around and then you look back at the three guys and you think, 'Alright, well it's just us, it's just a show.' And then I see my daughter on the side of the stage and I'm like 'Yeah, this is fuckin' cool.' It'll be alright." [1]

Grohl wasn't the only proud father to ignite the crowd at the Live

Earth concert. Taylor Hawkins, himself father to a new baby son –
Oliver Shane – joined forces with Roger Taylor of Queen, Cad
Smith of the Red Hot Chili Peppers and forty drummers from
around the world including the Dhol Foundation, Taiko drummers
and a drum corps from Shotts, in a one time drum supergroup
called the SOS Allstars. The drumming collective, built around the
lead trio of Hawkins, Taylor and Smith, delivered a track written
for the evening by Taylor and based on the Morse Code for SOS
before finishing with the drum intro to Queen's 'We Will Rock
You'. As fantasy drum master classes go, it was pretty untouchable.

By 2007, it was clear that the Foo Fighters had come a long way
since Grohl's first demo turned album. Despite continued attempts
by critics to keep the link alive, the band were now far removed
from the spectre of the Nirvana legacy. The Foo Fighters had
hooked into a generation of fans who cared little for his previous
band but did feel an affinity for the Foo Fighters' brand of melodic,
angsty rock. Presidents used their music for campaign rallies, sports
shows used their music as a soundtrack, daytime radio rocked to
their singles, MTV held special Foo Fighters weekends and their
Skin and Bones Hollywood show seemed to be broadcast continually
throughout the world. Like it or not, the band were now situated
squarely in the very public mainstream.

This position clearly reflected Grohl's state of mind. Now in his
late thirties, he had found a new sense of calm in his life. Happily
married with a beautifiul daughter, financially very secure, the
owner of the workplace of any musician's dreams, a list of
friendships with childhood heroes, a long standing extended Foos-
related family and shelves boasting far too many industry awards
than is usual for anyone, Grohl was in the enviable position of being
master of his own destiny.

Despite the ever-prying eyes of the internet and Grohl's
apparently easy going demeanour, the band revealed him to be a
very private person who only lets in the people that he wants. It is
perhaps this key aspect to his psychological make-up that has

helped Grohl survive for so long in such an insecure and fickle industry.

"I know a thousand people but I think maybe two of them know me," Grohl once explained. "I remember reading this horoscope when I was twelve or thirteen years old, that said you have to be careful not to alienate everyone because there's a great chance that you'll wind up completely alone later on in life. I have a tendency to do that. I can be cordial and polite and somewhat open to most people, but I don't want everyone to know me."

Another aspect of his private life that has helped him retain a very centered approach has been his sessions with therapists, arguing that he thinks it is important to have "someone with an objective opinion who's trained in 'the ways of the mind' to talk to."

Grohl sought the objective support of a therapist when his first marriage was in crisis. "I was seeing that therapist when Kurt died, so fortunately I had already established a relationship with this person so I had someone to talk to when that happened. I've never been on medication or anything like that and I've never been overly depressed, but there have been times when I need advice from someone else. I don't ask for advice that often." (5)

Grohl also revealed that he continued to see a therapist today to help him understand band problems, getting older, problems with the volume of work and general life changes. "You go, you talk to the person once a week for a couple of months and it helps for some reason. If you're a junkie, you go to a drug counsellor. If you're a rock musician, what do you do?" he said. (5)

Early in 2007 Grohl found his music being broadcast to approximately ninety million Americans who had tuned in to Super Bowl XLI. It was an unexpected airing, but one which raised a number of eyebrows. During his half-time performance, Prince delivered a high octane version of 'Best of You', in a belated response to the Foos 2003 cover of his 'Darling Nikki' (from his 1984 album, *Purple Rain*) and released it as a B-side on the Australian version of their 'Have It All' single (it eventually became a set–closing staple at Foo Fighters' 2004 shows).

Recording cover versions had become a standard thing for the band to do when they were winding down from recording an album; however, this particular cover allegedly did not meet with Prince's approval, with that star telling *Entertainment Weekly* he didn't appreciate the Foos (or anyone else) covering his work, and suggesting that Grohl and his band should "write [their] own tunes."

"We wanted to put it out here in the States, but Prince wouldn't let us," Hawkins said. "I heard that he didn't like our version. Or maybe he just didn't like us doing it."

On January 29, 2007 a studio version of Prince fusing 'All Along the Watchtower' with 'Best of You' made its worldwide debut on Howard Stern's Sirius satellite radio show. The medley was soon the subject of positive discussion in the blogosphere and a month later the Eighties legend was doing his thing on stage at Miami's ProPlayer Stadium when 'Best of You' was given a Prince style working out one more time.

"Dude, I have no idea why he did it, but I'd love to find out," Hawkins laughed at the time. "I mean, the thought went through my head that maybe he was doing it as a sort of 'Fuck you' to us, or maybe he really likes the song. Either way, it was pretty amazing to have a guy like Prince covering one of our songs – and actually doing it better than we did!"

With the Foo Fighters now embarking on the demos for their next album, rumour was rife that once again the band would cover a Prince song. But they had more important things to consider. The apparent fall out of the *Skin and Bones* album had left the band reconsidering their own music. Early demos for the new album revealed the acoustic sessions to have had a lasting impact, but the need for this next set was to bring the extremes together. To reunite the split personalities of their music and take the Foo Fighters to fresh creative highs.

With usual producer Nick Raskulinecz unavailable due to commitments producing the new Rush album, Grohl once again brought in Gil Norton, the producer behind what is still considered by many fans to be the band's finest album *The Color and the Shape* (which itself was reissued with extra tracks in 2007 as a tenth anniversary edition). However, if fans had hoped that the reuniting of band and producer would result in an album of power pop rock classics, then they were sadly mistaken. The resulting set, *Echoes, Silence, Patience And Grace* which arrived in September 2007, was the band's most complex, brooding and uncommercial outing yet. If the last seven years, from the beginning of the *Probot* project to the execution of the acoustic performances had been all about Grohl growing up in public, then *Echoes, Silence, Patience And Grace* was the sound of a man coming to terms with getting older. Finally his work had the maturity and sophistication to truly match his aspirations to be like Neil Young.

Yet the album was anything but the sound of contentment. Despite Grohl's public persona of the happy-go-lucky, grinning workaholic, on this album he appeared to be allowing the world in on his more private self. There was a sense of a man working through his dilemmas and confusions, both personally and musically. No longer afraid to reveal his true self in public, thanks largely to the strength he had gained from fatherhood. Furthermore, the band's own security from a musical perspective had grown through time spent in Studio 606, where they have been allowed to develop without the scrutiny of the public, and that had resulted in a less 'fan aware' sound. Some might call this self-indulgent, but by this stage in the band's career it is probably fairer to say that they'd developed a greater sense of *self-awareness*.

"At this point, having done it for as long as we have, it becomes a little more introverted. As a musician you need to do the things that satisfy yourself," Grohl suggested.

The end result was an occasionally harrowing, often moving journey through multi-hued, multi-textured terrain, where the light and dark, public and private melt into and support each other to create a sensitive but muscular powerhouse. An album which draws heavily on influences such as Neil Young in both his Crazy

Horse (especially on 'Summer's End') and acoustic incarnations, Todd Rundgren's early non-prog stuff (his 'Just One Victory' begs to be covered by the Foos) and even a hint of Paul McCartney's Wings.

"I think any rock 'n' roll album is inspired by McCartney and Lennon," Grohl explained, "I probably wouldn't be sitting here if it weren't for those guys. I grew up listening to The Beatles, I grew up listening to Neil Young, I grew up listening to Led Zeppelin, those classic rock guys as much as I was into the hardcore scene in the Eighties, so it's inevitable that those things shape the way you compose and arrange. We were down at Abbey Road a couple of weeks ago recording a song for the BBC – we were recording 'Band On The Run' and Paul McCartney showed up! To me that's like having the Pope walk into your living room or something. It was a real moment for me." [1]

From the controlled Zeppelin-esque power of the opener 'The Pretender' to the closing piano ballad 'Home', the album explores avenues that finds the Foos pushing themselves far beyond the riff and the hook and for the first time shows them to have real longevity. With tracks like mid-paced southern rocker 'Statues' you can truly imagine the band lasting long after fashion has left mainstream power rock behind.

"Five years ago those songs wouldn't have been on a Foo Fighters record because I would have been too concerned that it was too much of an abstract direction; it was too much of a shift in the band. And now, I just wanna make music. So a song like 'Statues', or a song like 'Home', I think those are two of the best songs that the band have ever written, just because after thirteen years it's still changing; the band is managing to evolve somehow – we'll just change rather than suffocate in the same fuckin' cage that a lot of bands get trapped in." [1]

There are less interesting moments where the band relax back into the tried and tested, like on 'Erase/Replace', 'Long Road To Ruin' and 'Cheer Up Boys (Your Make Up is Running)' where they again resort to powerhouse riffing with quiet, melodic verse and grinding, chanted chorus. 'Stranger Things Have Happened' also wanders through familiar territory, despite its acoustic form. And yet none of these songs can be viewed as fillers, more that they don't reinvent the template quite as willingly as other tracks.

One of the album's most poignant moments comes with the instrumental 'The Ballad Of The Beaconsfield Miners', which was written for and dedicated to two miners who were trapped for a fortnight in a collapsed gold mine in the town of Beaconsfield, Northern Tasmania in April 2006. While trapped, the miners sent up a request to have MP3 players with the Foo Fighters' music sent down to them. Grohl issued a message via fax that read, "Though I'm halfway around the world right now, my heart is with you both, and I want you to know that when you come home, there's two tickets to any Foos show, anywhere, and two cold beers waiting for you. Deal?" In October 2007, one of the miners took him up on the offer after a show at the Sydney Opera House.

"Music has obviously had a profound impact on my life over the years, but to consider something that I've done to have that same impact, that power, is strange, personally. I don't think about it that way. But when I heard about the Beaconsfield guys, someone sent me an email from Australia and told me what was going on, I mean the back story is incredible, but these guys are good guys, y'know? And they made it through a situation like that because they're good guys. So I was honoured to be able to put that song on the record.

And that was a huge moment for me because for once ... it was really the first time that I felt like what we do is maybe bigger than pyrotechnics and lasers and beers backstage. It felt like what we do had been legitimised. I was really touched, was very moved, and I wanted to pay tribute to honour these guys for giving me something that no one else has ever given me before.'" [3]

The track itself is a dueling picked guitars affair that has a touch of the film *Deliverance* about it. It reflects Grohl's need to express much wider concerns than on any previous record.

"When Violet was born, I suddenly had a picture of her as an adult standing by my deathbed. I was thinking, 'Who's going to be with me when I die? My daughter and maybe my grand-daughter?' I never used to think about these things. Most people think the world begins with their birth and ends with their death, but at some point you realise there's a much larger world out there that will continue existing long after you have made your exit. So I started to take in the big picture and these realisations had an influence on the new album. There are songs about birth, death and life because my perception of these things has changed radically." [2]

Perhaps the song more obviously affected by the birth of his daughter is the haunting 'Come Alive' with the lyrics over a plaintive acoustic round which grows towards a huge rolling crescendo.

The most interesting aspect of *Echoes, Silence, Patience And Grace* is that at no point do you imagine Nirvana in the proceedings. Indeed, their ghosts appear fully exorcised from Grohl's perspective on life. Lyrics on the track 'Let it Die' would, on previous outings, have sent Nirvana conspiracy theorists running to their blogs to argue about the presence of Cobain in the words. This has much to do with the deeper and more connected nature of the lyrics on this set. Previously any mention of life, death, disappointment and the other big issues in life would have jumped out at you. Here they're all up for discussion.

As a whole, *Echoes, Silence, Patience And Grace* represents the band's most accomplished album to date. Despite (and possibly due to) the lack of obvious hook heavy singles, it sits as an artifact unto itself. An album that needs to be enjoyed in its entirety and in that respect a record that harks back to the pre-download days of the album experience. To download only certain tracks from this set is to miss the whole picture and for the first time on any Foo Fighters album, the entire spectrum of that multi-coloured picture is essential to the enjoyment of the album.

In 2008, with *Echoes, Silence, Patience And Grace* following the global success enjoyed by their previous albums, the band find themselves in perhaps the best place they've ever been. Musically assured, with a stable line up and an ever growing army of fans who seem ready to take on the new directions the band throw at them. Thankfully these new directions are all pretty closely linked. There is little chance of the band discovering techno or pushing their brave new dubstep sound, but this only makes them stronger – their own men.

Today the Foo Fighters sit in an enviable position. They draw fans from all backgrounds and age groups. Their music sells to blue-collar workers as much as it does to white-collar professionals. They play in the mainstream arena but get full respect from the underground. They call some of the greatest musicians in rock their friends, but also enjoy links with rock's cutting edge newcomers. They're loved by daytime as much as specialist evening radio. They're uncomplicated enough to be mainstream stars, but deep enough to be awarded respect from even the most introverted music scholar.

Quite simply they're the mainstream every-Joes it's okay to like. As for Grohl? Today he exists in a place that few ever attain. He's as successful in his home and personal life as he is his work and creative worlds.

A few years back Grohl told me that in his wildest dreams he couldn't imagine still being in the Foo Fighters after ten years.

"I used to think I'd retire at 33, anything over that is too old. It's obscene. But now I just think 'I'll keep going – see what happens."
Now, thirteen years on from that first Foo Fighters album, Grohl is in the perfect place. Hell, he even got to play the part of the devil on drums in a Tenacious D video… How much more joy can one man get?

Dave Grohl is one of those rare people in the music world: a genuinely nice guy. No matter who you talk to or what feature you read, that one fact is crystal clear. He's cool. Yet beneath that outer surface, there lies a personality that makes him almost pathologically unable to see his own ability and worth. In his mind, he will always be a bit player, the one that no one notices, the guy that pales into insignificance next to the enigmatic personalities in his own bands and those he guests for.

Throughout his career, his ego has taken a backseat, while he has watched in awe as the Stahl Brothers, Skeeter Thompson, Kurt Cobain, Krist Novoselic, Pat Smear and Taylor Hawkins have done their thing. In fact, its even been suggested that he surrounds himself with these characters to take the spotlight away from himself. He is a fan boy. The one who always watches, but never gets involved.

And this is what is so frustrating about Dave Grohl. Quite simply, he has achieved an incredible amount. He is a world-renowned songwriter. Foo Fighters are one of the most popular bands across the globe and his face is known to millions of MTV viewers. Notwithstanding the fact that, of course, he was a third of one of the greatest bands ever, Nirvana. Far from being the unknown member of a band, his solo acoustic performances have proven that he can dominate a stage with consummate ease.

He has a natural charisma that is underpinned by his insecurity. As a result, he has turned self-mocking into an art form, almost to the point of derision. The same is true of his seemingly obsessive need to be seen as a normal person. The reality however is that he doesn't work nine-to-five in a job he hates just so he can pay the bills and support the kids. He lives an extraordinary life. One that involves travelling around the world doing something he loves and getting paid incredibly well for it. Furthermore he is worshipped by a legion of fans who look upon him in the same way as he views the musicians he admires himself.

The fact is that Dave Grohl hasn't been a normal Joe since that day he joined Scream. However, against the odds, he has somehow managed to keep grounded enough to retain a very down-to-earth worldview despite all the countless dramas around him. This is a rare quality in a musician at any level of popularity, let alone one so successful.

"Luxury to me is sleeping in the same bed for more than two and a half weeks at a time," he says simply. "That doesn't happen much in my life. Luxury to me is stability. You have the conflict between that and the opportunity of doing what I do. I'm given these amazing opportunities. And I've always said I'd like to do this while I'm still young. Well, I'm nearing the cusp. I don't feel old. I just feel like I should feel old."

Dave Grohl is one of the most driven people in music. He claims not to be career driven, but he has the ability to make the right decisions all of the time. Decisions that end up being career -enhancing. His ambition to become like Neil Young may be the fan boy's biggest and most aspirational fantasy. To "be like Young" he will need to be able to sit still for longer than ten minutes, work on albums for longer than two weeks, tour once in a blue moon and devote huge amounts of his time to family, farming and other none musical pursuits.

The reality is that Grohl is an addict when it comes to music. And giving up, or cutting back that particular drug may prove to be almost impossible. Reducing – or cutting out altogether – his Foo Fighters work may perhaps be a realistic option. Especially now that he has taken the band to the top. From here maybe there is nowhere else to go, but back underground, or simply to turn into the Rolling Stones.

"I can imagine a thousand things I'd rather do. Absolutely ... producing other bands or scoring films, learning to make furniture to learning to work on old cars. I have the luxuries and freedom to do them if I like. There are a few I'm really serious about and others that seem they're meant to take up time."

He may have the luxuries and freedoms to pursue other lifestyles, but whether or not he has the burning desire to follow such new paths remains to be seen. Meanwhile, he has his music. Fortunately, for the time being at least, so do we.

POST SCRIPT... A REFLECTION

What place for biographies like these? In these days of internet investigation no stone remains unturned, no rumour unreported for too long. Each morsel, each tiny bite of info is grabbed by the fan and posted for consumption on an imagined community of other online obsessives. Where once the myths surrounding music would emerge from the pages of the music press, today its fansite discussion boards and blogs that create the rumours, state the presumed facts. Today, like never before, stories and lies masquerading behind a mask of truth are published without consideration for reality.

In this collapse between truths and realities, lies and stories, any sense of unquestioned history becomes forgotten. What happened is less interesting than what might have happened, what was reported as having happened and what is disseminated as the version of how people might have hoped it had happened. Numerous histories emerge, histories on a verge of collapse through loss of critical voice.

Once these biographies attempted to be the conduits of truth. Once they would be the only places to glean the new knowledge and to explore the previously uncovered myth. Today, however, biographies have a different use. Today biographers are tour guides. We pick our way through the detritus of popular culture, explore the irrelevant, celebrate the facts, but above all attempt to find a path through the multiple versions of history, the histories that exist.

To this versioning of history we add a critical perspective – sure it's our opinion, but then enjoyment of music was always about opinion. Music journos are always the first to express those opinions. This is how it should be.

The biographer can never be outside of the story. We are implicated in every word, every story line followed and every fact written. Our opinions, backgrounds and ambitions colour these texts. We are critics and this is our work.

The stories, rumours and lies can take care of themselves on the internet. Biographers should attempt to grasp the burning embers from the fires of historical confusion and culturally locate them in the here and now.

Which is why Grohl is so fascinating to me. In many ways he seems to embody the cultural obsessions of the age in which we live. His music isn't overly deep, but instantly memorable and at times as deposable as pop. But then he delivers some of the most touching records on the commercial landscape. He comes over as a nice guy with few hidden depths, but then surprises us with his ability to cut to the quick with acute lyrical meaning. He seems politically unmotivated, a typical Generation X-er, but then he makes a statement, either musical or personal, that is steeped in the politics of people. In this age of celebrity he is a private man, but with celebrity leanings. He will turn up to awards ceremonies, gets pictures of his personal life in the pages of the celebrity press and yet he has little to do with the machinations of the throw-away PR machinery. Perhaps most interesting is the fact that at a time when family is in a state of breakdown, Grohl talks endlessly about exactly that, *family*. From his mum, to his wife and child, from his band to those people (techs to PRs) who have worked for him for years. All are his family. And that is a very revealing aspect to his moralities, ethics and ideologies.

He's the family guy and all of the confusions that this idea presents.

DISCOGRAPHY

FREAK BABY
DEMO (no label) 1984
Includes: Different

MISSION IMPOSSIBLE
DEMO (no label) 1985
Includes: Different (new version)

Single
SPLIT 7" with Lunchmeat (Sammich Records) 1985
Helpless/ Into Your Shell/ Am I Alone?

Compilation
ALIVE AND KICKING (WGNS/Metrozine)
Helpless/ I Can Only Try

DAIN BRAMAGE
DEMO #1 (no label) 1986
In The Dark/ Watching It Bake/ Cheyenne/ Space Cat/ Bend

DEMO #2 (no label) 1986
Flannery/ Give It Up/ The Log/ Eyes Open/ Home Sweet Nowhere/ We're An American Band/
...And There's A.../ Success/ Baltimore Sucks (But Booje Needs the Bucks)

Album
I SCREAM NOT COMING DOWN (Fart Blossom Records) 1987
The Log/ I Scream Not Coming Down/ Eyes Open/ Swear/ Flannery/ Drag Queen/ Stubble/
Flicker/ Give It Up/ Home Sweet Nowhere

SCREAM (with Grohl)
Single
Mardi Gras – 7" (DSI) 1990
Mardi Gras / Land Torn Down

Albums
NO MORE CENSORSHIP (RAS Records) 1988
Hit Me/ No More Censorship/ Fucked Without a Kiss/ No Escape/ Building Dreams/ Take It from
The Top/ Something in My Head/ It's About Time/ Binge/ Run to the Sun/ In the Beginning
Notes: Grohl drums on all tracks but 'Hit Me'. Grohl wrote 'In the Beginning)

LIVE AT VAN HALL IN AMSTERDAM (Konkurrel Records) 1989
Live At Van Hall In Amsterdam
Who Knows –Who Cares?/ U Suck A/ We're Fed Up/ Laissez Faire/ This Side Up/ Human
Behavior/ Iron Curtain/ Total Mash/ Still Screaming/ Chokeword/ Feel Like That/ Came Without
Warning/ Walk by Myself

FUMBLE (Dischord) [Recorded December 1989 – released July 1993)
Caffeine Dream / Sunmaker / Mardi Gras / Land Torn Down / Gods Look Down / Gas / Dying
Days / Poppa Says / Rain
Notes: Grohl wrote and sung "Gods Look Down". Album artwork by Grohl.

YOUR CHOICE LIVE SERIES O10 (Your Choice) 1990

C.W.W. PT. II / I.C.Y.U.O.D./ The Zoo Closes/ Hot Smoke and Sasafrass/ Fight/ American Justice/ Show and Tell/ Sunmaker/ No Escape/ Take It From the Top/ Dancing Madly Backwards/ Hit Me
Notes: Recorded live May 4, 1990 at Oberhaus in Germany

NIRVANA (with Grohl)
Singles
SMELLS LIKE TEEN SPIRIT (DGC) US 7"1991
Smells Like Teen Spirit/ Even in His Youth

SMELLS LIKE TEEN SPIRIT (DGC) US12"1991
Smells Like Teen Spirit/ Even in His Youth/ Aneurysm

SMELLS LIKE TEEN SPIRIT (DGC) UK 7"1991
Smells Like Teen Spirit/ Drain You

SMELLS LIKE TEEN SPIRIT (DGC) UK12"1991
Smells Like Teen Spirit (edit)/ Drain You/ Even in His Youth

SMELLS LIKE TEEN SPIRIT (DGC) UK CD1991
Smells Like Teen Spirit/ Drain You/ Even in His Youth/ Aneurysm

COME AS YOU ARE (DGC) UK/ Germany 7" 1992
Come as You Are/ Endless, Nameless

COME AS YOU ARE (DGC) US/ France7" 1992
Come as You Are/ Drain You (live)

COME AS YOU ARE (DGC) UK/ Germany 12" 1992
Come as You Are/ Endless, Nameless/ School (live)

COME AS YOU ARE (DGC) Australia/ Germany 12" 1992
Come as You Are / Endless, Nameless / Drain You (live)

COME AS YOU ARE (DGC) UK CD 1992
Come as You Are/ Endless, Nameless/ School (live)/ Drain You (live)

COME AS YOU ARE (DGC) US CD 1992
Come as You Are/ School/ Drain You (live)

LITHIUM (DGC) US/ Australia/ Germany CD/12" 1992
Lithium (4:16) / Been a Son (live 2:14) / Curmudgeon (2:58)

LITHIUM (DGC) UK CD 1992
Lithium (4:16) / Been a Son (live 2:14) / D-7 (3:48) / Curmudgeon (2:58)

IN BLOOM (DGC) UK/ Australia 7"
In Bloom / Polly (live)

IN BLOOM (DGC) UK/ Australia 12"/ CD 1993
In Bloom / Sliver (live) / Polly (live)

PUSS/OH, THE GUILT – Jesus Lizard/Nirvana split single (Touch&Go) 1993
Oh, the Guilt

HEART SHAPED BOX (DGC) UK 7" 1993
Heart-Shaped Box / Marigold

HEART SHAPED BOX (DGC) UK/ Australia 12"/ CD 1993
Heart-Shaped Box/ Milk It/ Marigold

ALL APOLOGIES/ RAPE ME (DGC) UK 7"/ 12"/ CD 1993
All Apologies/ Rape Me/ MV

ALL APOLOGIES/ RAPE ME (DGC) Australia CD 1993
All Apologies/ Rape Me/ Moist Vagina

ABOUT A GIRL (DGC) US/ Holland/ Australia CD1994
About A Girl/ Something In The Way

PENNYROYAL TEA (DGC) UK/ Europe 1994
Pennyroyal Tea (remix)/ I Hate Myself And Want To Die/ Where Did You Sleep Last Night? (In The Pines) – Unplugged version

NIRVANA SINGLES BOX SET (DGS) US/ Australia/ Germany 6 x CD set 1995
SMELLS LIKE TEEN SPIRIT: Smells Like Teen Spirit / Even In His Youth / Aneurysm
COME AS YOU ARE: Come As You Are / Endless, Nameless / School (live) / Drain You (live)
LITHIUM: Lithium / Been A Son (live) / Curmudgeon
IN BLOOM: In Bloom / Sliver (live) / Polly (live)
HEART-SHAPED BOX: Heart-Shaped Box / Milk It / Marigold
ALL APOLOGIES: All Apologies / Rape Me / Moist Vagina

Albums
NEVERMIND (DGC) 1991
Smells Like Teen Spirit/ In Bloom/ Come as You Are/ Breed/ Lithium/ Polly/ Territorial Pissings /
Drain You/ Lounge Act/ Stay Away/ On A Plain/ Something in the Way
+ Hidden track – Endless, Nameless

HORMOANING (DGC) 1992 – Australia only
Turnaround/ Aneurism/ D-7/ Son of a Gun/ Even in His Youth/ Molly's Lips

INCESTICIDE (DGC) 1992
With Grohl: Been a Son/ Turnaround/ Molly's Lips/ Son of a Gun/ (New Wave) Polly/ Aneurysm

IN UTERO (DGC) 1993
Serve The Servants/ Scentless Apprentice/ Heart-Shaped Box/ Rape Me/ Frances Farmer Will Have
Her Revenge On Seattle/ Dumb/ Very Ape/ Milk It/ Pennyroyal Tea/ Radio Friendly Unit Shifter/
tourette's/ All Apologies
+ Hidden track – Gallons Of Rubbing Alcohol Flow Through The Strip (3:50+7:33=31:32)

MTV UNPLUGGED IN NEW YORK (DGC) 1994
About A Girl/ Come As You Are/ Jesus Doesn't Want Me For A Sunbeam/ The Man Who Sold The
World/ Pennyroyal Tea/ Dumb/ Polly/ On A Plain/ Something In The Way/ Plateau/ Oh Me/ Lake
Of Fire/ All Apologies/ Where Did You Sleep Last Night

FROM THE MUDDY BANKS OF THE WISKAH (DGC) 1996
With Grohl: School/ Drain You/ Aneurism/ Smells Like Teen Spirit/ Been A Son/ Lithium/ Sliver/
Spank Thru/ Scentless Apprentice/ Heart Shaped Box/ Milk It/ Negative Creep/ tourette's/ Blew

NIRVANA (DGC) 2003
With Grohl: You Know You're Right/ About a Girl/ Smells Like Teen Spirit/ Come As You Are/ Lithium/ In Bloom/ Heart-Shaped Box/ Pennyroyal Tea/ Rape Me/ Dumb/ All Apologies/ The Man Who Sold the World.

LATE!
POCKETWATCH (Simple Machines) 1992
Pokey The Little Puppy/ Petrol CB/ Friend of a Friend/ Throwing Needles/ Just Another Story About Skeeter Thompson/ Color Pictures of a Marigold/ Hells Garden/ Winnebago/ Bruce/ Milk

DAVID GROHL
TOUCH SOUNDTRACK (Capitol / Roswell Records) 1997
Bill Hill Theme/ August Murray Theme/ How Do You Do/ Richie Baker's Miracle/ Making Popcorn/ Outrage/ Saints in Love/ Spinning Newspapers/ Remission My Ass/ Scene 6/ This Loving Thing (Lynn's Song)/ Final Miracle/ Touch

FOO FIGHTERS
Singles
THIS IS A CALL (Capitol / Roswell Records) UK CD1995
This Is A Call/ Winnebago/ Podunk

THIS IS A CALL (Capitol / Roswell Records) France CD 1995
This Is A Call/ Winnebago

THIS IS A CALL (Capitol / Roswell Records) Australian CD 1995
This Is A Call/ Winnebago/ Podunk (Cement Mix)

THIS IS A CALL (Capitol / Roswell Records Japan CD 1995
This Is A Call/ Winnebago

I'LL STICK AROUND (Capitol / Roswell Records UK CD1995
I'll Stick Around/ How I Miss You/ Ozone

I'LL STICK AROUND (Capitol / Roswell Records) Japan CD 1995
I'll Stick Around/ How I Miss You/ Ozone/ For All The Cows (Live)/ Wattershed (Live)

FOR ALL THE COWS (Capitol / Roswell Records) UK/ Holland CD1995
For All The Cows/ For All The Cows (Live)/ Wattershed (Live)

BIG ME (Capitol / Roswell Records) UK/ Australia/ Japan CD1996
Big Me/ Floaty (BBC Session)/ Gas Chamber (BBC Session)/ Alone + Easy Target (BBC Session)

BIG ME (Capitol / Roswell Records) US EP CD 1996
Big Me/ Winnebago/ How I Miss You/ Podunk/ Ozone/ For All The Cows (Live)/ Wattershed (Live)

BIG ME (Capitol / Roswell Records) France/ Holland CD 1996
Big Me/ Floaty (BBC Session)

MONKEY WRENCH (Capitol / Roswell Records) UK CD #1 1997
Monkey Wrench/ Up In Arms (Slow)/ The Colour And The Shape

MONKEY WRENCH (Capitol / Roswell Records) UK CD #2 1997

Monkey Wrench/ Down In The Park/ See You (Acoustic)

EVERLONG (Capitol / Roswell Records) UK CD #1 1997
Everlong/ Drive Me Wild/ See You (Live)

EVERLONG (Capitol / Roswell Records) UK CD #2 1997
Everlong/ Requiem/ I'll Stick Around (Live)

EVERLONG (Capitol / Roswell Records) Scandinavian/ Australian [ltd. Edition] CD 1997
Everlong/ Down In The Park/ See You (Acoustic)

MY HERO (Capitol / Roswell Records) UK CD 1998
My Hero/ Baker Street/ Dear Lover/ Enhanced Section

MY HERO (Capitol / Roswell Records) Japan CD 1998
My Hero/ Requiem/ Drive Me Wild/ Down In The Park/ Baker Street/ See You (Acoustic)/ For All
The Cows (Acoustic)

MY HERO (Capitol / Roswell Records) Australia CD 1998
My Hero/ Dear Lover/ For All The Cows (Acoustic)

WALKING AFTER YOU Split single with Ween (Elektra Records) 1998
Walking After You (New Version)

LEARN TO FLY (Roswell Records/ RCA) UK CD#1/ Australia 1999
Learn To Fly/ Iron and Stone/ Have a Cigar

LEARN TO FLY (Roswell Records/ RCA) UK CD#2 1999
Learn To Fly/ Make A Bet/ Have a Cigar

GENERATOR (Roswell Records/ RCA) UK CD 1999
Generator/ Ain't It The Life (Live Acoustic)/ Floaty (Live Acoustic)/ Fraternity/ Breakout (Live)

GENERATOR (Roswell Records/ RCA) Scandinavia CD 1999
Generator/ Ain't It The Life (Live Acoustic)/ Floaty (Live Acoustic)/ Breakout (Live)

GENERATOR (Roswell Records/ RCA) Australia CD 1999
Generator/ Learn To Fly (Live)/ Stacked Actors (Live)/ Breakout (Live)

BREAKOUT (Roswell Records/ RCA) UK #1 CD 2000
Breakout/ Iron & Stone/ Learn To Fly (Live)

BREAKOUT (Roswell Records/ RCA) UK #2 CD 2000
Breakout/ Monkey Wrench (Live)/ Stacked Actors (Live)

BREAKOUT (Roswell Records/ RCA) Australia CD 2000
Breakout/ Monkey Wrench (Live)/ Next Year (Live)

BREAKOUT (Roswell Records/ RCA) Japan CD 2000
Breakout/ Iron & Stone/ Ain't It The Life (Live Acoustic)/ Learn To Fly (Live)/ Stacked Actors (Live)

BREAKOUT - Live In Holland #1 (Roswell Records/ RCA) Holland CD 2000
Breakout/ Floaty (Live Acoustic)/ Ain't It The Life (Live Acoustic)/ Next Year (Live Acoustic)

NEXT YEAR (Roswell Records/ RCA) UK #1 CD 2000
Next Year/ Big Me (Live Acoustic)/ Next Year (Live Acoustic)

NEXT YEAR (Roswell Records/ RCA) UK #2 CD 2000
Next Year/ Baker Street/ Enhanced Section

NEXT YEAR (Roswell Records/ RCA) Australia CD 2000
Next Year/ Next Year (Remix)/ Monkey Wrench (Live)

NEXT YEAR (Roswell Records/ RCA) Japan EP CD 2000
Next Year/ Have A Cigar/ Make A Bet/ Floaty (Live Acoustic)/ Monkey Wrench (Live)

NEXT YEAR - Live In Holland # 2 (Roswell Records/ RCA) Holland CD CD 2000
Next Year/ My Hero (Live)/ For All The Cows (Live)/ Monkey Wrench (Live)

THE ONE (Roswell Records/ RCA) Australia CD 2001
The One/ Win Or Lose/ The One (CD-ROM Video)

ALL MY LIFE (Roswell Records/ RCA) UK #1/ Worldwide CD 2002
All My Life/ Sister Europe/ Win Or Lose/ All My Life (video – Director's Cut)

ALL MY LIFE (Roswell Records/ RCA) UK #2 CD 2002
All My Life/ Danny Says/ The One

TIMES LIKE THESE (Roswell Records/ RCA) UK Ltd Edition 7" 2002
Times Like These/ Life Of Illusion

TIMES LIKE THESE (Roswell Records/ RCA) UK #1 CD 2002
Times Like These/ Life Of Illusion/ Planet Claire (Live NYC)/ Enhanced section

TIMES LIKE THESE (Roswell Records/ RCA) UK #2 CD 2002
Times Like These/ Normal/ Learn To Fly (live)/ Enhanced section

LOW (Roswell Records/ RCA) UK #1 CD 2003
Low/ Enough Space (Live)/ Low (Video)

LOW (Roswell Records/ RCA) UK #2 CD 2003
Low/ Never Talking To You Again (Live)/ CDRom Extra

LOW (Roswell Records/ RCA) Australia CD 2003
Low/ Never Talking To You Again (Live)/ Enough Space (Live)/ Low (Video)/ Foo Fighters CD ROM (Bonus Clip)

LOW (Roswell Records/ RCA) Worldwide DVD EP2003
Low (Video)/ Times Like These (Video)/ Times Like These (UK Video)/ Times Like These (UK Acoustic Video)

BEST OF YOU (Roswell/ RCA) 2005
Best of You/ Fat Fucking/ Kiss the Bottle

DOA (Roswell/ RCA) 2005
CD1: DOA/ I Feel Free
CD2: DOA/ Skin and Bones (live backstage, T-In-The-Park 2005) / I Feel Free/ Best of You (Video)
7": DOA/ Razor

FIVE SONGS AND A COVER EP (exclusively distributed to Best Buy retail stores) 2005
Best of You" (live at The Quart Festival, Kristiansand, Norway, July 7th 2005)/ DOA" (demo) Skin and Bones (live backstage, T-In-The-Park 2005)/ World" (demo)/ I Feel Free" (Jack Bruce, Pete Brown/ FFL (aka Fat Fucking Lie)

RESOLVE (Roswell/ RCA), 2005
CD1: Resolve/ DOA (demo)
CD2: Resolve/ World (demo)/ Born on the Bayou/ Resolve (alternate video)
7": Resolve/ World" (demo)

NO WAY BACK/COLD DAY IN THE SUN (Roswell/ RCA) _2006
No Way Back/ Cold Day In The Sun/ Best of You (live at the Supertop, Auckland, New Zealand – 26th November 2005)

MIRACLE _PROMO ONLY (Roswell/ RCA), 2006
Miracle/ Suggested Callout Hook

THE PRETENDER ((Roswell/ RCA)) 2007
2-track CD: The Pretender/ If Ever
Maxi CD: The Pretender/ Come Alive (Demo)/ If Ever/ Monkey Wrench (Live from Hyde Park video)
7": The Pretender/ Bangin

LONG ROAD TO RUIN (Roswell/ RCA) 2007
2-track CD: Long Road to Ruin/ Seda
Maxi CD: Long Road to Ruin/ Keep the Car Running (Arcade Fire cover, live from Brighton 18th August 2007)/ Big Me" (Live from Wal-Mart Soundcheck)/ Long Road to Ruin" (video)
7": Long Road to Ruin/ Holiday in Cambodia

CHEER UP, BOYS (YOUR MAKE UP IS RUNNING) (Roswell/ RCA) 2008
Format tbc at time of writing

FOO FIGHTERS
Albums
FOO FIGHTERS (Capitol/ Roswell Records) UK/ US/ Europe1995
This Is A Call/ I'll Stick Around/ Big Me/ Alone + Easy Target/ Good Grief/ Floaty/ Weenie Beenie/ Oh, George/ For All The Cows/ X-Static/ Wattershed/ Exhausted

FOO FIGHTERS (Capitol/ Roswell Records) Japan 1995
This Is A Call/ I'll Stick Around/ Big Me/ Alone + Easy Target/ Good Grief/ Floaty/ Weenie Beenie/ Oh, George/ For All The Cows/ X-Static/ Wattershed/ Exhausted/ Winnebago/ Podunk

FOO FIGHTERS (Capitol/ Roswell Records) Australian Tour Pack 1995
CD#1: This Is A Call/ I'll Stick Around/ Big Me/ Alone + Easy Target/ Good Grief/ Floaty/ Weenie Beenie/ Oh, George/ For All The Cows/ X-Static/ Wattershed/ Exhausted
CD#2: Winnebago/ How I Miss You/ Podunk/ Ozone/ For All The Cows (Live)/ Wattershed (Live)

THE COLOUR AND THE SHAPE (Capitol/ Roswell Records) UK/ US/ Europe 1997
Doll/ Monkey Wrench/ Hey, Johnny Park!/ My Poor Brain/ Wind Up/ Up In Arms/ My Hero/ See You/ Enough Space/ February Stars/ Everlong/ Walking After You/ New Way Home

THE COLOUR AND THE SHAPE (Capitol/ Roswell Records) Australian Tour Pack) 1997

CD#1: Doll/ Monkey Wrench/ Hey, Johnny Park!/ My Poor Brain/ Wind Up/ Up In Arms/ My Hero/ See You/ Enough Space/ February Stars/ Everlong/ Walking After You/ New Way Home
CD#2: Down In The Park/ Drive Me Wild/ Baker Street/ Requiem

THE COLOUR AND THE SHAPE (Capitol/ Roswell Records) Japan CD 1997
Doll/ Monkey Wrench/ Hey, Johnny Park!/ My Poor Brain/ Wind Up/ Up In Arms/ My Hero/ See You/ Enough Space/ February Stars/ Everlong/ Walking After You/ New Way Home/ Dear Lover

THERE IS NOTHING LEFT TO LOSE (Roswell Records/ RCA) UK/ US/ Europe 1999
Stacked Actors/ Breakout/ Learn To Fly/ Gimme Stitches/ Generator/ Aurora/ Live-In Skin/ Next Year/ Headwires/ Ain't It The Life/ M.I.A

THERE IS NOTHING LEFT TO LOSE (Roswell Records/ RCA) Japan/ Australia 1999
Stacked Actors/ Breakout/ Learn To Fly/ Gimme Stitches/ Generator/ Aurora/ Live-In Skin/ Next Year/ Headwires/ Ain't It The Life/ M.I.A/ Fraternity

THERE IS NOTHING LEFT TO LOSE + VCD (Roswell Records/ RCA) Australia 2000
CD: Stacked Actors/ Breakout/ Learn To Fly/ Gimme Stitches/ Generator/ Aurora/ Live-In Skin/ Next Year/ Headwires/ Ain't It The Life/ M.I.A/ Fraternity
VCD: Learn To Fly (Video)/ Breakout (Video)/ Next Year (Video)/ Generator (Video)

ONE BY ONE (Roswell Records/ RCA) US/ UK/ Europe CD 2002
All My Life/ Low/ Have it All/ Time Like These/ Disenchanted Lullaby/ Tired Of You/ Halo/ Lonely As You/ Overdrive/ Burn Away/ Come Back

ONE BY ONE (Roswell Records/ RCA) Japan CD 2002
All My Life/ Low/ Have it All/ Time Like These/ Disenchanted Lullaby/ Tired Of You/ Halo/ Lonely As You/ Overdrive/ Burn Away/ Come Back/ Danny Says

ONE BY ONE (Roswell Records/ RCA) CD Norway 2003
CD#1: All My Life/ Low/ Have it All/ Time Like These/ Disenchanted Lullaby/ Tired Of You/ Halo/ Lonely As You/ Overdrive/ Burn Away/ Come Back
CD#2 Live: Snoof (aka Grohl trying to speak Norwegian)/ Times Like These/ Low/ Aurora/ Monkey Wrench

ONE BY ONE (Roswell Records/ RCA) UK Ltd. Edition 2x10" 2002
Label: Roswell / RCA Records
Side A: All My Life/ Low/ Have It All
Side B: Times Like These/ Disenchanted Lullaby/ Tired Of You
Side C: Halo/ Lonely As You/ Overdrive
Side D: Burn Away/ Comeback

IN YOUR HONOR (Roswell/ RCA) CD 2005
CD1: In Your Honor/ No Way Back/ Best of You/ DOA/ Hell/ The Last Song/ Free Me/ Resolve/ The Deepest Blues Are Black/ End Over End
CD2: Still/ What If I Do?/ Miracle/ Another Round/ Friend of a Friend/ Over and Out/ On the Mend/ Virginia Moon/ Cold Day in the Sun/ Razor

IN YOUR HONOR (Roswell/ RCA) UK Vinyl version 2005
CD1: In Your Honor/ No Way Back/ Best of You/ DOA/ Hell/ The Last Song/ Free Me/ Resolve/ The Deepest Blues Are Black/ End Over End/ The Sign
CD2: Still/ What If I Do?/ Miracle/ Another Round/ Friend of a Friend/ Over and Out/ On the Mend/ Virginia Moon/ Cold Day in the Sun/ Razor

SKIN AND BONES (Roswell/ RCA) 2006
Razor/ Over and Out/ Walking After You/Marigold/ My Hero/ Next Year/ Another Round/ Big Me/ Cold Day in the Sun/ Skin and Bones/ February Stars/ Times Like These/ Friend of a Friend" – 4:01/ Best of You/ Everlong
iTunes Bonus Tracks & Videos
Ain't It the Life/ Skin and Bones – video

LIVE IN HYDE PARK (audio download only) 2006
In Your Honor/ All My Life/ Best Of You/ Times Like These/ Learn To Fly/ Breakout/ Shake Your Blood/ Stacked Actors/ My Hero/ Generator/ DOA/ Monkey Wrench/ Everlong

ECHOES, SILENCE, PATIENCE & GRACE (Roswell/ RCA) 2007
The Pretender/ Let It Die/ Erase/Replace/ Long Road to Ruin/ Come Alive/ Stranger Things Have Happened/ Cheer Up, Boys (Your Make Up Is Running)/ Summer's End/ Ballad of the Beaconsfield Miners/ Statues/ But, Honestly/ Home

ECHOES, SILENCE, PATIENCE & GRACE (Roswell/ RCA) UK 2007
The Pretender/ Let It Die/ Erase/Replace/ Long Road to Ruin/ Come Alive/ Stranger Things Have Happened/ Cheer Up, Boys (Your Make Up Is Running)/ Summer's End/ Ballad of the Beaconsfield Miners/ Statues/ But, Honestly/ Home/ Once & for All (demo)

ECHOES, SILENCE, PATIENCE & GRACE (Roswell/ RCA) Japan 2007
The Pretender/ Let It Die/ Erase/Replace/ Long Road to Ruin/ Come Alive/ Stranger Things Have Happened/ Cheer Up, Boys (Your Make Up Is Running)/ Summer's End/ Ballad of the Beaconsfield Miners/ Statues/ But, Honestly/ Home/ Once & for All (demo)/ Seda
iTunes Bonus Tracks
Once & for All (demo)/ Seda
live @ Wal-Mart Soundcheck Bonus Tracks
The Pretender/ My Hero

DVDs
EVERYWHERE BUT HOME (Roswell/ RCA) 2003
Toronto section
All My Life/ My Hero/Breakout/ Have It All/ Generator/ Learn To Fly/ For All The Cows/ Stacked Actors/ Low/ Hey, Johnny Park!/ Monkey Wrench/ Times Like These" (Acoustic)/ Aurora/ Tired of You/ Everlong
Washington, D.C. section
Doll/ See You (Acoustic)/ For All The Cows (Acoustic)/ Everlong (Acoustic)
Slane Castle section
All My Life/ Everlong
Reykjavik (Audio Only section)
All My Life/ The One/ Times Like These/ My Hero/ Learn To Fly/ Have It All/ For All The Cows/ Breakout/ Generator/ Stacked Actors/ Low/ Hey, Johnny Park/ Monkey Wrench/ Aurora/ Weenie Beenie/ Tired Of You"
Everlong
Dublin (Hidden Concert)
Introduction/All My Life/ Breakout/ The One/ My Hero/ Aurora/ Low/ Everlong"
Dublin (Hidden Audio Content)
Can be accessed by following these steps: Go to the main menu/ Select "Slane Castle"/ Press 3, wait for the red arrow to reappear/ Press 8, wait for the red arrow to reappear/ Repeat the previous steps for 2, 5, 4, and 6.

SKIN AND BONES (Roswell/ RCA) 2006
DVD 1: Live in Hollywood (USA)
Intro/ Razor/ Over and Out/ On the Mend/ Walking After You/ Still/ Marigold/ My Hero/ Next Year/ Another Round/ See You/ Cold Day in the Sun/ Big Me/ What If I Do/ Skin And Bones/ Ain't It the Life/ February Stars/ Times Like These/ Friend of a Friend/ Best of You/ Everlong
DVD2: Live in Hyde Park (UK)
In Your Honor/ All My Life/ Best Of You/ Times Like These/ Learn To Fly/ Breakout/ Shake Your Blood/ Stacked Actors/ My Hero/ Generator/ DOA/ Monkey Wrench/ Everlong

SIDE PROJECTS AND COLLABORATIONS
BUZZ OSBORNE
KING BUZZO (Boner Records) 1992
Isabella/ Porg/ Annum/ Skeeter

BACKBEAT BAND
BACKBEAT SOUNDTRACK (Virgin Records) 1994
Money/ Long Tall Sally/ Bad Boy/ Twist And Shout/ Please Mr. Postman/ C'mon Everybody/ Rock 'N' Roll Music/ Slow Down/ Road Runner/ Carol/ Good Golly Miss Molly/ 20 Flight Rock

MIKE WATT
BALL HOG OR TUG BOAT? (Columbia Records) 1995
With Grohl: Big Train/ Against The 70's/ Forever – One Reporters Opinion

HARLINGTOX A.D.
HARLINGTOX A.D. (Laundry Room Records) 1996
Treason Daddy Brother in Crime Real Patriots Type Stuff/ Orbitting Prisons in Space/ Recycled Children Never to Be Grown/ Obtaining a Bachelors Degree/ Open Straigtedge Arms

PUFF DADDY
Been Around the World (Bad Boy Records) 1997
Been Around The World/ It's All About The Benjamins (Rock Remix #1)/ It's All About The Benjamins (Rock Remix #2)

IT'S ALL ABOUT THE BENJAMINS (Arista/ Bad Boy Records) 1997
It's All About The Benjamins (Rock Remix #1)/ It's All About The Benjamins (Album Version)/ It's All About The Benjamins (Rock Remix #2)/ It's All About The Benjamins (DJ Ming & FS Drum 'N' Bass Mix)

JOHN DOE
FOR THE REST OF US EP (Kill Rock Stars) 1998
A Step Outside/ Let's Get Lost/ The Unhappy Song/ Bad, Bad Feeling/ This Loving Thing (from Touch Soundtrack)

THE EARTHLINGS?
THE EARTHLINGS? (Efa/ Caroline) 1998
Nothing/ Saving Up For My Spaceship/Illuminate/ Reaper (Don't Fear This Child)/ Cavalry/ Happiest Day Of My Life/ Conversing Among Misfits/ Mars On Fire/ Stungun/ The Dreaded Lovelies/ Icy Halls Of Sobriety (I Dare Not Tread)/ Triumphant March Of The Buffoons

TOMMY IOMMI
IOMMI (Priority / Divine Records) 2000

Written by and featuring Grohl: Goodbye Lament

DAVID BOWIE
HEATHEN (Iso/ Columbia) 2002
With Grohl: I've Been Waiting For You

CAT POWER
YOU ARE FREE (Matador) 2002
With Grohl: Speak for Me/ Shaking Paper/ He War

QUEENS OF THE STONE AGE
SONGS FOR THE DEAF
You Think I Ain't Worth A Dollar, But I Feel Like A Millionaire/ No One Knows/ First It Giveth/ A Song For The Dead/ The Sky Is Fallin'/ Six Shooter/ Hangin' Tree/ Go With The Flow/ Gonna Leave You/ Do It Again/ God Is In The Radio/ Another Love Song/ A Song For The Deaf/ Mosquito Song/ Everybody's Gonna Be Happy

KILLING JOKE
THE DEATH AND RESURRECTION SHOW (Zuma) 2003
The Death & Resurrection Show/ Total Invasion/ Asteroid/ Implant/ Blood On Your Hands/ Loose Cannon/ You'll Never Get To Me/ Seeing Red/ Dark Forces/ The House That Pain Built

PROBOT
PROBOT (Southern Lord Records) 2004
Centuries of Sin/ Red War/ Access Babylon/ Silent Spring/ Ice Cold Man/ The Emerald Law/ Big Sky/ Dictatosaurus/ My Tortured Soul/ Sweet Dreams/ I Am the Warlock (Hidden Track)

NINE INCH NAILS
WHITE TEETH (Interscope/ Nothing) 2005
With Grohl: All the Love in the World/ You Know What You Are?/ The Collector/ Every Day Is Exactly the Same/ Getting Smaller/ Sunspots/ The Line Begins to Blur

GARBAGE
BLEED LIKE ME (Warner Brothers) 2005
With Grohl: Bad Boyfriend

PETE YORN
THE NIGHTCRAWLER (Coumbia) 2006
With Grohl: For Us

JULIETTE AND THE LICKS
FOUR ON THE FLOOR (Hassle Records) 2007
Smash and Grab/ Hot Kiss/ Sticky Honey/ Killer/ Death of a Whore/ Purgatory Blues/ Get Up/ Mind Full of Daggers/ Bullshit King/ Inside The Cage/ Are You Happy? (Bonus Track)/ Lucky For You (Hidden Bonus Track)

INDEX OF ARTICLES REFERENCED

Unless otherwise stated, all interviews by Martin James. Some chapters also feature unpublished interviews by Victoria Segal and Ian Winwood.

CHAPTER 1: 1. Dave Grohl Feature by Eric Brace (www.unomas.com); 2. I Was A Teenage Punk Rocker (Kerrang!) 1997; 3. Dave Grohl Feature by Eric Brace; 4. Dance of Days – Two Decades of Punk in the Nations Capital by Mark Anderson and Mark Jenkins (Soft Skull Press) 2001; 5, 6 & 7. unknown; 8. Dain Bramage biography by Keith Richmond (www.pooldrop.com) 1998; 9. Dave Grohl: His Life So Far by Tommy Udo (Metal Hammer) 2003; 10. Interview with Scream (Touch and Go)1982; 11. Interview with Scream (Thrill Seeker2)1982; 12. Flipside #36 -1982; 13. ibid; 14. Dave Grohl Feature by Eric Brace; 15, 16. & 17. ibid

CHAPTER 2: 1. unknown; 2. Bleached Wails by Everett True (Melody Maker) October 21 1989; 3. Sup Pop – Seattle: Rock City by Everett True (Melody Maker) March 16 1989; 4. 'Love Buzz' Review by Everett True (Melody Maker) February 18 1989; 5. Kills All Known Germs by Edwin Pouncey (NME) September 2 1989; 6. Bleach review by Edwin Pouncey (NME) July 8 1989; 7. Verse Chorus Verse: The Recording History of Nirvana by Gillian G. Gaar (Goldmine)1997; 8. ibid; 9. Eat, Drink, Breathe (and Sometimes Sleep) Music An Interview with Dave Grohl by Fish Rock and Tim Holsopple (www.manateebound.com) 2001; 10. Dave Grohl Feature by Eric Brace; 11. Unknown; 12. Heaven Can Wait by Push (Melody Maker) December 15 1990; 13 ibid; 14. Nevermind Ten Years After by David Fricke (Rollingstone.com) 2001; 15. Verse Chorus Verse: The Recording History of Nirvana by Gillian G. Gaar (Goldmine)1997; 16. ibid; 17. Nevermind Ten Years After by David Fricke (Rollingstone.com) 2001; 18. Unknown; 19. Nevermind review by Everett True (Melody Maker) September 14 1991; 20. Nevermind review by Steve Lamacq (NME) September 21 1991; 21. Nevermind review by Ira Robbins (Rollling Stone) October 1991; 22. Nevermind Ten Years After by David Fricke (Rollingstone.com) 2001; 23. Dark Side of the Womb by The Stud Brothers (Melody Maker) August 21 1993; 24. Verse Chorus Verse: The Recording History of Nirvana by Gillian G. Gaar (Goldmine)1997; 25. Nevermind Ten Years After by David Fricke (Rollingstone.com) 2001; 26. Dark Side of the Womb by The Stud Brothers (Melody Maker) August 21 1993; 27. Dave Grohl Feature by Eric Brace (www.unomas.com/features/foofighters.html) ; 28. Nevermind Ten Years After by David Fricke (Rollingstone.com) 2001; 29. Unknown; 30. Love Will Tear Us Apart by Keith Cameron (NME) August 29 1992

CHAPTER 3: 1 Territorial Pissings - The Battles Behind Nirvana's New Album by Michael Azzerad (Musician) 1993; 2. In My Head I'm So Ugly by Everett True (Melody Maker) July 1992; 3. Love Will Tear Us Apart by Keithe Cameron (NME) August 1992 ; 4. ibid; 5. Eyewitness Nirvana: The Day-By-Day Chronicle by Carrie Borzillo-Vrenna (Thunders Mouth/ Carlton Books) 2000; 6. news item by Carrie Borzillo-Vrenna (Rollingstone.com) April 10, 2003; 7. Come As You Are – The Story of Nirvana by Michael Azzerad (Main Street Books)1993; 8. Verse Chorus Verse: The Recording History of Nirvana by Gillian G. Gaar (Goldmine)1997; 9, 10, 11 & 12. ibid; 13 Dance of Days- Two Decades of Punk in the Nations Capital by Mark Anderson and Mark Jenkins (Soft Skull Press) 2001; 14. news item, no bi-line (Washington Post)1993; 15 Dave Grohl Feature by Eric Brace (www.unomas.com/features/foofighters.html) ; 16 ibid; 17 Womb at the Top by Sharon O'Connell (Melody Maker) September 1993.; 18 Nevermind Ten Years After by David Fricke (Rollingstone.com) 2001; 19. Verse Chorus Verse: The Recording History of Nirvana by Gillian G. Gaar (Goldmine)1997; 20 Dave Grohl Feature by Eric Brace (www.unomas.com/features/foofighters. html)

CHAPTER 4: 1 Unknown; 2 It's a band, damn it. (And don't mention the "N" word), author unknown (Rolling Stone) Oct 1995; 3 Foo Fighters Press Biog 1995; 4 Foo Fighters Feature, author unknown (NME) 23/30 December, 1995; 5. It's a band, damn it. (And don't mention the "N" word) author unknown (Rolling Stone) Oct 1995; 6 Nirvana Legacy – Foo Fighters Carry the Alt Standard Forward by Alan Sculley (www.aceweekly.com) 1996; 7 Foo Fighters Feature, author unknown

(NME) 23/30 December, 1995.; 8. My House is Haunted, no bi-line (Kerrang!) June, 1996.; 9 Feels Like The First Time, author unknown, (Alternative Press) 1996; 10, 11 & 12, ibid; 13 The Chosen Foo by Everett True (Melody Maker) Nov 1995; 14 It's a band, damn it. (And don't mention the "N" word), author unknown (Rolling Stone) Oct 1995; 15 Triple J Interview (Triple JJJ) December 28, 1995; 16 Foo Fighters feature, author unknown, (Raw Magazine) Dec 6-19 1995. ; 17 News item – no bi-line (Kerrang!) 1995; 18 The Chosen Foo by Everett True (Melody Maker) Nov 1995; 19, 20, 21 & 22, ibid; 23 Foo Fighters Feature, author unknown (NME) 23/30 December, 1995; 24 news item – no bi-line (Kerrang!) 1995.

CHAPTER 5: 1, 2 & 3,. Foos on the road feature by Mike Peak (Kerrang!) April 1997 ; 4. news item, no bi-line, (Melody Maker). April 19, 1997; 5. Dave Grohl feature, author unknown (Guitar Magazine) 1998; 6. Foos on the road feature by Mike Peak (Kerrang!) April 1997; 7. Unknown; 8. Foos on the road feature by Mike Peak (Kerrang!) April 1997; 9. ibid; 10. Eat, Drink, Breathe (and Sometimes Sleep) Music An Interview with Dave Grohl by Fish Rock and Tim Holsopple (www.manateebound.com/features/grohl.html) 2001; 11. Dave Grohl Feature by Eric Brace (www.unomas.com/features/foofighters.html); 12. ibid; 13. unknown

CHAPTER 6: 1. Foo Man New, author unknown (Maximum Guitar) January 1998; 2. Eat, Drink, Breathe (and Sometimes Sleep) Music An Interview with Dave Grohl by Fish Rock and Tim Holsopple (www.manateebound.com/features/grohl.html) 2001; 3.I'll Be Home For Christmas, author unkown (CMJ New Music) December 1999; 4. Foo Man New, author unknown (Maximum Guitar) January 1998; 5. Dave Grohl Feature by Eric Brace (www.unomas.com/features/foofighters.html) ; 6. When I Think About Rock Stars Today, I Think They're Arseholes! , author unknown (Metal Hammer) June 1998; 7. ibid; 8. Rocktropolis premiere of the X-Files soundtrack, author unknown; 9. Eat, Drink, Breathe (and Sometimes Sleep) Music An Interview with Dave Grohl by Fish Rock and Tim Holsopple (www.manateebound.com/features/grohl.html) 2001; 10. Get In The Van, author unknown (Metal Hammer) May 1998; 11. ibid; 12. Eat, Drink, Breathe (and Sometimes Sleep) Music An Interview with Dave Grohl by Fish Rock and Tim Holsopple (www.manateebound.com/features/grohl.html) 2001; 13. Foo Fighters Always On the Move, author unknown (Circus)1998; 14 & 15, ibid; 16. Eat, Drink, Breathe (and Sometimes Sleep) Music An Interview with Dave Grohl by Fish Rock and Tim Holsopple (www.manateebound.com/features/grohl.html) 2001; 17. Foo For Thought, author unknown (Spin) December 1999; 18 Eat, Drink, Breathe (and Sometimes Sleep) Music An Interview with Dave Grohl by Fish Rock and Tim Holsopple (www.manateebound.com/features/grohl.html) 2001; 19 ibid; 20 Foo Fighters Always On the Move, author unknown (Circus)1998; 21. Eat, Drink, Breathe (and Sometimes Sleep) Music An Interview with Dave Grohl by Fish Rock and Tim Holsopple (www.manateebound.com/features/grohl.html) 2001; 22. Foo Fighters Always On the Move, author unknown (Circus)1998

CHAPTER 7: 1 Men Behaving Badly author unkown (Kerrang!) June 2000; 2 Eat, Drink, Breathe (and Sometimes Sleep) Music An Interview with Dave Grohl by Fish Rock and Tim Holsopple (www.manateebound.com/features/grohl.html) 2001; 3 ibid; 4 news item, no bi-line (NME) 2001; 5 news item, no bi-line (Kerrang!) October 27 2001; 6 We Have Lift Off, author unknown (Kerrang!) June 2001; 7 ibid; 8 ibid; 9 Nick Oliveri counts his blessings as Dave Grohl rocks the royal family by Joe Rosenthal (Rolling Stone) May 3, 2002; 10 ibid; 11 Dave Grohl His Life So Far by Tommy Udo(Metal Hammer) 2003; 12 Foo Fighters feature by Paul Hagen (Big Cheese) January 2003; 13, 14, 15 & 16, One by One Review sidebar, author unknown (Rock Sound) November 2002

CHAPTER 8
1. Building The Perfect Probot by Jason Adams (LISTEN2THIS) 2004; 2. Metal Gods (Kerrang!) 2004; 3. Returning To His Roots With Probot by Ken Micallef (Modern Drummer) 2004; 4. Release the Probot by Ben Thompson (Independent) 2004; 5. Q: Are We Not Metal? A: We Are Probot! (Spin) 2004; 6. I, Probot by Jon Wiederhorn (Revolver) 2004; 7. Man of Steel by Dan Epstein (Guitar World) 2004; 8. The New Metallers In Town by James Doorn (Bizarre) 2004; 9. Dave Grohl's League

Of Extraordinary Gentlemen by Marion Garden (Terrorizer) 2004; 10. The Fan Has Won by Jochen Schliemann (Visions) 2004; 11. Reinventing The Steel by Ian Winwood (Kerrang!) 2003; 12. NME, 2005

CHAPTER 9

1. Punk'd Rock (Blender), 2005; 2. Kicking Drums by Mark van Schaick (Drummer), 2005; 3. How The Other Half Lives (Guitar World Acoustic); 4. Foo Fighters: Their most outrageous interview ever! (Kerrang!) ; 5. A Life Less Ordinary by Ben Mitchell (Q), 2005; 6. Learnt To Fly by Jamie Hibbard_(Metal Hammer). 2005; 7. "I'm A Geek. I'm the Guy Next Door. Alright, Alright! I'm The Luckiest Bastard In The World!" by Ian Winwood (NME) 2005; 8. In the studio with Foo Fighters by Lisa Johnson (Clash) 2005; 9. Street Fighting Man by Jessica Hundley (Dazed & Confused) 2005; 10. Foo For Thought – Dave Grohl; My Story (Metal Hammer Presents...Foo Fighters), 2005; 11. The Maverick – Chris Shiflett; My Story (Metal Hammer Presents...Foo Fighters), 2005; 12. Lucky Man – Taylor Hawkins; My Story (Metal Hammer Presents...Foo Fighters), 2005; 13. The Quiet One – Nate Mendel; My Story (Metal Hammer Presents...Foo Fighters), 2005; 14. Grohl With It by Craig McLean (The Independent Magazine) 2005; 15. Into The Void by Dom Lawson (Kerrang!) 2005; 16. Riders On The Storm by Mörat (Kerrang!) 2005; 17. Twice As Nice by J Bennett (Rock Sound) 2005

CHAPTER 10

1.Let There Be Foo (Clash) 2007; 2. Life, Death and Rock 'n' Grohl (Hot Press) 2007; 3. Inside The Lives Of One Of Rock's Biggest Bands. (Total Guitar) 2007; 4. Into The Void by Dom Lawson (Kerrang!) 2005; 5. A Life Less Ordinary by Ben Mitchell (Q), 2005

While every attempt has been made to credit all references to author and publication title, this has at times been impossible. In these rare instances we have credited the source as unknown. If you are the author of any uncredited quotes please contact the publisher so that future versions of this book can be altered.

PICTURE CREDITS

Colour Plates:
1 – Sipa Press/Rex Features; Dave Allocca/Rex Features
2 – Ross Hodgson/Rex Features
3 – Erik Pendzich/Rex Features
4 – Stewart Cook/Rex Features; Ross Hodgson/Rex Features
5 – Modica/Canitano/Rex Features
6 – c.New line/Everett/Rex Features; NBCUPHOTOBANK/Rex Features
7 – Patrick Rideaux/Rex Features
8 – Richard Young/Rex Features

Black and White Plates:
1 – C. Cuffarol/Everett/Rex Features
2 – Ian Tilton/Retna Ltd; Charles Peterson/Retna ltd
3 – Stephen Meddle/Rex Features
4 – Erik Pendzich/Rex Features; Alfie Korda/BBees
5 – Zach Cordner/Retna Ltd; Brian Rasic/Rex Features
6 – Raymonds Press/Rex Features; Raymonds Press/Rex Features
7 – Brian Rasic/Rex Features; Sharok Hatami/Rex Features
8 – Brian Rasic/Rex Features